STUDIES IN IMPERIALISM

general editor John M. MacKenzie

Established in the belief that imperialism as a cultural phenomenon had as significant an effect on the dominant as on the subordinate societies, Studies in Imperialism seeks to develop the new socio-cultural approach which has emerged through cross-disciplinary work on popular culture, media studies, art history, the study of education and religion, sports history, and children's literature. The cultural emphasis embraces studies of migration and race, while the older political, and constitutional, economic and military concerns will never be far away. It will incorporate comparative work on European and American empire-building, with the chronological focus primarily, though not exclusively, on the nineteenth and twentieth centuries, when these cultural exchanges were most powerfully at work.

Colonial masculinity

'Mrinalini Sinha is clearly one of the best of a new generation of feminist scholars whose attention to the nuances of political history add a welcome dimension to the examination of gender, race and imperialism. In this careful and richly detailed study of the political and cultural significance of masculinity for the colonial enterprise, she does a splendid job of bringing together the cultural politics of gender and the political culture of British imperialism in India.'

Philippa Levine, University of Southern California

Colonial masculinity breaks new ground by placing masculinity at the centre of colonial and nationalist politics in the late nineteenth century in India. Mrinalini Sinha situates the analysis very specifically in the context of an imperial social formation, examining colonial masculinity not only in the context of social forces within India, but also as framed by and framing political, economic, and ideological shifts in Britain

STUDIES IN IMPERIALISM

Propaganda and empire
The manipulation of British public opinion, 1880–1960   John M. MacKenzie

Imperialism and popular culture
ed. John M. MacKenzie

'At duty's call'
A study in obsolete patriotism   W. J. Reader

Images of the army
The military in British art, 1815–1914   J. W. M. Hichberger

The empire of nature
Hunting, conservation and British imperialism   John M. MacKenzie

Imperial medicine and indigenous societies
ed. David Arnold

Imperialism and juvenile literature
ed. Jeffrey Richards

Asia in western fiction
ed. Robin W. Winks and James R. Rush

Empire and sexuality
The British experience   Ronald M. Hyam

Imperialism and the natural world
ed. John M. MacKenzie

Emigrants and empire
British settlement in the dominions between the wars   ed. Stephen Constantine

Revolution and empire
English politics and the American colonies in the seventeenth century   Robert M. Bliss

Air power and colonial control
The Royal Air Force 1919–39   David E. Omissi

Acts of supremacy
The British Empire and the stage, 1790–1930   J. S. Bratton et al.

Policing the Empire
Government, authority and control, 1830–1940   ed. David Anderson, David Killingray

Policing and decolonisation
Nationalism, politics and the police, 1917–65   ed. David Anderson, David Killingray

Popular imperialism and the military, 1850–1950
ed. John M. MacKenzie

The language of empire
Myths and metaphors of popular imperialism, 1880–1918   Robert H. MacDonald

Travellers in Africa
British travelogues, 1850–1900   Tim Youngs

Unfit for heroes
Reconstruction and soldier settlement in the empire between the wars   Kent Fedorowich

Colonial masculinity
The 'manly Englishman' and the 'effeminate Bengali' in the late nineteenth century   Mrinalini Sinha

Colonial masculinity

THE 'MANLY ENGLISHMAN' AND THE 'EFFEMINATE BENGALI' IN THE LATE NINETEENTH CENTURY

Mrinalini Sinha

MANCHESTER UNIVERSITY PRESS
Manchester and New York

Distributed exclusively in the USA and Canada by
ST. MARTIN'S PRESS

Copyright © Mrinalini Sinha 1995

Published by Manchester University Press
Oxford Road, Manchester M13 9NR, UK
and Room 400, 175 Fifth Avenue, New York, NY 10010, USA

*Distributed exclusively in the USA and Canada
by* St. Martin's Press, Inc.,
175 Fifth Avenue, New York, NY 10010, USA

British Library Cataloguing-in-Publication Data
A catalogue record for this book is available from the British Library

Library of Congress Cataloging-in-Publication Data
Sinha, Mrinalini, 1960–
    Colonial masculinity : the manly Englishman and the effeminate Bengali / Mrinalini Sinha.
      p. cm. — (Studies in imperialism)
    Revision of thesis (doctoral)—State University of New York at Stony Brook.
Includes index.
      ISBN 0–7190–4285–2. — ISBN 0–7190–4653–X (pbk.)
   1. Men—India—History—19th century. 2. Men—Great Britain–
–History—19th century. 3. Men—India—Psychology. 4. Men—Great Britain—Psychology. 5. Masculinity (Psychology)—India–
–History—19th century. 6. Masculinity (Psychology)—Great Britain–
–History—19th century. 7. Great Britain—Colonies—Asia–
–Administration. I. Title. II. Series: Studies in imperialism (Manchester, England)
HQ1090.7.I4S56 1995
305.32′0942—dc20   94–41728
                                                                                                         CIP

ISBN 0 7190 4285 2 *hardback*
     0 7190 4653 X *paperback*

First published 1995
99 98 97 96 95   10 9 8 7 6 5 4 3 2 1

Photoset in Trump Medieval
by Northern Phototypesetting Co. Ltd., Bolton
Printed in Great Britain
by Redwood Books, Trowbridge

CONTENTS

General editor's introduction — *page vii*

Acknowledgements — *ix*

Introduction — *1*

1 Reconfiguring hierarchies: the Ilbert Bill controversy, 1883–84   33

2 Containing crisis: the native volunteer movement, 1885–86   69

3 Competing masculinities: the Public Service Commission, 1886–87   100

4 Potent protests: the Age of Consent controversy, 1891   138

Conclusion — *181*

Index — *187*

GENERAL EDITOR'S INTRODUCTION

A distinguished British historian remarked at the 1994 Anglo-American conference in London that it was 'time to play the imperial card'. Many of the papers at that conference indicated that, at last, British historians are indeed beginning to recognise the significance of imperial history for the full understanding of social and cultural developments in the United Kingdom between the eighteenth and twentieth centuries, not least in the formation of the complex of national characteristics that brought English, Scots, Welsh and Irish together. The contributors to this series have of course been aware of these important interactive dimensions of the study of the British Empire for ten years and more. With this book by Mrinalini Sinha we have an excellent example of the genre.

She uses images of masculinity in Bengal in the late nineteenth century to illuminate much wider issues of gender, imperial rule, and British domestic social and cultural history. In that period, British and Bengali were delineated by sharp stereotypical distinctions – on the one hand, a supposed masculine ideal identified by a love of sports, particularly hunting, a disdain for the 'bookworm', a celebration of general competence ('trained for nothing, ready for anything'), a vigorous pursuit of play and 'japes' as well as work in its proper place, a chivalric (and therefore distancing) approach to women, all contributing to the 'manly character' which was seen as the well-nigh unique mark of the Briton.

The Bengali *babu* was viewed as the almost complete foil to this: effeminate, bookish, over-serious, languorous, lustful and lacking in self-discipline. As Dr Sinha so convincingly demonstrates, these stereotypes underpinned many of the legislative and administrative controversies of British India in the 1880s and 1890s: those connected with the Ilbert Bill, the native volunteer movement, the Public Service Commission and the revision of the age of consent. But issues of masculinity never operate within a vacuum: these crises were equally infused with feminine stereotypes, with broader issues of both imperial rule and domestic self-image, and also the interleaving of nationalist and traditionalist/patriarchal policies. Thus, although the focus is on Bengal, this book deals with significant areas of gender, culture and politics of much wider significance. Moreover, it is a major contribution to the notion that aspects of metropolitan culture and of class and gender relations were formed at the so-called imperial periphery. As such, it represents an important illustration of the necessarily interactive character of the study of the British Empire and its capacity to illuminate British social and cultural history.

It is hard to resist a footnote which illustrates the manner in which these interactions can take a deeply personal form. When travelling in India a few years ago, I found myself searching for my name on the platform notice-board which allocated sleeping accommodation on the night train for Delhi. Thinking that I had been missed off the list, I was relieved to find it rendered as John M. Mukherji. Somebody's handwriting had led to a perfectly natural Indianisation – or indeed Bengalisation – of my Scottish surname. Now, symmetrically, I learn

GENERAL EDITOR'S INTRODUCTION

from Mrinalini Sinha's book (p. 86) that in the 1920s a station master on the Bengal Assam Railway had changed his name from Satish Chandra Mukherji to Sydney Kenneth Mackenzie in order to join the volunteer force and secure a rifle so that he could hunt the tigers which infested his area.

These reversals of identity have very different resonances in the twentieth century. The assimilation of my name struck me as agreeable, flattering almost, and I resolved to think of Mukherji as my South Asian surrogate. Satish Chandra, however, sought a practical outcome, a Eurasian route to acceptability in the Volunteer Force and the opportunity to take on the European hunting mantle. He was of course found out and rejected, for in the period which Mrinalini Sinha studies, such shadings of identity were scarcely possible.

John M. MacKenzie

ACKNOWLEDGEMENTS

The project was begun as a doctoral dissertation at the State University of New York at Stony Brook. I am very grateful to the Department of History at Stony Brook for institutional, financial, and intellectual support during the early years of the project. For their intellectual generosity and constructive advice I would especially like to thank the following people at Stony Brook: Bernard Semmel, William Taylor, Herman Lebovics, and John Williams. To Bernard Semmel, under whose guidance I began this project, I offer my sincerest gratitude for his encouragement and his personal example of intellectual enquiry. His magnanimous support and his critical advice over the years have sustained this project in many ways. Geraldine Forbes of SUNY Oswego has been another mentor to me. To Gerry I shall remain ever thankful for reading through several early drafts, offering insightful criticism, alerting me to numerous new references, and, most of all, for being a true friend, colleague, and critic ever since. Joan Scott has also been there for me from the very beginning. She was one of the first to share my excitement about the topic and to encourage me to pursue it further. As one of my readers, she offered me instructive comments on improving the project; over the years, moreover, she has continued to have a profound impact on my work both through her own scholarship and her warm and generous support.

I have received financial assistance from the following institutions for this project: American Institute of Indian Studies; Taraknath Das Foundation Grant, Columbia University; Altrusa International Women's Grant; and SUNY Stony Brook. A Faculty Fellowship from Boston College allowed me the time off from teaching to complete the book. This book would not have been possible without the support and co-operation of the staff of the India Office Library and Records, the British Museum and Library, the National Archives of India, the National Library in Calcutta, the Nehru Memorial Museum and Library in New Delhi, and the libraries at the School of Oriental and African Studies, Jawaharlal Nehru University, the University of Illinois at Urbana-Champaign, the University of Chicago, Harvard University, SUNY at Stony Brook, Boston College, and Southern Illinois University. An early version of Chapter 1 has appeared in Nupur Chaudhuri and M. Strobel, *Western Women and Imperialism* (Indiana University Press, 1991); and an early version of Chapter 4 has appeared both in M. Kimmel, *Changing Men: New Directions in Research on Men and Masculinity* (Sage, 1987) and in T. Stewart (ed.), *Shaping Bengali Worlds: Public and Private* (University of Michigan, 1989). Certain portions of Chapter 4 have also been incorporated in an article forthcoming in *Genders*.

My colleagues at Boston College have been very supportive of my work and of my leave from teaching to complete this book. I would like to thank Paul Breines, Sherry Broder, Jim Cronin, Robin Fleming, Roberta Manning, Karen Miller, David Northrup, Ginny Reinberg, Jenny Sharpe, Judy Smith, Karen Spalding, Peter Weiler, and Larry Woolf for their intellectual companionship. I

ACKNOWLEDGEMENTS

have also learned a lot from my students at Boston College. They have not only patiently borne early versions of this project with only the faintest sign of revolt, but also forced me to strive for greater clarity in presenting my ideas. Over the years, the following people have left their mark in one way or another on my thinking: Taisha Abraham, Saurabh Dube, Eric Hoffman, Margaret Schragge, Ann Geneva, Mala Mathrani, Monomita Roy, Ena Singh, Mita Chaudhury, Amita Bhatla, Yasmin Tambiah, S. Krishna, Kathinka Kerkhoff, Bob Post, Shanta Rao, Umaa Hiremath, Imtiaz Ahmad, and Janaki Nair. The 'Cultural Studies Reading Group' at Southern Illinois University at Carbondale helped me keep my sanity during the final stages of the writing. The project has been sustained in great measure by the reassuring presence and constancy of family and friends: Manisha, Karsten, Binu, Ken, Bish, Nags, Didi, Eulogio, Munnu, Gigi, Janmejaya, Bill, Carolyn, my parents, my grandfather, my adopted grandparents, the Chatterjees, and the children, Anjali, Raul, Ambuj, Vinayak, Megan, and Neal. My parents, to whom this book is dedicated, I owe more than I can ever acknowledge. My interest in history was first awakened by the long discussions over bed-tea led by my father; his many books and articles have always been an inspiration to me. My mother taught me early how to dream and to go after my dream. From her I also learned both a healthy scepticism and passion for a cause. Together they are in every way the true inspiration for this book. Finally, I thank Clem, whose imprint is everywhere on this book. Without his friendship, emotional support, and intellectual companionship, this project could not have been completed. I am especially grateful to him for bearing with good humour, even when I could not, the massive disruption to our lives created by my manuscript and his.

For my parents

INTRODUCTION

This book is about the processes and practices through which two differently positioned elites, among the colonisers and the colonised, were constituted respectively as the 'manly Englishman' and the 'effeminate Bengali' in nineteenth-century India. In *Colonial Masculinity: The 'manly Englishman' and the 'effeminate Bengali' in the late nineteenth century*, I argue that the emerging dynamics between colonial and nationalist politics in the 1880s and 1890s in India is best captured in the logic of colonial masculinity. For colonial masculinity points towards the multiple axes along which power was exercised in colonial India: among or within the colonisers and the colonised as well as between colonisers and colonised. Neither the colonisers nor the colonised represented homogenous groups; there were not only important internal hierarchies of class, gender, and status within each group, but also alliances across various axes that in fact helped fashion the opposition between colonial and nationalist politics. Indeed, *Colonial Masculinity* reframes, from the perspective of the uneven and contradictory intersection of various axes of power, the dynamics between colonialism and nationalism, on the one hand, and between colonial Indian and metropolitan British society, on the other. It thus recontextualises some of the major colonial controversies of the late nineteenth century in India. The book traces the impact of colonial masculinity in four specific controversies: the 'white mutiny' against the Ilbert Bill in 1883, the official government response to the Native Volunteer movement in 1885, the recommendations of the Public Service Commission of 1886, and the Indian opposition to the Age of Consent Bill in 1891.

The argument of the book proceeds from two basic assumptions. The first is that the categories of the coloniser and colonised are not fixed or self-evident categories.[1] Although these categories may appear to have represented 'natural' differences of race or national origin, there was nothing natural or fixed about them. There was a constant need, therefore, to define and redefine the coloniser and the colonised. Moreover, since the coloniser and colonised were themselves historically constructed categories, the relations between the two were neither fixed nor given for all time. Indeed, the relations between the coloniser and colonised were constantly rearticulated in accordance with the continually changing political and economic imperatives of colonial rule. It follows, then, that the figures of the 'manly Englishman' and the

INTRODUCTION

'effeminate Bengali' must be examined in relation to 'specific practices of ruling', rather than as products of a universalised or generalised colonial condition.[2] The second assumption of the book is that the contours of colonial masculinity were shaped in the context of an imperial social formation that included both Britain and India.[3] The figures of the 'manly Englishman' and the 'effeminate Bengali' were thus constituted in relation to colonial Indian society as well as to some of the following aspects of late nineteenth-century British society: the emergence of the 'New Woman'; the 'remaking of the working class'; the legacy of 'internal colonialism'; and the anti-feminist backlash of the 1880s and 1890s. This focus on the imperial social formation points not only to the intersection of the imperial with the categories of nation, race, class, gender, and sexuality, but also to the essentially uneven and contradictory nature of that intersection. *Colonial Masculinity* thus examines the politics of masculinity in the late nineteenth century from what Rosemary Hennessy has called a 'global social analytic'. Such an analytic is global in two senses: first, it focuses on a world-system fashioned by imperialism; and, second, it understands the 'social' as the intersection of the political, economic, and ideological, none of which can be reduced to any of the others.[4]

The following contemporary account of the 'effeminate Bengali *babu*' in *The Times* in London demonstrates a surprising perspicacity about historicising colonial constructs: 'the old East India Company did not develop the Bengali babu – the old East India Company left the Bengali as it found him – a cringing subserviant eye servant, to be made use of as circumstances or occasion required. The Crown took the Babu in hand and developed the babu into his present state of loquacity and disloyalty.'[5] The author's definition of the 'Bengali *babu*' alludes to a quite specific historical ordering of colonial masculinity. By the late nineteenth century, the politics of colonial masculinity was organised along a descending scale: senior British officials associated with the administrative and military establishment, and elite non-officials, those not directly related to the colonial administration, occupied positions at the top of the scale. Other groups and classes that made up colonial society supposedly shared some, though not all, of the attributes associated with the figure of the 'manly Englishman'. In this colonial ordering of masculinity, the politically self-conscious Indian intellectuals occupied a unique place: they represented an 'unnatural' or 'perverted' form of masculinity. Hence this group of Indians, the most typical representatives of which at the time were middle-class Bengali Hindus, became the quintessential referents for that odious category designated as 'effeminate *babus*'. The major emphasis of this book is to examine how colonial masculinity, in the context of the changes in the

INTRODUCTION

imperial social formation in the late nineteenth century, produced and exploited such categories.

The figures of the 'manly Englishman' and the 'effeminate Bengali *babu*' were produced by, and helped to shape, the shifts in the political economy of colonialism in the late nineteenth century: the changing imperatives in the strategies of colonial rule as well as the altered conditions for the indigenous elite's collaboration with colonial rule. The colonial cliché of the 'effeminate Bengali *babu*' was thus tied to the entire ensemble of political, economic, and administrative imperatives that underpinned the strategies of colonial rule in the late nineteenth century. The sheer lucrativeness of colonial domination over India was perhaps never more evident than in the closing decades of the last century. India, for long regarded as the 'Jewel in the Crown', was the linchpin of Britain's economic and political pre-eminence in the world. India served as a source of raw materials for British manufactures, as a captive market for British industrial products, and as a field for British overseas investments in agriculture, extractive industries, and in public works like the railways that had a guaranteed rate of profit. Moreover, Britain's unfavourable balance of trade with the rest of the world – a result of the 'protectionist' policies of many of Britain's trading partners in the second half of the century – was financed through India's export surplus with other countries. The transfer of surplus from India to Britain was managed through the complex system of 'Home Charges' for civil and military expenditures, guaranteed interest on railways, interest on the India Debt accumulating in England, and charges for such 'invisible services' as shipping, insurance, and so on; early Indian nationalists aptly termed this process the 'drain of wealth'.[6] Furthermore, imperial banks in India handled British overseas trade, 'coolie' labour from India was used as cheap labour on British economic concerns in different parts of the British Empire, and Indian troops, paid for by the Indians, were used to secure and extend British control overseas.[7] The province of Bengal was in many ways the key to this entire structure of British economic and political domination in India.

If the 'high imperialism' of the late nineteenth century was a reminder of the enormous political and economic stakes in the colonial domination of India, it was also an era in which colonial administrators faced a crisis of confidence in existing forms and practices of colonial rule. The 'illusion of permanence' that historians have identified in the colonial attitudes of the last quarter of the century was secured only after a shift in the practices of colonial rule in India.[8] In the early nineteenth century the colonial administration, drawing upon British Evangelical and Utilitarian thought, had embarked on a conscious programme of restructuring the existing colonial administration. This

INTRODUCTION

development was marked by the victory of the Anglicist over the Orientalist school of colonial administration; the latter favoured rule through supposedly indigenous or traditional means.[9] But the Great Revolt of 1857 eroded much of the early nineteenth-century confidence in the Anglicist programme. The expression of Indian discontent in 1857 was seen as a warning against the radical restructuring of 'traditional' Indian society. The suppression of the rebellion and the transfer of India from the East India Company to the British Crown in 1858 ushered in a new era of caution: the colonial administrators henceforth sought allies in the traditional landholding classes and orthodox religious leaders who were seen as the main forces behind the rebellion of 1857.[10] The problem of 'educated Indians', though far less dramatic, was an equally important factor in the rethinking of colonial policies in the second half of the century. The colonial administration was faced with the daunting task of accommodating a growing number of Western-educated Indians within the existing colonial administrative and political structures without threatening the exclusive rights and privileges to which generations of colonial officials and non-officials in India had grown accustomed.[11]

Both of these factors led to a shift in the dominant administrative perspective from the second half of the century onwards. The mid-century Anglicist perspective began to be tempered by a revival of the Orientalist perspective. There was a growing acceptance of the view that India could be best governed only through a judicious use of its supposedly indigenous traditions. These so-called indigenous traditions of rule, as various scholars have pointed out, were themselves a product of an earlier phase of colonial administration: in the late eighteenth century colonial administrators-cum-scholars, also known as Orientalists or Indologists, had through such practices as the codification of indigenous laws contributed to the construction of a specifically colonial understanding of indigenous tradition.[12] This colonial construction of indigenous traditions had enabled a trading company, recently entrusted with the task of rule, to exercise what was in essence a new and 'alien' form of authority in the name of continuity with Indian traditions.[13] The return to these supposedly traditional Indian forms of rule in the second half of the nineteenth century and the courting of more orthodox or traditional Indian groups signalled a marked shift from the Anglicist goal of creating a 'class of persons Indian in colour and blood, but English in tastes, in opinions, in morals and in intellect'.[14] The earlier policy of relying on Western-educated Indians as the most trusted allies of the government began to falter as these groups began demanding a share in the exclusive privileges of the British colonial elite. The new attitude towards this group of Indians was reflected in the colonial 'discourse' that characterised them as an 'artificial' and 'unnatural' class of persons: in short, 'effeminate *babus*'.[15] It was these changes in colonial rule that came to a head in the 'white mutiny' against the Ilbert Bill in 1883. In my discussion of the Ilbert Bill controversy, I argue that the British or Anglo-Indian opposition to the Ilbert Bill rearticulated the broader shifts in colonial economic, political, and administrative imperatives in the politics of colonial masculinity: it substituted for a straightforward defence of racial exclusivity a supposedly more 'natural' gender hierarchy between 'manly' and 'unmanly' men.

The indigenous elite's own investment in colonial masculinity, moreover, was also shaped by, and shaped, the realignment of the colonial political economy. The changes of the late nineteenth century had an impact not only on the transfer of surplus from India to Britain, but also on the modification and intensification of class hierarchies within India. The transformation in the economic prospects of the Bengali middle class, for example, fostered the self-perception of Bengali effeminacy. For, as Tanika Sarkar reminds us, 'manhood' in colonial society was based on a particular relationship to property; it was this relationship to property that was gradually eroded for the Bengali middle class in the second half of the nineteenth century.[16] From the heyday of the early decades of the century, there was a decline of Indian economic competitiveness in the modern economic sector in Bengal. The Bengali elites found themselves squeezed out of the dynamic economic sector as the new economic arrangements of the second half of the century came to be dominated almost entirely by the European managing agency system; there was little compensation for Bengali elites in the less prestigious local trade and business activities either, for these were already in the hands of Marwaris, an immigrant native group from western India.[17] Added to this was the declining fortune of the significant *rentier* class of Bengali elites. In 1793 the British, under the terms of the Permanent Settlement, had fixed the revenue obligations of landlords in Bengal; this had allowed the growth of a *rentier* class who made a considerable fortune from rural and urban ground rent.[18] From the 1870s onwards, however, the Bengali *rentier* class witnessed a decrease in revenue from landholdings as a result of a combination of factors: increase in population, land fragmentation, and lack of agricultural improvements. Furthermore, new tenancy regulations as well as the peasant resistance of the last quarter of the nineteenth century made dents in the untrammelled power that landlords had exercised over the countryside under the terms of the Permanent Settlement.[19] The Bengali elites were being defined more and more through administrative and professional employment. Indeed, the majority of the Bengali middle class found their horizons severely contracted by *'chakri'*, or petty clerical work.[20] This ignominious experience of *'chakri'*, according to Sarkar, underpinned the self-perception of effeminacy among the Bengali elites.

Furthermore, the Bengali elite's simultaneous investment in, and contestation of, colonial masculinity also reflected the new contradictions in elite politics: the changes in the conditions of elite collaboration with colonial rule. As many historians have recognised, there was a shift in elite politics in Bengal from collaboration to criticism of specific colonial policies in the last quarter of the nineteenth century. Yet the constraints of the colonial political economy in Bengal also limited any substantial modification in the role of Bengali elites as mediators between a colonial import-export sector and a largely subsistence peasant economy.[21] It was this contradiction that haunted the change that historians have noted in elite Bengali politics in the last quarter of the nineteenth century: the rise of two distinct groups within the Bengali *bhadralok*, or 'respectable' society, from the erosion of the hierarchical ties between an older aristocratic elite and newer social groups within *bhadralok* society. In discussing elite politics in Bengal in the post-1870 period, therefore, the historian Rajat Kanta Ray identifies a 'triangular' pattern of interaction between senior European officials and non-officials, an Indian aristocratic or gentry class, and a new western-educated Indian middle class.[22] There exists a long controversy in the historiography of colonial India, however, over identifying the newly visible group in *bhadralok* society in the late nineteenth century as a distinct social class; for, as Michelguglielmo Torri has argued, the changes suggest instead a transformation or mutation in the role of intellectuals – both the western-educated and the vernacular literati – as spokespersons for the powerful landed magnates and notables who together made up the indigenous elites.[23]

The various anomalies in elite politics in late nineteenth-century Bengal are nicely captured in the politics of colonial masculinity. For, despite important economic and cultural ties to the older landholding or *rentier* Indian elite, the newly visible group of intellectuals did define themselves as a distinct *sikhita madhyabitto*, or educated middle class. Their world was defined against both the more traditional or orthodox Indian elites and the vast majority of Indians, the peasants and the urban poor. By the 1870s they had set up their own political organisations, like the Indian League and the Indian Association, distinct from the British Indian Association and other such organisations of an older landed and titled Indian elite; they also had their own newspapers and journals like the *Amrita Bazar Patrika* and the *Bengalee*, distinct from older newspapers like the *Hindoo Patriot*, which represented the views of an older elite.[24] It is the anomaly in their struggle for legitimacy – which Partha Chatterjee has called the paradox of the 'subalternity' of an elite – that provides the background for the Bengali elite's investment in colonial masculinity in the late nineteenth century.[25] On the one hand, as Sarkar has suggested, the self-perception of effeminacy was itself an expression of the hegemonic aspirations of the Bengali elite: for the degeneration of the body of the elite Hindu male became the symbol of the negative impact of colonial rule on indigenous society as a whole.[26] On the other hand, the self-perception of effeminacy also facilitated a challenge, however limited and contradictory, to the dominance of the colonising elites: for the emasculation of Indians was also the basis for challenging specific colonial policies. I demonstrate the tension in the Bengali elite's investment in colonial masculinity in the native volunteer movement of 1885. For though the demand for native volunteering by the elites also provided a more radical critique of the impact of expensive colonial financial and military policies on the majority of Indians, this challenge was recuperated in the obsessive concern over the 'demilitarisation' of the elite Indian male. The Bengali elites thus both accepted and resisted the colonial politics of masculinity that cast them in the unenviable position of 'effeminate *babus*'.

Studying colonial masculinity from a densely historicised context does indeed open up new ways of situating not only colonial and nationalist politics but also metropolitan British and colonial Indian developments. One contribution of *Colonial Masculinity* is thus to demonstrate that late nineteenth-century notions of English/British masculinity or Bengali/Indian effeminacy cannot be understood simply from the framework of discrete 'national' cultures; instead, they must be understood in relation to one another, and as constitutive of each other. Hence the point of my discussion of colonial masculinity is not to stage an encounter between discrete British and Indian conceptions of masculinity. Rather, it is to understand the prior significance of imperialism in the construction of both 'national' British and 'colonial' Indian politics of masculinity in the late nineteenth century. My emphasis on the imperial constitution of the politics of masculinity, therefore, marks a point of departure from such pioneering works on masculinity and the psychology of colonialism as Ashis Nandy's *The Intimate Enemy*. Nandy connects the development of a post-Enlightenment notion of modern 'Western' masculinity and colonial domination.[27] Unlike Nandy, however, my focus is much more on the material, historical specificity of colonial masculinity in the late nineteenth century rather than on broad historical generalisations. Nandy's discussion of the politics of masculinity, moreover, emphasises the impact of modern Western notions of masculinity on the reordering of more traditional conceptions of masculinity in India; the historical approach of my book, however, is meant precisely to complicate either notions of modern Western masculinity or of traditional Indian conceptions of masculinity as discrete or mutually exclusive categories by a recognition of their mutual implication in imperial politics. To offer one example: the colonial government, in rejecting the Indian demands for a native volunteer force, claimed to be perpetuating an Indian tradition that distinguished between so-called 'martial' and 'non-martial' Indian castes. But as various scholars of colonial India have demonstrated, the popular understanding of the Indian caste system and the colonial invention of the criterion of 'martial' and 'non-martial' Indian races for recruitment in the post-1857 colonial army were both products of a peculiarly colonial understanding of an indigenous Indian institution.[28] The distinction between supposedly distinct 'martial' and 'non-martial' Indian races that was at stake in the colonial response to the native volunteer movement did not reflect a 'traditional Indian organization of masculinity' but a colonial understanding of the ways in which certain attributes of masculinity were supposedly distributed in traditional Indian society. Equally important for my purposes is to note that the colonial preference for 'martial' over 'non-martial' Indians did not simply reflect the priorities of a discrete British/Western masculinity, but that nineteenth-century British masculinity was itself implicated in the history of British imperialism.

A sustained focus on the imperial constitution of colonial masculinity, therefore, serves also to refine the standard historical scholarship on nineteenth-century British masculinity. For though recent studies of the politics of masculinity in Britain have gone beyond the narrow institutional focus on the 'great English public schools' and 'Oxbridge' to explain the changing ideals of 'manliness', their broader sociological explanations still remain limited because of the predominantly metropolitan British frame of reference. A reticence in engaging the imperial social formation has limited even such important contributions to the understanding of nineteenth-century British masculinity as George Mosse's study of masculinity, middle-class respectability and nationalism in nineteenth-century Britain and Germany; Catherine Hall and Leonore Davidoff's examination of the 'separate spheres ideology' of masculinity and femininity in British middle-class formation; Keith McClelland's essay on masculinity and the politics of work in British artisanal culture; Jeffrey Weeks's account of the historical construction of gender and the regulation of sexuality in late nineteenth-century Britain; and Brian Harrison's examination of male bonding in the politics of the opponents of female suffrage in Britain.[29] For a historical and materialist understanding of 'British' masculinity from

INTRODUCTION

the perspective of the political, economic, and ideological developments of the nineteenth century does in fact require extending the exclusive 'national' frame of reference to recognise its location in a larger imperial social formation. My discussion of the late nineteenth-century politics of colonial masculinity is meant precisely to challenge the traditional frames of reference in accounts of metropolitan British or colonial Indian masculinity.

The most obvious case to be made for locating the metropolitan British context in a larger imperial social formation is that the extended frame of reference can shed new light on even such tried and true topics as the masculine ethos of the all-male, elite English public schools. There is a general consensus among scholars about the historical evolution of public-school 'manliness' in the nineteenth century: the meaning of manliness in the public schools changed from Thomas Arnold's 'godliness and goodlearning' in the 1830s to the 'vigorous muscular Christianity' of the mid-Victorian period, associated with men such as Charles Kingsley and Thomas Hughes, and, finally, to the games-mania or 'athleticism' of the 1870s which fed the recruiting campaigns for imperial projects in the late nineteenth century.[30] Yet there is little consensus on the relation of these changes to broader social forces; it is only in passing that various explanations such as the 'gentrification' of the middle class in Britain, the consolidation of a new bourgeois culture in Victorian Britain, or the instrumental needs of an imperial class have been offered to make sense of the masculine ethos of the public schools. My discussion of the Public Service Commission of 1886 that finally secured 'Oxbridge' domination of the civil service in India demonstrates how the imperial context extends the analysis of the function of the public-school ideal of manliness in the nineteenth century. For the changes recommended by the Commission suggest that the connection between the imperial context and such institutions as the public schools and 'Oxbridge' was not limited to the latter providing the functionaries of empire with the proper 'imperial' attributes. Rather, the connection also suggests that the consolidation in the schools and universities of a *national* representation of 'English' masculinity for the British was itself tied to a strictly *provincial* representation of 'native' masculinity for Indians.

The more important case to be made for going beyond the strictly 'national' frame of reference for colonial masculinity is that it provides new ways of understanding the relation between 'imperial' and 'national'. For even today few historians have carried out the kind of 'centripetal' analysis of imperial influence recommended by John MacKenzie to replace the dominant 'centrifugal' analysis of the radiation of imperial influence from Britain to her colonies overseas.[31]

INTRODUCTION

Curiously, therefore, even the proliferation of recent works devoted quite specifically to an analysis of British masculinity as a dimension of class, race, sexual, and imperial politics have failed to address the full implication of the imperial constitution of British masculinity.[32] Ironically, although these studies examine the predominantly imperial themes in such supposedly metropolitan British staples as public-school culture and such juvenile literature as boys' papers and adventure stories, they seldom accord the colonial domain full analytical weight. By and large, the colonial context serves only a limited function: it is either the backdrop for the full flowering of British masculinity or else the arena where gender or class domination in Britain is simply extended outwards for the purpose of imperial domination in the colonies. As Gauri Viswanathan rightly suggests, this mode of understanding the relation between 'imperial' and 'national' leads to an easy and unproblematic conflation of the two terms.[33] Typically, therefore, the 'imperial' gets conceptualised simply as an extension of the 'national,' or at best a shadowy presence in the making of the 'national'. The full constitutive impact of the colonial experience in the making of British masculinity – despite the proliferation of studies on British masculinity and imperialism – remains insufficiently acknowledged. Catherine Hall's essay on competing definitions of white, British masculinity in the controversy arising out of British administration in Jamaica is one of the few attempts to take seriously the impact of the colonial experience on the metropolitan debate on British masculinity.[34] The further point, however, is that we also need to go beyond demonstrating the intersection of the metropolitan with the colonial. For to heed Viswanathan's call for the reinsertion of 'imperial' in 'national' without conflating the two, it is necessary also to demonstrate the essentially uneven and contradictory impact of the intersection between metropolitan and colonial histories. It is the unevenness in the metropolitan and colonial contexts that motivates my discussion of the controversy over the Indian Consent Bill of 1891. I show how colonial politics mediated the 'crisis' of British and Indian masculinity to produce quite different and contradictory results in Britain and India. Although the context of embattled masculinities brings the debate over the British Consent Bill and the Indian Consent Bill within the same field of study, it also underscores the incommensurability of the two debates. For, as I argue, it was precisely the differences in the terms of the two debates that allowed the redefinition of female consent in both Britain and in India to be recuperated in the politics of colonial masculinity. The discussion of the Indian consent controversy indeed cautions against either overlooking the imperial context or simply conflating the metropolitan with the colonial: in

INTRODUCTION

short, it underscores the importance of historicising adequately.

Another contribution of *Colonial Masculinity* is to demonstrate that the gendered constructs of the 'manly Englishman' and the 'effeminate Bengali' were in fact 'overdetermined' by various intersecting late nineteenth-century ideologies of race, ethnicity, class, religion, and sexuality.[35] By focusing on colonial masculinity as the site for understanding the organisation of power in colonial India, therefore, I do not confine my analysis simply to the gender or sexual politics of colonial rule; rather, I focus on colonial masculinity to get at the multiple axes of domination and subordination in colonial Indian society as a whole. Here I am drawing upon recent feminist scholarship that has extended analysis of the 'sex–gender system' to understand much more than simply the history of women and sexuality. Gender, in this view, serves as a 'useful category of analysis' for elucidating the many ways in which relations of power are constructed and represented in society.[36] On the one hand, then, *Colonial Masculinity* makes what should by now (after the more favourable reception in recent years of the contributions of women of colour, 'Third-World' women, and lesbians to feminist scholarship) be a more obvious point: that gender was an important axis along which colonial power was constructed, and that, at the same time, the category of gender itself was never distinct from national, class/caste, and racial categories. The most persuasive formulation of this argument has been made by feminist historians Kumkum Sangari and Sudesh Vaid. They argue that all aspects of reality are gendered and that gender must serve as a mode of questioning that undergirds all efforts at historical reconstruction; but, at the same time, they argue that since the experience of gender itself is deeply implicated in other categories such as class/caste, race, nation, and sexuality, an exclusive focus on gender can never be adequate for a feminist historiography.[37] The ways in which the politics of gender itself was complicated by its intersection with other categories is brought out, for example, in my discussion of the politics of masculinity in the Ilbert Bill controversy. In this racial controversy, an effort was made to construct an alternative politics – what one white woman in India called the 'pride of womanhood'. This effort, however, foundered on the issue of the different ways in which British women and Indian women understood such a politics. For British women, the pride of womanhood legitimated the participation of white women in the predominantly male colonial public sphere as well as confirmed the role of white women in a masculinist colonial society by stressing the need for the 'protection' of white women by white men through the preservation of exclusive white privileges. To middle-class Indian women or *bhadramahila*, the pride of womanhood underscored their solidarity with Indian men of their class and opened up a space for the separate contributions of Indian women to a unified nationalist front against the British.

On the other hand, however, *Colonial Masculinity* also makes a further point: it attempts to complicate the a priori prioritisation of gender or of any one category of analysis over another in the construction of the colonial politics of the 'manly Englishman' and the 'effeminate Bengali'. The controversies examined in this book do indeed underscore the many different axes for the construction of colonial masculinity in the late nineteenth century. Whereas my discussion of the Ilbert Bill controversy, for example, highlights gender identities as an important context for colonial masculinity, the native volunteer controversy highlights the role of class identities. *Colonial Masculinity* suggests that such an overdetermined context for analysing colonial masculinity in fact broadens the significance of a feminist historiography. For, as I demonstrate in recontextualising the Indian opposition to the Consent Bill, it brings the concerns of feminist politics to the very centre of the study of nationalist politics. It is significant to note, therefore, that elite Indian nationalism did not simply rejuvenate itself at the price of a more patriarchal politics in the Indian opposition to the Consent Bill: the nationalist challenge itself, rather, was sacrificed in the patriarchal opposition to the Bill.

Finally, and most importantly, *Colonial Masculinity* contributes to the understanding of the exercise of colonial power in late nineteenth-century India. In recent years, the discursive aspect of colonial rule has begun to receive almost as much attention from scholars as the standard focus on the political and economic aspects of colonial rule. Edward Said's *Orientalism* has perhaps been the most influential text in thus expanding our understanding of colonialism and imperialism.[38] Said argues that the political and economic enterprise inaugurated by late eighteenth-century European imperialism was accompanied by a massive project that reconstructed 'knowledge' about the Orient for the exercise of imperial power. This project of collecting and disseminating knowledge about the Orient, what Said calls 'Orientalism', was both a product of the political and economic imperatives of modern European imperialism and itself created the conditions necessary for imperialism. Although several scholars have modified Said's important thesis since the first publication of his book in 1978, the two basic insights of *Orientalism* – that under the political and economic imperatives of imperialism a certain 'knowledge' of the Orient was constituted for the exercise of imperial power and that this invention also had a generative impact in producing what would henceforth become the Orient – remain pertinent to my project. Yet my historical and materialist analysis of the ways in which in the late nineteenth century the

INTRODUCTION

colonisers constructed knowledge of the colonised, and, equally crucially, the ways in which the colonised contributed to as well as resisted this knowledge, necessarily engages with some of the more specific critiques of Said's analysis of the power/knowledge nexus in the colonial domain.

My book draws upon recent scholarship that re-thinks the 'Orientalist' enterprise and the critiques of Orientalism from a historical materialist perspective. For such a perspective cautions against substituting a universalising account of colonial race relations for a more historical account of the transformation of the imperial social formation in the late nineteenth century as the basis for understanding the historicity of the 'manly Englishman' and the 'effeminate Bengali'. Central to this project, therefore, is the effort to locate the 'Orientalist' enterprise more securely as part of broader social transformations. Imperialism in the modern era was not, as Joseph Schumpeter would argue, simply an 'atavistic' phenomenon, but was an integral part of the historical contradictions in the development of capitalism and the birth of the 'modern'.[39] Despite the trappings of older forms, therefore, modern European imperialism and its attendant 'Orientalist' enterprise were never simply a throwback to the imperialisms of ancient civilisations; they were more integrally connected to the social transformations of their time. The relation between imperial centres and the imperialised peripheries, especially from the late eighteenth century onwards, began to emerge gradually as qualitatively different from the past; for the complex mechanism for the transfer of surplus from the periphery to the centre, which went beyond the simple extraction of surplus, eventually led to a restructuring of all the societies within its orbit. The need and the ability to restructure societies that accompanied modern capitalist imperialism provided the context for the development of the discourse that Said has rightly identified as 'Orientalism'. Hence to trace the genesis of this Orientalism, as Said's critics have accused him of doing in his book, to the ways in which ancient Greeks or medieval Europeans perceived racial or cultural 'others' is to miss the historical specificity of the material conditions for modern European imperialism and the Orientalist enterprise.[40] This lack of clarity about the historicity of the Orientalist enterprise has led several scholars, following Said, to examine the construction of racial Others in the nineteenth century as little more than an intensified version of an ancient European tendency. But the Orientalist enterprise was not a simple intensification of ancient prejudices; it marked a crucial break in the strategies by which 'knowledge' about cultures and civilisations was constructed. The changed material conditions of modern European imperialism should caution us against analysing the racialising

[13]

INTRODUCTION

procedures that it inaugurated as simply an extension or intensification of a timeless and universal human predeliction for depicting racial and cultural others.

The recognition of the historical and material conditions to which racialising procedures respond, moreover, is crucial precisely to avoid replicating the very assumptions of the Orientalist enterprise. For, as Aijaz Ahmad argues, even otherwise sensitive critics of Orientalism have often ended up sharing in the assumptions of Orientalism: while these critics rightly point out that the 'Orient' produced in Orientalist discourse was an ahistorical construct that conveniently elided the imperial political and economic conditions that underlay this conceptual production, they do not explore the full implications of this insight.[41] Many of them, as Ahmad demonstrates, subscribe to an equally ahistorical concept of the 'West', whose genealogy is traced in an unbroken continuum from 'Athens to Albion'. But as various scholars, most notably Martin Bernal, have demonstrated, there was in fact a major 'historiographical shift' in the understanding of the 'West' in the early nineteenth century. This shift, ignoring what generations of previous European scholars had acknowledged, minimised the contributions of West Asia and Northern Africa in the making of Ancient Greece in order to construct a racially 'pure' genealogy for the modern West in a conveniently 'Aryanised' Ancient Greece.[42] This effort to trace the idea of a racially distinct 'West' in an unbroken line from ancient Greece to modern-day Europe was itself part of the imperatives of modern capitalist imperialism that initiated a massive reordering of knowledge in terms of racial essences. A critic of modern European imperialism, therefore, must recognise that the historical specificity of the Orientalist enterprise was not simply that the 'Orient' was constructed as the racial or cultural Other of Europe; but, even more importantly, that both 'Europe' and the 'Orient' were constructed in the realm of ideas or racial essences, the function of which was to suppress the more complicated material history of the regions now designated as 'Europe' and the 'Orient'. This should caution us against critiques of racial politics that eschew an integrated political, economic, and cultural analysis.

Indeed, *Colonial Masculinity* demonstrates that it was precisely because colonial race relations were constantly rearticulated in response to changes in material conditions that a universalising account of colonial racial politics cannot be adequate for understanding the colonial constructs of the 'manly Englishman' and the 'effeminate Bengali *babu*'. The construct of the 'effeminate Bengali *babu*', for example, was substantially modified to respond to the political and economic shifts of the last quarter of the nineteenth century. It may be

INTRODUCTION

conceded that broad generalisations about the mild-mannered and effete nature of inhabitants of certain regions in India or believers of certain Indian religions were long part of the stock of ideas held by Europeans, and even by some Indians themselves. John Rosselli notes that the European perception of Indians as a passive and effeminate people goes back at least to the early days of colonial rule: Richard Orme in the 1770s had observed in his *History of the Military Transactions of the British Nation in Indostan* that all natives showed 'effeminacy of character' but that the Bengalis were 'still of weaker frame and more enervated character'.[43] In the 1820s Bishop Heber noted that Bengalis were regarded as 'the greatest cowards in India' and that the 'term Bengali [was] used to express anything which was roguish and cowardly'. Other major early nineteenth-century ideologues of imperialism, such as the Evangelical Charles Grant and the Utilitarian James Mill, also had recourse to arguments about the passive and effeminate character of Bengali Hindus. For Mill, Hindus 'possess[ed] a certain softness both in their persons and in their address' that distinguished them from the 'manlier races' of Europe.[44] Thomas Babington Macaulay, the Law Member for India in the 1830s, is perhaps the most famous and often-cited source on Bengali effeminacy. In his Essay on Robert Clive, the famous conqueror of Bengal, Macaulay gave the following description of Bengalis:

> The men by whom this rich tract was peopled, enervated by a soft climate and accustomed to peaceful employments, bore the same relation to other Asiatics which the Asiatics generally bear to the bold and energetic children of Europe. The Castillians have a proverb that in Valencia the Earth is water and the men women; the description is at least equally applicable to the vast plain of the Lower Ganges. Whatever the Bengali does he does languidly. His favourite pursuits are sedentary. He shrinks from bodily exertion; and though voluble in dispute, and singularly pertinacious in the war of chicane he seldom engages in personal conflict, and scarcely ever enlists as a soldier. There never perhaps existed a people so thoroughly fitted by habit for a foreign yoke.[45]

The 'feebleness' of the Bengalis served to justify their loss of independence to the British. For Macaulay, this feebleness also had important implications for the moral character of the inhabitants of Bengal. To quote once again from Macaulay:

> The physical organization of the Bengalee is feeble even to effeminacy. He lives in a constant vapour bath. His pursuits are sedentary, his limbs delicate, his movements languid. During many ages he has been trampled upon by men of bolder and more hardy breeds. Courage, independence,

veracity are qualities to which his constitution and his situation are equally unfavourable.[46]

Yet Macaulay's eloquent characterisation of the effeminacy of the inhabitants of Bengal not only became more widespread and virulent, but also acquired a more specific meaning in the late nineteenth-century stereotype of the 'effeminate Bengali *babu*'. If in the past effeminacy loosely characterised all the inhabitants of Bengal, in the second half of the century it was used quite specifically to characterise the Indian middle class, or a section of this class identified as *babus*. In Bengal itself, therefore, effeminacy came to be associated only with a small percentage of its total population. The majority of Bengalis, the labouring classes, and certain low-caste groups such as the Gops and the Gwalas, were quite specifically exempted from the charge of effeminacy. The Muslims in Bengal, who as a group had a slight numerical advantage over Hindus, were similarly usually exempted from the popular elaboration of Bengali effeminacy.[47] The vast majority of the Muslims in Bengal were among the labouring classes and were also under-represented in the Western-educated community. In the words of one British official in India, 'it is not known that many, outside the purely writer and *zemindar* class, acknowledge themselves to be Bengalis and no Mahommedan, although born in the province, does'.[48]

Over time, effeminacy had evolved from a loosely defined attribute associated with the entire population of Bengal, and sometimes by extension of all of India, to an attribute associated very specifically with Western-educated Indians, a large majority of whom were Bengali Hindus. On the one hand, the concept of Bengali effeminacy had been narrowed to refer quite specifically to this group of *babus*. On the other hand, the concept of Bengali effeminacy was also greatly expanded to include the politically discontented middle-class 'natives' from all over India. As an editorial in the *Amrita Bazar Patrika* noted, 'if any one of the dumb millions gets his tongue, he becomes a babu at once and then it is only a babu who speaks'.[49] Similarly the *Bengalee* claimed that 'in Anglo Indian parlance [the English educated natives of the country] are all babus, whether they be Parsees or Sikhs or Mahrattas or Madrasis'.[50] The Indian National Congress, formed in 1885 as an umbrella organisation that brought the various new Indian political associations from all over India under its ambit, was often dubbed the quintessential *babu* organisation. The concept of the 'effeminate *babu*' in the last quarter of the nineteenth century emerged out of both a narrowing and a widening of earlier notions of Bengali effeminacy. The concept reflected the new development in colonial society: the political challenge posed by the Indian middle class to certain exclusive British rights and privileges in

INTRODUCTION

India. It was the shift in British colonial attitudes towards Western-educated Indians, from mediators between the colonial administration and the rest of the Indian population to an unrepresentative and artificial minority representing nothing but the anomalies of their own situation, that was signalled by the late nineteenth-century concept of the 'effeminate *babu*'.

The evolution in the British use of the word '*babu*' similarly demonstrates the rearticulation of colonial racial politics in changed material conditions. The *babu*, an old Bengali word of Persian origin, did not always have negative connotations for the British. In fact, well up to the second half of the century, as several scholars have noted, the term was used as a title of respect for men who had no other titles, very like its English equivalents 'Mr' or 'Esquire'.[51] The origins of a more negative meaning of the word, as Christine Baxter points out, can be traced to the works of early nineteenth-century Bengali social satirists. These early Bengali social commentators used the term '*babu*' to satirise the culture of the *nouveau riche* in Bengali society; the term was associated with Bengali parvenus who had adopted Persianised and later Anglicised manners for upward economic and social mobility.[52] When the British first adopted this negative usage of the *babu*, its connotation of social-climbing or money-grubbing continued as an important theme in British satires of the Bengali *babu*. Dave Carson's famous song, 'Bengalee Baboo', immortalised this generation of money-making '*babus*':

> I very good Bengali Baboo
> in Calcutta I long time stop
> Ramchand Tunda Ghosh my name
> Radha Bazar I keep my shop.[53]

The thrust of Carson's satire of the Bengali *babu*, despite the mockery of the *babu's* stilted mannerisms, was still aimed mainly at the economic acquisitiveness of the *babus* as shopkeepers, petty traders, clerks, and so on.

By the late nineteenth century, however, there was a new economic underpinning in the colonial understanding of the 'effeminate *babu*'. The thrust of the colonial satire of the *babu* came to be directed more pointedly against the grandiose pretensions and the economic impotence of the potentially disloyal Anglicised or English-educated Indian in particular. The racial exclusivity that gave European-owned businesses in Bengal an edge over Indian economic competitors was obscured in the popular colonial perception that effeminate Bengali *babus* lacked the entrepreneurial initiatives of the British or of other Indian groups, like the Parsis in Bombay, who had retained a share in the modern economic sector. The Bengali *babus'* reliance on professional or administrative employment, entry into which was determined by English education, thus became an indispensable part of the stereotype of the effeminate *babu*. Hence the *Hobson-Jobson*, a glossary of British words and phrases in India compiled in the 1880s, suggests that in the popular colonial imagination the word *babu* had come to mean primarily a 'native clerk who writes in English'. As the editors of this volume noted, the word was used with 'a slight savour of disparagement, as characterizing a superficially cultivated but too often effeminate Bengali'.[54]

The historical shifts in the construct of the 'effeminate Bengali *babu*' suggest the need to go beyond Homi Bhabha's otherwise perceptive analysis of colonial stereotypes. Despite Bhabha's contention that the coloniser and colonised are socially or culturally constituted, his model of the colonial subject does not explain adequately the historical processes that constituted the 'effeminate *babu*' in the late nineteenth century. Bhabha, for example, makes sense of the colonial stereotype in the context of the 'ambivalence', which results from the simultaneous identification with and alienation from the colonial Other in the formation of the colonial subject. Bhabha's model of the colonial subject thus extends the psychosexual dynamics in the formation of gendered subjects (specific to the Western bourgeois family) to the arena of colonial race relations.[55] Bhabha's notion of 'ambivalence' as constitutive of the colonial subject has been extremely useful in complicating accounts of the coloniser and colonised in terms of simple binary oppositions; but it does not do justice to the full complexity of the concept of 'effeminacy' in colonial politics.[56] However useful his explanation may be for conceptualising the nature of colonial contradictions – it takes us well beyond generalisations about the gendering of the 'Orient' as female and about the feminisation of the colonised – it does not address adequately the range of historical developments that shaped, and were shaped by, the construct of the 'effeminate *babu*'. A model of the colonial subject based on the supposedly universal gender and sexual dynamics of identity-formation, moreover, offers too limiting a context for the construct of colonial 'effeminacy'; for the construct of the 'effeminate *babu*' was overdetermined by the intersection of a variety of different late nineteenth-century historical developments.[57] My discussion of the Age of Consent Act controversy of 1891, for example, suggests at least one such overdetermined context for the concept of 'effeminacy': the intersection of notions of Bengali effeminacy with contemporary discourses about the regulation of sexual practices and sexual identities in Britain. The British demonstrated the Bengali's lack of 'manly self-control' in arguments about the excessive sexual indulgence of the

INTRODUCTION

Bengali male, represented by the premature consummation of marriage as well as by the overtly sexual atmosphere of the Bengali home that allegedly led to such practices as masturbation. As further indication of the unevenness in the intersection of metropolitan and colonial contexts, moreover, the elaboration of the debilitating sexuality of the Bengali male intersected in complex ways with the elaboration of a distinct homosexual personality in contemporary medical and scientific discourses in Britain. It is interesting, for example, that in the popular colonial imagination homosexual practices were associated with the favoured 'manly' and 'virile' native races rather than with the effeminate Bengali, the object of colonial derision. This apparent paradox, as Lewis D. Wurgaft has pointed out, fascinated many a 'manly' colonial official: colonial officials were intrigued that homosexual practices could exist among 'the most resolute characters'; indeed, among those very Indians who symbolised to them 'the last words in daring and reckless courage'.[58] The colonial focus on effeminacy to distinguish the sexually enervated Bengali male from the sexually virile frontier tribesmen in India exposed the contradictions of a discourse that attempted to link homosexual practices with a distinct homosexual personality defined in terms of effeminacy and lack of manly virility. It is the multiple determinants for the concept of colonial effeminacy that also get elided in prematurely closing off a historical analysis of colonial contradictions.

Furthermore, a historical analysis of the concept of effeminacy in colonial India also demonstrates that Orientalist discourse was neither monolithic nor unidirectional, but much more complex and heterogenous in its construction.[59] Not only did the specifics of the British Orientalist enterprise change over time and differ from the Orientalisms of other European nations, but there were also significant differences in the ways in which different parts of the so-called Orient were constructed in the Orientalist enterprise.[60] The production of 'knowledge' about India in British Orientalist discourse, for example, was grounded in the nature and history of the British colonial enterprise in India. It was the particular history of British colonialism in India that gave rise to dominant British explanations of contemporary Indian society in terms of decline or effeminacy. The pervasiveness of explanations of decline and effeminacy in British accounts of India reflected the popular distinction that several British scholars made between Indian 'barbarity' and so-called African 'savagery'.[61] The 'barbarism' of contemporary Indian society was commonly perceived as the barbarism of early stages of European civilisation. Hence Sir Henry Maine, whose association with India derived both from his tenure as Law Member of the Viceroy's Council and his influential scholarly treatises on early

Indian institutions, suggested that the barbarism of the contemporary social state of India was the barbarism 'of the very family of mankind to which we belong'.[62] The British acceptance of a commonality between ancient Indian and European civilisations drew upon the work of classical philologists who had established that Sanskrit, the ancient Indian language, belonged to a common Indo-European family of languages. In the hands of some nineteenth-century European scholars this linguistic commonality was extended spuriously to suggest a common racial origin of the early Europeans and Indians. The Aryan theory of ancient Indian civilisation, based on misinterpreting the word *'arya'* in ancient Indian Vedic texts in racial terms, provided an incentive for colonial scholars to study the society of ancient India.[63] Although the theory of a common Aryan origin of Europeans and Indians was not universally accepted among scholars and was only occassionally elaborated by colonial officials themselves, it contributed, together with the administrative imperatives of early colonial rule, to the voluminous scholarship on the ancient Indian past produced by colonial scholars and administrators. This scholarship had very little impact on actual race relations in colonial India, but it formed the basis for popular colonial explanations of contemporary Indian society in terms of a fall or decline from the glories of an ancient Aryan past.

The concept of effeminacy embodied these notions about the decline and degeneration of contemporary Indians. Various explanations such as diet, the hot and humid climate of India, the social or economic organisation of Indian society (the insecurity of property relations, the caste system, or Hinduism, for example) were offered as explanations for the stifling of the 'manly independence' of the early Aryans of India.[64] Even with the application of supposedly 'scientific' theories of race to the concept of effeminacy in the second half of the century, the predominant theme remained that of decline and degeneration. Herbert Risley, an amateur British ethnologist and physical anthropologist who did much to popularise pseudo-scientific studies of Indian races in the second half of the century, was another source for theories of the supposed decline or effeminacy of Bengalis. Risley's scientific study of noses found that Bengalis were mainly from a Mongolo-Dravidian racial stock; his further scientific observations also established that Bengalis, more than other Indians, were slenderly built, small-boned, and of low and stunted stature. Yet his major explanations of Bengali effeminacy had more to do with the 'relaxing climate', the 'enfeebling diet', and the premature maternity of women that had resulted in the birth of a weak and stunted race in Bengal.[65] Whether effeminacy was explained in terms of social or economic factors or such supposedly scientific factors as climate, biology, or the non-Aryan or mixed Aryan–Dravidian

INTRODUCTION

descent of the Bengalis, the emphasis was inevitably on decline and degeneracy.

The popularity that notions of decline and effeminacy acquired in colonial society, moreover, was not simply a reflection of British colonial priorities: it intersected in significant ways with the interests of Indian elites themselves. The anomalous political project of the Indian middle class itself contributed to the perpetuation of notions of decline and effeminacy in the characterisation of contemporary Indian society. The self-perception of effeminacy, as Rosselli has pointed out, was recognised by Bengali intellectuals and political leaders to be a peculiarly middle-class phenomenon. They offered various explanations for Bengali effeminacy: the decline of native physical pursuits under the material security provided by British rule; the elites' scorn for indigenous pastimes and obsession with everything English; the excessive concentration on studies leading to 'brain fever' and 'feeble development of muscles'; the Bengali diet of rice; the hot and enervating climate; early parenthood, and so on.[66] In the second half of the century, middle-class Bengalis made several efforts to combat the problem of the emasculation of the Bengali male. Rosselli has demonstrated the various efforts in the second half of the nineteenth century in Bengal to revive the culture of *akharas* or gymnasiums in order to cultivate and instill a sense of pride in the physical prowess of Bengalis.[67] Prominent nineteenth-century Bengali intellectuals were indeed concerned about the consequences of effeminacy. In the 1860s the famous Tagores of Jorasanko and the organisation with which they were most closely associated, the *Adi Brahmo Samaj*, launched a concerted drive for the physical regeneration of Bengalis.[68] Bankimchandra Chatterjee, one of the most famous Bengali writers, oscillated between mocking the modern *babu* and attempting to answer the charge of Bengali effeminacy which he called *Bharat Kalanka* or the *Indian Stigma*.[69] Bengali social and religious reformer, Swami Vivekanand, was similarly a great proponent of cultivating a 'manly' physique; in his most quoted words on the subject he is reported to have remarked: 'You will be nearer to God through football than through the *Bhagwad Gita*.'[70] Sarala Debi, a prominent woman among mostly male nineteenth-century Bengali nationalist leaders, played an important part in the 1890s in arousing Bengali youth to the pursuit of a militant and nationalistic culture. By the turn of the century, Rosselli notes that the physical culture movement in Bengal had become a base for terrorist organisations against the British.[71]

The popularity of notions of decline, embodied in the concept of effeminacy, does indeed illustrate the essentially interactive process in the deployment of the discursive mechanisms of colonial rule. For the

INTRODUCTION

obsessive concern with the emasculation of the Bengalis among the Bengali middle class cannot be attributed solely to the power of British colonial propaganda. Power in colonial India was seldom held unilaterally by the colonisers; the production of colonial knowledge in India was always a two-way process, constructed out of the contestation and collaboration of certain sections of the Indian elite with the British.[72] The appeal of the colonial politics of masculinity and effeminacy, therefore, was equally symptomatic of the efforts of the Indian middle class to establish their own hegemony in colonial society: these efforts were directed both at the native society whose leaders or representatives they wished to become and at British domination of colonial society which denied basic rights of citizenship to all Indians. The dual fronts on which the Indian middle class struggled to establish its hegemony under colonial conditions resulted in a simultaneous identification with the interests of colonial rule as well as resistance to specific racist and exclusivist policies and attitudes of the colonial regime. In this context, the interrelated arguments about the achievements of ancient India, the dubious 'Aryan' origin for Indians and Europeans, and the decline or effeminacy of contemporary Indians served a variety of political purposes: for middle-class Indian nationalists, appalled at the contemporary state of Indian society, the arguments of India's decline from a venerable past afforded a justification for the reform and restructuring of contemporary society to revive the glories of the past as well as for Indian demands for equality with the British; for elite and upper-caste Hindus, moreover, these arguments also buttressed supposedly scientific rationales for hierarchical relations within contemporary Indian society: notably, the caste system which sanctioned the domination of the upper castes, seen as descendants of the original Aryans, over the lower castes, supposed descendants of the indigenous peoples or Dravidians.[73] Historians, most notably Chatterjee, have noted similar contradictions in official Indian nationalist thought, which rejected certain colonialist generalisations about India but, nevertheless, continued to subscribe to many of the basic assumptions of the colonial 'Orientalist' paradigm.[74] No account of the colonial stereotypes of the 'manly Englishman' and the 'effeminate *babu*' can afford to overlook the stakes of the Indian middle class themselves in arguments about the decline and emasculation of contemporary Indians.

The chapters in this book have been organised both chronologically and thematically. Starting from the consolidation of Anglo-Indian public opinion in the Ilbert Bill controversy in 1883 to the recuperation of Indian nationalist politics in the Indian opposition to the Age of Consent Bill in 1891, each of the four chapters examines the implica-

INTRODUCTION

tions of colonial masculinity and effeminacy in a separate colonial controversy. Chapter 1 discusses the intersections of the politics of masculinity with the politics of womanhood in the Ilbert Bill controversy of 1883. The Bill was meant to empower Indian civil servants with criminal jurisdiction over European British subjects in *mofussil* or country stations. The 'white mutiny' against the Bill, however, forced several modifications that dissipated the original intention of the Bill. Chapter 2 is about the intersection of colonial masculinity with the politics of class in the Native Volunteer Movement of 1885. Although the struggle of middle-class Bengalis for the right to bear arms gave rise to the emergence of a new critique of colonial policies as having emasculated the Bengali male, it also exposed the limits of a nationalist politics based on the bid of a propertied class to reclaim their masculinity. The discussion of the Public Service Commission of 1886 in Chapter 3 demonstrates the impact of the policy of 'divide and rule', which fostered discrete linguistic, ethnic, provincial, and 'communal' (religious) representations of native masculinity. The subsequent fragmentation of the native-dominated civil service along provincial lines, as recommended by the Commission, intervened in the claims of certain sections of the native elites to the representational status of 'Indians'. Chapter 4 examines the controversy over the Age of Consent Act of 1891, which aimed at protecting young girls in India from the premature consummation of child marriage. By making visible the politics of colonial masculinity in the controversy over the Indian Consent debate, this chapter qualifies substantially the role of the Indian opposition to the Bill in revitalising nationalist politics.

I would like to clarify my use of certain terms in the proceeding chapters. For the sake of convenience, I have retained certain nineteenth-century usages of terms designating the British and the Indians in colonial India. I use the term 'Anglo-Indian' to refer to British officials and non-officials in India. Although by the 1920s and 1930s the term came to designate the offsprings of mixed European and Asian or Eurasian descent, throughout the nineteenth century it was used more generally for any Briton who came out to India for an extended period of time, either in an official or a non-official capacity. The domiciled European population in India was also included in this category; but, by the late nineteenth century, those among the domiciled European population who were of Eurasian descent were more often excluded from the category 'Anglo-Indian'. I have also retained the nineteenth-century term 'native' in speaking of the inhabitants of India. The term 'native', of course, had a more explicitly contested meaning even in nineteenth-century colonial society. The British emphasised what they considered to be irreconcilable differences of caste, religion, and community among

INTRODUCTION

the inhabitants of India. Consequently, they were loath to consider any one of the native groups as representative 'Indians'. Indeed, the term 'Indian', as in Indian civilian or Indian army officer, was commonly used to refer to the Anglo-Indians serving in India. By mid-century, however, various native groups had begun to resent the term 'native' and preferred to call themselves 'Indians'. I have used the two terms interchangeably, preferring at times one over the other, for purposes of clarity as well as for retaining the sense in which 'Indian' – and even 'India' – were historical constructs. I thus retain the term 'native', despite its connotations, in the spirit of the following editorial comment on the use of the term in the *Amrita Bazar Patrika*: 'it does not matter what they call us so long as we can compel them to respect us'.[75]

It is also necessary for me to clarify the geographical entity symbolised by 'Bengal'; for in the nineteenth century Bengal could refer to three quite different entities. On one level was the Bengal Presidency, which included almost all of northern India from the mouth of the Brahmaputra to the borders of Afghanistan. This region was garrisoned by the Bengal Army and administered by members of the Bengal Civil Service.[76] For much of the nineteenth century, however, this meaning had become obsolete; it was used more for administrative convenience rather than to refer to a specific geographical entity. I use the term 'Bengal' to refer broadly to the actual administrative division that came under the Lt.-Governor of Bengal, but more specifically to only one of the four regions in this division, known as Bengal Proper or Lower Bengal. The administrative division under the control of the Lt.-Governor of Bengal in the nineteenth century comprised the following regions: Bihar; Orissa; Chota Nagpur; and Bengal Proper, the largest and most important region which included the nineteenth-century capital of British India, Calcutta. The region of Bengal Proper was unified by the use of the 'Bengali' language; yet the consolidation and standardisation of a separate social and cultural identity around a common 'Bengali' language itself occurred in the course of the nineteenth century and remained an essentially uneven process. For the consolidation of a 'chaste' Bengali in the nineteenth century, as many scholars have pointed out, had the effect of setting the Bengali elites apart from the more 'vulgar' language used by women and the common people of Bengal.[77] In using the term 'Bengal', I am referring in particular to the administrative and cultural unit that was being defined through the Bengali language. There is even greater ambiguity surrounding the term 'Hindu'. For, as Romila Thapar has demonstrated, 'Hinduism' as the unified name for different ancient Indian religions and the 'Hindu' as a recently consolidated religious identity bore even more directly the traces of the colonial impact.[78] It is to this identity, as consolidated

[24]

INTRODUCTION

under the aegis of colonialism, that I refer in speaking of 'Hindus' in the late nineteenth century.

Notes

1. Ann Stoler's work has been the most influential in directing attention to the historical construction of the categories of coloniser and colonised. See her 'Rethinking Colonial Categories: European Communities and the Boundaries of Rule', *Comparative Studies in Society and History*, 31:1 (Jan. 1989), 134–201; and 'Making Empire Respectable: The Politics of Race and Sexuality in 20th-Century Colonial Cultures', *American Ethnologist*, 16:4 (Nov. 1989), 634–60.
2. I owe this point to the discussion in Chandra Mohanty, 'Cartographies of Struggle', in C. Mohanty, A. Russo, and L. Torres (eds.), *Third World Women and the Politics of Feminism* (Bloomington: Indiana University Press, 1991), pp. 14–15.
3. A similar argument for the 'coincidences and contradictions' in the consolidation of British middle classes and Indian middle classes in the first half of the nineteenth century has been made by Kumkum Sangari. See Kumkum Sangari, 'Relating Histories: Definitions of Literacy, Literature, Gender in Early Nineteenth-Century Calcutta and England', in Svati Joshi (ed.), *Rethinking English: Essays in Literature, Language, History* (New Delhi: Trianka, 1991), pp. 32–123.
4. Rosemary Hennessy, *Materialist Feminism and the Politics of Discourse* (London: Routledge, 1993).
5. *The Times* (London), 1 Jan. 1888, quoted in *English Opinion on India: A Monthly Magazine Containing Select Extracts From English Newspapers on Indian Subjects* (Poona), vol. 1 (Feb. 1888), p. 22.
6. For a discussion of the economic critique of colonialism by early Indian nationalists, see Bipan Chandra, *The Rise and Growth of Economic Nationalism in India: Economic Policies of Indian National Leadership 1880–1905* (New Delhi: People's Publishing House, 1966). The controversy over the 'drain' theory is discussed in J. R. McLane, 'The Drain of Wealth and Indian Nationalism at the Turn of the Century', in T. Raychaudhuri (ed.) *Contributions to Indian Economic History*, vol. 2 (Calcutta, 1963). Also see Sunanda Sen, *Colonies and the Empire, India 1890–1914* (Calcutta: Orient Longman, 1992). For a debate on the 'de-industrialisation' of India under colonial rule, see M. D. Morris *et al.*, *Indian Economy in the Nineteenth Century: A Symposium* (Delhi: IESH Association, 1969). See also a review of current scholarship on the political economy of British India, Irfan Habib, 'Studying a Colonial Economy – Without Perceiving Colonialism', *Modern Asian Studies*, 19:3 (1985), 355–81. For a general discussion of the contribution of colonial domination to the development of Western capitalism, see Shreeram Krishnaswami, 'Colonial Foundations of Western Capitalism', *Economic and Political Weekly*, 27:30 (25 July 1992), PE81-PE89.
7. This summary is from Sumit Sarkar, *Modern India 1885–1947* (New Delhi: Macmillan India Ltd, 1983), ch. 2; Rajat Kanta Ray, *Social Conflict and Political Unrest in Bengal 1875–1927* (Delhi: Oxford University Press, 1984), pp. 11–21; and John R. McLane, *Indian Nationalism and the Early Congress* (Princeton: Princeton University Press, 1977), pp. 21–4. For a general account of India's role in Britain's rise as an industrial power, see Eric Hobsbawm, *Industry and Empire, The Making of Modern English Society, Volume 2, 1750 to the Present Day* (New York: Pantheon Books, 1968); for the growing importance of India to the British economy in the late nineteenth century, see S. B. Saul, *Studies in British Overseas Trade 1870–1914* (Liverpool: Liverpool University Press, 1960), ch. 8.
8. Francis G. Hutchins, *The Illusion of Permanence: British Imperialism in India* (Princeton: Princeton University Press, 1967).
9. I have drawn from Romila Thapar's perceptive analysis of the continuities and changes in the interpretation of early India in the colonial historical traditions of both Orientalists and Anglicists. See Romila Thapar, *Interpreting Early India* (Delhi: Oxford University Press, 1992), esp. ch. 1. For a discussion of the Orientalist tradition

INTRODUCTION

in late eighteenth- and early nineteenth-century India, see David Kopf, *British Orientalism and the Bengal Renaissance: The Dynamics of Indian Modernization, 1773–1835* (Berkeley: University of California Press, 1969). Also see B. Cohn, 'The Command of Language and the Language of Command', in R. Guha (ed.), *Subaltern Studies 4: Writings on South Asian History and Society* (Delhi: Oxford University Press, 1985), pp. 276–329; and Jenny Sharpe, 'The Violence of Light in the Land of Desire; or, How William Jones Discovered India', *boundary 2*, 20:1 (1993), 26–46.

10 For a discussion of the change in British policy after 1857, see Thomas Metcalf, *The Aftermath of Revolt, India 1857–1870* (Princeton: Princeton University Press, 1964).

11 For the problem of the 'educated Indians' in the late nineteenth century, see Briton Martin Jr, *New India, 1885* (Berkeley: University of California Press, 1969); and S. Gopal, *British Policy in India 1858–1905* (Madras: Orient Longman, 1975).

12 For the codification of indigenous laws under the British, see J. D. M. Derrett, 'The Administration of Hindu Law by the British', *Comparative Studies in Society and History*, 4 (1961), 10–52; and *Religion, Law and the State in India* (London: Faber & Faber, 1968). Also see Rosanne Rocher, 'British Orientalism in the Eighteenth Century: The Dialectics of Knowledge and Government', in C. A. Breckenridge and P. van der Veer (eds.), *Orientalism and the Postcolonial Predicament: Perspectives on South Asia* (Philadelphia: University of Pennsylvania Press, 1993), pp. 215–59. As Lata Mani has argued, the reliance on sacred Indian texts in the codification of indigenous laws produced a 'textualised' view of Indian traditions. See Lata Mani, 'Contentious Traditions: The Debate on *Sati* in Colonial India', in Kumkum Sangari and Sudesh Vaid (eds.), *Recasting Women: Essays in Indian Colonial History* (New Brunswick: Rutgers University Press, 1989), pp. 88–126.

13 British rule was new and alien not because the British came from outside the Indian sub-continent, but because, unlike any previous rule in India, British rule had to serve interests that were external to the sub-continent. Revisionist historical work, however, has tended to emphasise a greater continuity between pre-colonial and early colonial India. For a criticism of this revisionist approach, see P. Chatterjee, *The Nation and its Fragments: Colonial and Postcolonial Histories* (Princeton: Princeton University Press, 1993), pp. 27–34.

14 Lord Macaulay was the author of the famous Minute on Education of 2 February 1835; for key passages of Macaulay's Minute, see W. M. Theodore de Barry (ed.), *Sources of Indian Tradition* (New York: Columbia University Press, 1966) vol. 2, p. 49; and G. M. Young (ed.), *Macaulay: Prose and Poetry* (London: Hart-Davis, 1952), p. 722. For a discussion of the role of English education in India, see Gauri Viswanathan, *Masks of Conquest: Literary Study and British Rule in India* (New York: Columbia University Press, 1989); also Krishna Kumar, *Political Agenda of Education: A Study of Colonialist and Nationalist Ideals* (New Delhi: Sage, 1991).

15 The concept of 'discourse' is from Michel Foucault. Foucault defines 'discourse' not just as 'things said', but as 'practice'. Hence, according to him, the crucial emphasis is on the fact that 'something is formed' in language. See *The Archaeology of Knowledge*, trans. Alan Sheridan (New York: Pantheon Books, 1972), pp. 44–55; also 'Politics and the Study of Discourse', *Ideology and Consciousness*, 3 (1978), 7–26. I owe my understanding to Hennessy, *Materialist Feminism*, ch. 2.

16 See Tanika Sarkar, 'The Hindu Wife and the Hindu Nation: Domesticity and Nationalism in Nineteenth-Century Bengal', *Studies in History*, 8:2 (1992), 213–35.

17 For Bengali entrepreneurship in the first half of the nineteenth century, see Blair B. Kling, 'Entrepreneurship and Regional Identity in Bengal', in David Kopf (ed.), *Bengal Regional Identity* (East Lansing: Michigan State University Press, 1969), pp. 75–84; and his 'Economic Foundations of the Bengal Renaissance', in Rachel Van M. Baumer (ed.), *Aspects of Bengali History and Society* (Hawaii: University of Hawaii Press, 1975), pp. 26–42. For the late nineteenth-century decline, see R. K. Ray, *Social Conflict and Political Protest*; and *Urban Roots of Indian Nationalism: Pressure Groups and Conflict of Interest in Calcutta City Politics, 1875–1939* (New Delhi: Vikas Publishing House, 1979).

18 For the Permanent Settlement, see Ranajit Guha, *A Rule of Property for Bengal* (Paris:

INTRODUCTION

Mouton, 1963). Also see P. J. Marshall, *Bengal: The British Bridgehead, Eastern India 1740–1828* (Cambridge: Cambridge University Press, 1987), pp. 93–136.

19 See T. Sarkar, 'The Hindu Wife and the Hindu Nation', pp. 222–3. For peasant and tribal unrest in the second half of the nineteenth century in India, see Ranajit Guha, *Elementary Aspects of Peasant Insurgency* (New Delhi: Oxford University Press, 1983).

20 For the Bengali middle-class's despair at *chakri*, see Sumit Sarkar, ' "Kaliyuga", "Chakri" and "Bhakti": Ramakrishna and His Times', *Economic and Political Weekly*, 27:29 (18 July 1992), 1543–66.

21 See Ray, *Social Conflict and Political Unrest*, pp. 13–15.

22 *Ibid.*, p. 84.

23 For a review of the historiographical debate on the category of the Western-educated middle class, see Michelguglielmo Torri, '"Westernized Middle Class", Intellectuals and Society in Late Colonial India', *Economic and Political Weekly*, 25:4 (27 Jan. 1990), PE 2–11. For some arguments in defence of the Western-educated Indians as a new class in the late nineteenth century, see R. Ray, 'Three Interpretations of Indian Nationalism', in B. R. Nanda (ed.), *Essays in Modern Indian History* (Delhi: Oxford University Press, 1980), pp. 1–39.

24 For changes within *bhadralok* society, see S. N. Mukherjee, '*Daladali* in Calcutta in the Nineteenth Century', *Modern Asian Studies*, 9 (1975), 59–80, and '*Bhadralok* in Bengali Language and Literature: An Essay on the Language of Class and Status', *Bengal Past and Present* (July-Dec. 1976), 225–37. Also John McGuire, *The Making of a Colonial Mind: A Quantitative Study of the Bhadralok in Calcutta 1857–1885* (Canberra: Australian National University, 1983). For an account of the development of specifically middle-class political organisations, see Sudhir Chandra, 'The Indian League and the Western Indian Association', *Indian Economic and Social History Review*, 8:2 (June 1971), 73–98; and C. Furedy, ' "New Men" Political Club in Calcutta in the 1870s and 1880s: A Colonial Mix of Self Interest and Ideology', *Indian Journal of Politics*, 13 (Ap./Aug. 1979), 63–73.

25 See Partha Chatterjee, 'A Religion of Urban Domesticity: Sri Ramakrishna and the Calcutta Middle Class', in P. Chatterjee and G. Pandey (eds.), *Subaltern Studies 7, Writings on South Asian History and Society* (Delhi: Oxford University Press, 1993), p. 42. Scholars associated with the 'Subaltern Studies' project on South Asian history find Antonio Gramsci's concept of the 'subaltern' useful to characterise the relation between elites and non-elites in the political and economic conditions of the Indian sub-continent. However, the term, as used by the scholars of the 'Subaltern Studies' collective, does not refer to any one homogenous social group. Rather, it represents a category of difference which signifies opposition to the elites or ruling classes. See Ranajit Guha, 'On Some Aspects of the Historiography of Colonial India', in R. Guha (ed.), *Subaltern Studies 1: Writings on South Asian History and Society* (Delhi: Oxford University Press, 1982), pp. 1–8.

26 See T. Sarkar, 'The Hindu Wife and the Hindu Nation', pp. 219–20.

27 Ashis Nandy, *The Intimate Enemy: Loss and Recovery of Self Under Colonialism* (Delhi: Oxford University Press, 1983).

28 For a discussion of the ways in which caste was transformed under colonial rule, see Nicholas Dirks, 'Castes of Mind', *Representations*, 37 (Winter 1992), 56–78; also A. Appadurai, 'Putting Hierarchy in its Place', *Current Anthropology*, 3:1 (Feb. 1988), 36–49; Rashmi Pant, 'The Cognitive Status of Caste in Colonial Ethnography', *Indian Economic and Social History Review*, 24 (1987), 145–62. For a materialist analysis of the caste system, also see Irfan Habib, *Interpreting Indian History*, Zakir Hussain Memorial Lecture Series (Shillong: North-Eastern Hill University Publications, 1985), pp. 15–21. For the invention of 'martial' and 'non-martial' races and its usefulness for British recruitment policies in the army, see David Omissi, '"Martial Race": Ethnicity and Security in Colonial India, 1858–1939', *War and Society*, 9:1 (1991), 1–27. For the preference of 'martial' races in colonial employment more generally, see also David Arnold, 'Bureaucratic Recruitment and Subordination in Colonial India: The Madras Constabulary, 1859–1947', in R. Guha (ed.), *Subaltern Studies 4: Writing on South*

INTRODUCTION

Asian History and Society (Delhi: Oxford University Press, 1985), pp. 1–53.

29 George Mosse, *Nationalism and Sexuality: Respectability and Abnormal Sexuality in Modern Europe* (New York: H. Fertig, 1985); Catherine Hall and Leonore Davidoff, *Family Fortunes: Men and Women of the English Middle Class, 1780–1850* (Chicago: University of Chicago Press, 1987); Keith McClelland, 'Masculinity and the "Representative" Artisan in Britain, 1850–80', in M. Roper and J. Tosh (eds.), *Manful Assertions: Masculinities in Britain Since 1800* (London: Routledge, 1991), pp. 44–73; Jeffrey Weeks, *Sex, Politics, and Society: The Regulation of Sexuality Since 1800* (New York: Longman, 1981); and Brian Harrison, *Separate Spheres: The Opposition to Women's Suffrage in Britain* (London: Croom Helm, 1978). The above in no way pretends to be an exhaustive list of books that examine the nineteenth-century politics of British masculinity from a broader historical perspective.

30 See Norman Vance, 'The Ideal of Manliness', in B. Simon and I. Bradley (eds.), *The Victorian Public School: Studies in the Development of an Educational Institution* (Dublin: Gill & Macmillan, 1975), pp. 115–28. See also David Newsome, *Godliness and Goodlearning: Four Studies on a Victorian Ideal* (London: John Murray, 1961); Norman Vance, *The Sinews of the Spirit: The Ideal of Christian Manliness in Victorian Literature and Religious Thought* (Cambridge: Cambridge University Press, 1985); J. A. Mangan, *Athleticism in the Victorian and Edwardian Public Schools* (Cambridge: Cambridge University Press, 1981); J. R. de S. Honey, *Tom Brown's Universe: The Development of the English Public School in the Late Nineteenth Century* (New York: Quadrangle/New York Times Book Co., 1977); and Malcolm Tozer, 'Manliness: The Evolution of a Victorian Ideal' (unpublished Ph.D. dissertation, University of Leicester, 1978). For imperial manliness in other domains, as in the Boy-Scout movement, see Michael Rosenthal, *The Character Factory: Baden-Powell and the Origins of the Boy Scout Movement* (New York: Pantheon Books, 1984); in the world of popular journalism, see H. John Field, *Toward a Programme of Imperial Life: The British Empire at the Turn of the Century*, (New Haven, CT: Greenwood Press, 1982).

31 John MacKenzie, *Propaganda and Empire: The Manipulation of British Public Opinion 1880–1960* (Manchester: Manchester University Press, 1984), p. 2.

32 For some examples of recent scholarship on masculinity, see M. Roper and J. Tosh (eds.), *Manful Assertions*; J. A. Mangan and J. Walvin (eds.), *Manliness and Morality: Middle-Class Masculinity in Britain and America, 1800–1940* (Manchester: Manchester University Press, 1987); Lynne Segal, *Slow Motion: Changing Masculinities, Changing Men* (London: Virago, 1990); Peter N. Stearns, *Be a Man! Males in Modern Society* (New York: Holmes & Meier, 1979); R. W. Connell, *Gender and Power* (Cambridge: Polity, 1987); R. Chapman and J. Rutherfords (eds.), *Male Order: Unwrapping Masculinity* (London: Lawrence & Wishart, 1988); A. Easthope, *What a Man's Gotta Do* (London: Paladin, 1986); David Jackson, *Unmasking Masculinity* (London: Unwin Hyman, 1990); M. Kaufman (ed.), *Beyond Patriarchy: Essays by Men on Pleasure, Power and Change* (Toronto: Oxford University Press, 1987); M. Kimmel (ed.), *Changing Men: New Directions in Research in Men and Masculinity* (London: Sage, 1987); Victor J. Seidler, *Rediscovering Masculinity: Reason, Language and Sexuality* (London: Routledge, 1989); and Paul Hoch, *White Hero, Black Beast: Racism, Sexism and the Mask of Masculinity* (London: Pluto Press, 1979).

33 Gauri Viswanathan, 'Raymond Williams and British Colonialism', *Yale Journal of Criticism*, 4:2 (Spring 1991), 47–66.

34 Catherine Hall, 'The Economy of Intellectual Prestige: Thomas Carlyle, J. S. Mill and the Case of Governor Eyre', *Cultural Critique*, 12 (Spring 1989), 167–96. Unfortunately, Graham Dawson's *Soldier Heroes: British Adventure, Empire and the Imaging of Masculinity* (London: Routledge, 1994) appeared too late for consideration here.

35 The concept of overdetermination is from Louis Althusser. Althusser uses the concept to suggest that reality is irreducibly complex and subject to multiple causation or is overdetermined; any 'contradiction' therefore, is shaped by, and shapes, different *levels* and *instances* of the social formation. See L. Althusser, *For Marx*, trans. Ben

INTRODUCTION

Brewster (New York: Vintage Books, 1970), Part Three: 'Contradiction and Overdetermination', pp. 87–127.

36 See Joan Scott, 'Gender: A Useful Category of Historical Analysis', *American Historical Review*, 91 (Dec. 1986), pp. 1053–75.
37 See 'Recasting Women: An Introduction', in Sangari and Vaid (eds.), *Recasting Women*, p. 1–27.
38 Edward Said, *Orientalism* (New York: Vintage Books, 1978).
39 See Joseph Schumpeter, *Imperialism and Social Classes*, trans. Heinz Norden, ed. Paul Sweezey (New York: Augustus M. Kelley, Inc., 1951). For a re-examination of the Lenin versus Schumpeter debate on imperialism, see Eric Stokes, 'Late Nineteenth-Century Colonial Expansion and the Attack on the Theory of Economic Imperialism: A Case of Mistaken Identity', *Historical Journal*, 13:2 (1969), 205–301. For a historical survey of the different stages of a modern world system shaped by imperialism, see L. S. Stavrianos, *Global Rift: The Third World Comes of Age* (New York: William Morrow, 1981).
40 I owe this point to Aijaz Ahmad's critical reading of Said. See '*Orientalism* and After: Ambivalence and Metropolitan Location in the Work of Edward Said', in Ahmad, *In Theory: Classes, Nations, Literatures* (London: Verso, 1992), pp. 159–220.
41 See Ahmad, *In Theory*, pp. 159–220. For an earlier reminder of the need to historicise further Said's Orientalism thesis, see Lata Mani and Ruth Frankenburg, 'The Challenge of Orientalism', *Economy and Society*, 14:2 (1985), 174–93.
42 See Martin Bernal, *Black Athena: The Afroasiatic Roots of Classical Civilization*, vol. 1 (New Brunswick: Rutgers University Press, 1987). See discussion of Bernal in Ahmad, *In Theory*, p. 183; and in Said, *Culture and Imperialism* (New York: Alfred A. Knopf, 1993), pp. 15–19. For the implications of Bernal's insight for critiques of Orientalist writings on India, also see Clement Hawes, 'Leading History By the Nose: The Turn to the Eighteenth Century in *Midnight's Children*', *Modern Fiction Studies*, 39:1 (Spring 1993), 147–68.
43 Richard Orme, *A History of the Military Transactions of the British Nation in Indostan, from year 1745, to which is prefixed a dissertation on the establishment made by Mahomedan conquerors in Hindustan*, vol. 2 (Madras: Pharoah & Co., [1763] 1861), p. 5, cited in John Rosselli, 'The Self-Image of Effeteness: Physical Education and Nationalism in Nineteenth-Century Bengal', *Past and Present*, 86 (Feb. 1980), p. 123. See also Percival Spear, *The Nabobs* (London: Oxford University Press, 1963), pp. 198–9.
44 Bishop Heber, quoted in Ketaki Kushari Dyson, *A Various Universe: A Study of the Journals and Memoirs of the British Men and Women in the Indian Sub-Continent, 1765–1856* (Delhi: Oxford University Press, 1978), p. 49. James Mill, *The History of India*, vol. 2 (London: James Madden & Co., 1858), p. 149. See also A. R. H. Copley, 'Projection, Displacement and Distortion in Nineteenth Century Moral Imperialism – A Re-Examination of Charles Grant and James Mill', *The Calcutta Historical Journal*, 7:2 (Jan.-June 1983), 1–27.
45 Quoted in Sir John Strachey, *India, Its Administration and Progress* (London: Macmillan & Co., (1888) 1911), pp. 449–50.
46 T. B. Macaulay, 'Warren Hastings', quoted in Strachey, *India*, p. 450.
47 There were, however, Bengali Muslim leaders who were equally concerned about the effeminacy of the Muslims in Bengal. See Abdus Salam, *Physical Education in India* (Calcutta: W. Newman & Co., 1895) cited in Joseph S. Alter, 'Celibacy, Sexuality, and the Transformation of Gender into Nationalism in Northern India', *Journal of Asian Studies*, 53:1 (Feb. 1994), 45–66. For a study of the Muslims in Bengal, see Rafiuddin Ahmad, *The Bengal Muslims, 1871–1906: A Quest for Identity* (Delhi: Oxford University Press, 1981).
48 Charles Tyre, *Side Khals* (Calcutta: Newman & Co., 1900), p. 25.
49 *Amrita Bazar Patrika* (Calcutta), 27 Mar. 1887, p. 3.
50 *Bengalee* (Calcutta), 10 Oct. 1891, p. 485.
51 See Mukherjee, '*Bhadralok* in Bengali Language and Literature', pp. 233–5.
52 Christine Baxter, 'The Genesis of the Babu: Bhabanicharan Bannerji and *Kalikata*

INTRODUCTION

Kamalalay', in Peter Robb and David Taylor (eds.), *Rule, Protest, Identity, Aspects of Modern South Asia* (London: Curzon Press, 1978), pp. 193–206.

53 Quoted in Sir D. E. Wacha, *Shells from the Sands of Bombay: Being My Recollections and Reminiscences 1860–1875* (Bombay: Bombay Chronicle Press, 1920), pp. 350–2. A satire, 'The Bengalee Baboo or One Way to a Fortune', with a very similar theme, was performed by the 60th Regiment Bengal Infantry in Simla in the 1870s. See Col. Thomas Nicholas Walker, *Through the Mutiny: Reminiscences of Thirty Years' Active Service and Sport in India, 1854–83* (London: Gibbergs & Co., 1907), pp. 45–6. The '*babu*' satires performed by Anglo-Indians, especially during and after the Ilbert Bill controversy, had already acquired a very different emphasis.

54 Henry Yule and A. C. Burnell, *Hobson-Jobson*, (ed.) William Crooke (Delhi: Munshiram Manoharlal, (1903) new edn. 1968), pp. 44–45.

55 See Homi Bhabha, 'Of Mimicry and Man: The Ambivalence of Colonial Discourse', *October*, 28 (Spring 1984), 125–33; 'The Other Question – The Stereotype and Colonial Discourse', *Screen*, 24:6 (Nov./Dec. 1983), 18–36; 'Sly Civility', *October*, 34 (Fall 1985), 71–80. I have benefited from the discussion of Bhabha's theory of alterity in Rosemary Hennessy and Rajeswari Mohan, 'The Construction of Woman in Three Popular Texts of Empire: Toward a Critique of Materialist Feminism', *Textual Practice*, 3:3 (Winter 1989), 323–59.

56 Nandy also makes the important point that colonial culture revolved not so much around the opposition between masculinity and femininity, but, rather, that between masculinity and effeminacy. See Nandy, *Intimate Enemy*, p. 8. Sara Suleri's efforts to complicate similarly the binary opposition of coloniser and colonised by the concepts of 'homosociality' and 'homoeroticism' have some of the same strengths and weaknesses of Bhabha's notion of 'ambivalence'; see Suleri, *The Rhetoric of English India* (Chicago: University of Chicago Press, 1992).

57 I owe this point to Hennessy and Mohan, 'The Construction of Woman', p. 328. For a criticism of Bhabha's use of sexual difference as an analogy for racial difference, see also Christine Anne Holmlund, 'Displacing Limits of Difference: Gender, Race, and Colonialism in Edward Said and Homi Bhabha's Theoretical Models and Marguerite Duras's Experimental Films', *Quarterly Review of Film and Video*, 13:1–3 (1991), 1–22.

58 Quoted in Lewis D. Wurgaft, *The Imperial Imagination: Magic and Myth in Kipling's India* (Connecticut: Wesleyan University Press, 1983), p. 50. See also George Mac Munn, *The Underworld of India* (London: Jarrolds, 1933), p. 201. The intrepid Sir Richard Burton in his famous essay on 'Pedarasty' included the Punjab, Sind, and Kashmir in what he called the 'Sotadic Zones' of the world, cited in Fawn M. Brodie, *The Devil Drives: A Life of Sir Richard Burton* (New York: W. W. Norton & Co., 1967), pp. 305–6. For a study of sexuality simply in terms of the 'sexual opportunities' available to the white male, see Richard Hyam, *Sexuality and Empire: The British Experience* (Manchester: Manchester University Press, 1990); also see the criticism of Hyam in Mark T. Berger, 'Imperialism and Sexual Exploitation', *Journal of Imperial and Commonwealth History*, 17:1 (1988), 83–9.

59 This point has been made in Kumkum Sangari, 'Introduction: Representation in History', *Journal of Arts and Ideas*, 17 and 18 (June 1989), 3–7.

60 For some comparisons of British and French Orientalisms, see Lisa Lowe, *Critical Terrains: French and British Orientalisms* (Ithaca: Cornell University Press, 1991). For a modification of Said's Orientalism thesis as it applies to British discourses on India, see B. J. Moore-Gilbert, *Kipling and 'Orientalism'* (London: Croom Helm, 1986); Javed Majeed, *Ungoverned Imaginings: James Mill's The History of British India and Orientalism* (Oxford: Clarendon Press, 1992); Breckenridge and van der Veer (eds.), *Orientalism and the Postcolonial Predicament*; and Richard G. Fox, 'East of Said', in Michael Sprinker (ed.), *Edward Said: A Critical Reader* (Cambridge: Blackwell, 1992), pp. 144–56. For the construction of British knowledge of Indian society, see Bernard Cohn, *An Anthropologist Among Historians and Other Essays* (Delhi: Oxford University Press, 1987); and his 'The Command of Language and the Language of Command'.

INTRODUCTION

61 I owe this point to Joan Leopold, 'British Applications of the Aryan Race Theory of Race to India, 1850–1870', *English Historical Review*, 89:352 (1974), 578–603.

62 Quoted in Joan Leopold, 'British Applications of the Aryan Race Theory', p. 586. For a discussion of Henry Maine's works, see George Feaver, *From Status to Contract: A Biography of Sir Henry Maine, 1822–1888* (London: Longman, 1969). For the impact of the theory of the 'Aryan' origins of Indians, see Nilakantha Majumdar, *Are We Aryans?* (Calcutta: 1886), in *India Office Tracts*, vol. 666, India Office Library and Records, London. James Crawfurd, President of the London Ethnological Society, was one of the main critics of the common Aryan race theory; cited in Nemai Sadhan Bose, *Racism, Struggle for Equality and Indian Nationalism* (Calcutta: Firma KLM Pvt. Ltd, 1981), p. 227.

63 For a discussion of the intellectual origins of the 'Aryan Race Theory' in the works of British Indologists, see Romila Thapar, 'Ideology and the Interpretation of Early Indian History', in *Interpreting Early India*, pp. 1–23. Also Leopold, 'British Applications of the Aryan Theory of Race'; and Partha Mitter, 'The Aryan Myth and British Writings on Indian Art and Culture', in B. Moore-Gilbert (ed.), *Literature and Imperialism* (Roehampton: Roehampton Institute of Higher Education, 1983), pp. 69–92.

64 See Mill quoted in Hutchins, *Illusion of Permanence*, pp. 64–6; also Monier Williams, *Modern India and the Indians: Being a Series of Impressions, Notes and Essays* (London: Trubner & Co., 1878), pp. 233–5.

65 See Sir Herbert Risley, *The People of India* (Calcutta: Thacker, Spink & Co., 1908), pp. 39, 55. I owe this reference to Rosselli, 'The Self-Image of Effeteness', p. 134.

66 See Rosselli, 'The Self-Image of Effeteness', pp. 121–48.

67 *Ibid.* For a discussion of the 'male body' and Indian nationalism in the early twentieth century, see Alter, 'Celibacy, Sexuality, and the Transformation of Gender.

68 See *Bengalis as They Are and as They Ought to Be*, A Discourse Read at the Young Men's Literary Association by U.N.T. (Calcutta: Presidency College, 1854), *India Office Tracts*, vol. 866, India Office Library and Records, London. Also Rosselli, 'The Self-Image of Effeteness', pp. 127–8.

69 Cited in K. M. Purkayastha (ed.), *Short Selections from Bankimchandra* (Calcutta: Sirbhumi Pub. Co., 1935). Also see the discussion of Bankimchandra in Rachel R. Van Meter, 'Bankim Chandra's View of the Role of Bengal in Indian Civilization', in D. Kopf (ed.), *Bengal Regional Identity*, pp. 61–72; and Partha Chatterjee, *Nationalist Thought and the Colonial World: A Derivative Discourse?* (London: Zed, 1986), ch. 3.

70 Swami Nikhilananda, *Vivekananda: A Biography* (New York: Ramakrishna Center, 1953), p. 167, quoted in Barbara Southard, 'Neo-Hinduism and Militant Politics in Bengal 1875–1910' (unpublished Ph.D dissertation, University of Hawaii, 1971), p. 279. For a discussion of football in early twentieth-century Bengal, see Tony Mason, 'Football on the Maidan: Cultural Imperialism in Calcutta', *International Journal of the History of Sport*, 7:1 (1990), 85–96; and Brian Stoddart, 'Sport, Cultural Imperialism and Colonial Response in the British Empire', *Comparative Studies in Society and History*, 30:4 (Oct. 1988), 649–73.

71 See Sarala Debi, *Jibaner Jharapata* ('Scattered Leaves of Life') cited in Rosselli, 'The Self-Image of Effeteness', pp. 123 and 136–8.

72 This point has been argued in Lata Mani's analysis of the construction of colonial knowledge on *sati*. See her 'Contentious Traditions'; and 'Production of an Official Discourse on *Sati* in Early Nineteenth-Century Bengal', *Economic and Political Weekly*, 21:17 (26 Apr. 1986), WS 32–40.

73 For Indian appropriations of the Aryan race theory, see Joan Leopold, 'The Aryan Theory of Race in India 1870–1920: Nationalist and Internationalist Visions', *The Indian Economic and Social History Review*, 7 (1970), 271–97; also Sucheta Mazumdar, 'Racist Responses to Racism: The Aryan Myth and South Asians in the U.S.', *South Asia Bulletin*, 9:1 (1989), 47–55; and V. Kaiwar, 'Racism and the Writing Of History, Part 1', *South Asia Bulletin*, 9: 2 (1989), 32–56.

74 The point has been made most effectively in Chatterjee, *Nationalist Thought and the Colonial World*.

75 *Amrita Bazar Patrika*, 5 Sept. 1889, pp. 5–6.

INTRODUCTION

76 See George Chesney, *Indian Polity: A View of the System of Administration in India* (London: Longmans, Green & Co., 1868), p. 60.
77 For the consolidation of a chaste Bengali in the nineteenth century, see Sumanta Banerjee, 'Bogey of the Bawdy – The Changing Concept of "Obscenity" in Nineteenth – Century Bengali Culture', *Economic and Political Weekly*, 22:29 (18 July 1987), 1197–1206; also 'Marginalization of Women's Popular Culture in Nineteenth-Century Bengal', in Sangari and Vaid (eds.), *Recasting Women*, pp. 127–79.
78 Romila Thapar, 'Imagined Religious Communities? Ancient History and the Modern Search for a Hindu Identity', *Modern Asian Studies*, 23 (1989), 209–32. Also see John Stratton Hawley, 'Naming Hinduism', *Wilson Quarterly*, 15:3 (Summer 1991), 20–34.

CHAPTER ONE

Reconfiguring hierarchies: the Ilbert Bill controversy, 1883–84

On 9 February 1883, the Law Member of the Government of India, C. P. Ilbert, introduced a bill in the Legislative Council to amend the Code of Criminal Procedure of the Indian Penal Code. The Bill, popularly called the Ilbert Bill, proposed to give various classes of native officials in the colonial administrative service limited criminal jurisdiction over European British subjects living in the *mofussil*, or country towns in India.[1] The Ilbert Bill, which was widely interpreted as a challenge to the control European capitalists exercised over sources of raw material and labour in the interiors of India, provoked a 'white mutiny' from Anglo-Indian officials and non-officials alike.[2] The opposition secured a victory when the Viceroy Lord Ripon was forced into an agreement or 'concordat' to get a modified bill passed on 25 January 1884, which undermined the original principle of the Ilbert Bill. Although the new Act accorded native magistrates criminal jurisdiction over European British subjects in the *mofussils*, the special legal status of European British subjects was preserved. The European British subjects in the *mofussils* won the right to demand trial by a jury of whom at least half were European British subjects or Americans.

As a crucial moment in the consolidation of a unified Anglo-Indian public opinion in India, the Ilbert Bill controversy has received its share of attention from scholars. Yet while scholars have examined the impact of the Ilbert Bill controversy on the racial polarisation between Anglo-Indians and Indians and on the development of an all-India nationalist sentiment, they have scarcely begun to explore the impact of its intersecting gender and racial ideologies on imperialist and nationalist politics in the second half of the nineteenth century.[3] The stereotypes of the 'manly Englishman' and the 'effeminate Bengali *babu*' that structured the Ilbert Bill controversy emerged out of, and helped shape, important shifts in racial and gender ideologies that accompanied the political and economic transformations of the imperial social formation in the late nineteenth century. The politics of colonial masculinity in the Ilbert Bill controversy not only reflected the intersection of racial and gender ideologies, but also enabled those hierarchies to be reconfigured in new ways.

Contemporaries readily acknowledged the gender politics in the racial arguments against the Ilbert Bill. According to the Head of Police Intelligence in Bengal, the agitation against the Bill was instigated by the 'capitalists' in Bengal, but in order to 'make the grievance a general one, they raised the cry of danger to European women and so the agitation spread'.[4] Opponents of the Bill, moreover, expressed their disdain of native civil servants by likening them to 'sweet girl graduates from Girton'.[5] The gender politics of the Anglo-Indian agitation was no doubt underpinned by a patriarchal construct of womanhood. At the same time, however, the Ilbert Bill controversy also witnessed an impressive and unprecedented mobilisation of white women in India. The contribution of white women in India, the *memsahibs* as they were popularly called, provoked a mixed admiration from Anglo-Indian men: 'one circumstance hitherto unexampled in Indian history ... is that Englishwomen have for the first time thought it necessary to descend into the arena of political controversy'.[6] The *Englishwoman's Review*, one of the leading women's journals in Britain, was more unequivocal in its praise of the racist agitation against the Ilbert Bill for providing Englishwomen in India an opportunity to prove their 'interest in politics'.[7]

Such tensions around women's roles were grist to the mill of an intensified politics of colonial masculinity. For it was precisely the unevenness in the intersection of racial and gender ideologies that gave the politics of colonial masculinity its particular significance in the Ilbert Bill controversy. On the one hand, the agitation against the Ilbert Bill recuperated the challenge of racial equality by rearticulating racial difference in the terms of a pre-given gender hierarchy. On the other, it recuperated the feminist challenge of gender equality by harnessing even a 'New' gender ideology to the agenda of racial hierarchy. Indeed, the impact of the Ilbert Bill controversy was not simply to consolidate traditional racial and gender hierarchies. Rather, the true significance of colonial masculinity in the Ilbert Bill controversy was precisely in rearticulating traditional racial and gender hierarchies to preserve imperial interests in a new guise.

At the first, and perhaps most obvious level, the stereotype of 'effeminacy' performed important ideological service in the Ilbert Bill controversy: it presented the racial privileges of the Anglo-Indians in more acceptable and naturalised gendered terms. The attempt to rationalise racial hierarchy on a supposedly more natural gender hierarchy was based not on homology but on difference. Sir Lepel Griffin, a senior Anglo-Indian official, in his essay entitled 'The Place of Bengalis in Politics' published in 1892 emphasised this difference. He had the following to say of the 'feminine' traits shared by Englishwomen and Bengali men:

> The characteristics of women which disqualify them for public life and its responsibilities are inherent in their sex and are worthy of honour, for to be womanly is the highest praise for a woman, as to be masculine is her worst reproach, but when men, as the Bengalis are disqualified for political enfranchisement by the possession of essentially feminine characteristics, they must expect to be held in such contempt by stronger and braver races, who have fought for such liberties as they have won or retained.[8]

According to Griffin, Englishwomen and Bengali men were disqualified from playing an active part in politics because they both possessed 'feminine' traits; but whereas 'feminine' traits were 'natural' for the former and made them the 'ornaments of life', for the latter it was 'unnatural', and made them the objects of ridicule.

The stereotype of the 'effeminate Bengali *babu*' worked precisely by invoking simultaneously the Victorian British gender ideology and the increasingly embattled status of this ideology: on the one hand, therefore, it invoked the logic of a gender system that associated masculinity with maleness and femininity with femaleness and found in them the basis for the 'natural' division of society into male and female spheres; and, on the other, it also invoked the pressures on the classical bourgeois male public sphere from the inclusion of new social actors, like women and the working class.[9] For as Griffin points out, the 'unnaturalness' of the demands of 'effeminate *babus*' was parallel to the 'unnaturalness' of British feminist demands. To quote Griffin once again:

> Although it would be both impertinent and paradoxical to compare Englishwomen – the most courageous, charming and beautiful of the daughters of Eve – with Bengali agitators, yet it is a curious fact that the question of admitting Bengalis to political power, occupies in British India, the same place that in England is taken by the question of the extension of the vote to women, both may be advocated on somewhat similar grounds and both may be refused in compliance with the necessities of the same arguments.[10]

It was this 'unnaturalness' that was being invoked in the displacement of the racial politics of the Ilbert Bill on to a different register: the supposedly natural division of the sexes.

The need for such a displacement of racial politics was touched off by a debate on the central contradiction of British colonial policy in India: a racial equality that was both promised and endlessly deferred. Although the Bill was initiated innocuously enough as a minor administrative measure, it quickly became the touchstone of the racial policy of the colonial authorities in India. The measure was designed to overcome certain anomalies in the exercise of criminal jurisdiction following the Code of Criminal Procedure of 1872. The Code of 1872 had brought European British subjects in the *mofussils* under the jurisdiction of the *mofussil* courts for the first time; in the past European British subjects in the *mofussils* had to be taken to the High Courts in the Presidency towns for trial on criminal offences. Since an act of 1869 had previously given natives the right to be appointed as Justices of Peace in the *mofussils*, the non-official European population in the *mofussils* were willing to be brought under the *mofussil* courts only if they were to be tried by European British subjects alone. In exchange for being brought under the jurisdiction of the *mofussil* courts, the European British subjects were guaranteed that they would be tried only by Justices of Peace who were themselves European British subjects.[11] The anomalies in the 1872 Code, however, became apparent as natives in the elite Indian civil service gained enough seniority to be appointed as District Officers in the *mofussils*. A native District Magistrate or Sessions Judge, for example, could not try a European British subject in the *mofussil*, but would have to call upon his subordinate, a European Joint Magistrate, to exercise jurisdiction over the case. Moreover, native civilians, who as Presidency Magistrates could exercise jurisdiction over European British subjects in the Presidency towns, would be forced to give up this privilege on promotion as District Officers in *mofussil* towns.

The need for a change in the 1872 Code had been apparent for some time, but the Government decided to proceed cautiously. Hence Act Ten of 1882, which was meant to review the 1872 Code, proposed no changes. Instead, the Government of India decided to take up the issue in a separate amendment to the Code. The proposal for an amendment had been initiated by a Bengali member of the Indian civil service, Behari Lal Gupta.[12] Gupta urged the government to remove the racial disqualification against native members of the senior or 'covenanted' branch of the Indian civil service. Gupta's note of 30 January 1882 was approved by the then Lt.-Governor of Bengal, Sir Ashley Eden, as a 'matter of general policy' and 'administrative convenience'.[13] The Government of India followed up on Eden's recommendation by sending Gupta's proposal for the opinion of other local administrations in India, with the exception of Bengal, whose Lt.-Governor had already approved the proposal. Despite a handful of dissenting opinions from diehard Anglo-Indian officials, there was an 'overwhelming consensus of opinion' that it was time to reconsider the special privilege reserved for Anglo-Indians in the *mofussils* by the Code of 1872.[14] The proposal to amend the 1872 Code was sent to Lord Hartington, the Secretary of State in London; Hartington approved the Government of India's proposal, although he failed to inform the Viceroy of the considerable hostility to the change from some members of his Council, such as Sir Henry Maine.[15] The Viceroy subsequently instructed his Legislative Department to draft a bill incorporating Gupta's proposal; the Bill, now known as the Ilbert Bill, was introduced in the Council on 9 February 1883. Ilbert's Bill, however, went beyond Gupta's original proposal in empowering not just natives in the senior or 'covenanted' branch of the civil service, but various other classes of native civil servants as well.

The Ilbert Bill became the occasion for one of the most significant mobilisations of Anglo-Indian opinion ever in India, even though the changes it proposed would have a very limited impact for many years. For despite the more comprehensive scope of Ilbert's bill, there were too few Indians of sufficient seniority in the civil service actually to qualify to try European British subjects in the *mofussils*. The Government of India, moreover, was willing to concede that at least for some time to come the extension of privilege would be limited only to natives in the senior or 'covenanted' branch of the Indian civil service. The vast majority of Indians in the civil service were not in the 'covenanted', but in the 'uncovenanted' or lower rungs of the administrative service. Native entry into the more prestigous 'covenanted' branch of the civil service was limited, either through the expensive and time-consuming procedure of taking the open competitive examination held in London since 1859 or through government nomination in accordance with the Government of India Act of 1870, which provided for the appointment of 'qualified' natives as 'statutory' civilians to covenanted posts.[16] In 1883 in all of India there were only eleven Indians who had entered the covenanted branch of the Indian civil service through open competition in London. One had left the service, one was dead, two were posted in Bombay, one was posted in the North-West Provinces, and six were posted in Bengal. Even with the inclusion of 'statutory' civilians, the number of Indians in the covenanted civil service was small; and the numbers senior enough to be affected by the change even smaller. In Bengal, for example, including both 'competition' and 'statutory' civilians there was a total of only twelve Indians in the covenanted branch of the civil service.[17] In all of India there were only two Bengali 'competition' civilians who would immediately qualify for the privileges under the Ilbert Bill: S. N. Tagore, of the Bombay civil service, and R. C. Dutt, of the Bengal civil service. Both held appointments as District Magistrates and Sessions Judge and hence confronted the issue of jurisdiction over European British subjects in the *mofussil*. The only other 'competition' civilian with sufficient seniority was B. L. Gupta, who was a Presidency Magistrate in Calcutta. On being moved from Calcutta to a district appointment, Gupta would also have to face the issue of exercising jurisdiction over British subjects. In the next five years only two others, K. G. Gupta and Brajendranath De, both 'competition' civilians serving in Bengal, would be eligible for appointments as District Officers and hence for jurisdiction over European British subjects in the *mofussils*. For another ten years, only nine Indian covenanted civilians, competition and statutory, would qualify for the proposed jurisdiction. Even if the Bill extended the jurisdiction to all classes of native officials, including those in the covenanted as well as the uncovenanted branch of the service, there would be for a long time to come only thirty-seven Indians in all of India able to qualify for the privilege.[18]

The howl of protest from the Anglo-Indian community over the Ilbert Bill thus had less to do with the Bill itself as with the general challenge it posed to the principle of Anglo-Indian racial exclusivity in India. Taken together with other recent measures, the Ilbert Bill was seen as the unfolding of the dubious promise of racial equality made to the colonial subjects. As the *Englishman*, a newspaper of the Anglo-Indian business community in Calcutta, claimed: 'the cause for . . . alarm is to be found in the tendency of the times as exemplified in the (Ilbert) Bill, much more than in the four corners of the Bill itself'.[19] The Government of India was committed, in rhetoric at least, to a policy of racial equality as enunciated in the Charter Act of 1833 and the Queen's Proclamation of 1858. As the time came to fulfil some of these liberal promises, however, the colonial Government found its rhetoric increasingly at odds with the special privileges reserved for Anglo-Indians in India. These underlying contradictions came to a head during the Viceroyalty of Lord Ripon. Ripon, who was an appointee of the Liberal Gladstone Government in Britain, had hoped to cement the loyalty of the Western-educated Indian middle class by removing some of the more glaring racial disqualifications against natives enacted by his predecessors.[20] Ripon's policy, however, set him on a collision course with the vested interests of Anglo-Indian officials and non-officials in India. Members of the Calcutta Bar were enraged that Ripon had appointed a native judge, R. C. Mitter, as the Acting Chief Justice in Calcutta. Ripon's other measures, such as the repeal of the Vernacular Press Acts and the passage of the Local Self-Government Act, were perceived by the Anglo-Indian population as a threat to their exclusive privileges in India. The *Englishman* and the *Civil and Military Gazette* of Lahore blamed Ripon's initiatives for converting India into a 'theatre on which actors play to Radical audiences in England'.[21] Ripon himself was acutely aware of the larger issues at stake in the Anglo-Indian opposition to the Ilbert Bill. In his note to the Secretary of State in London, he admitted that the opposition to the Bill goes 'beyond the Bill and brings into discussion some of the fundamental principles of British policy in India'.[22]

It was indeed precisely these 'fundamental principles of British policy in India' that were at stake in the Ilbert Bill controversy. By the second half of the century, both 'liberal' and 'conservative' Anglo-Indian administrators and intellectuals were forced to reconsider the promise of racial equality as the guiding principle of British policy in India. The pressure for the reconsideration of British colonial policy was over-determined by various economic and political changes in the second half of the nineteenth century: the threat to Britain's economic position from other European nations; the massive increase in British financial investments abroad; and the growing challenge of an Indian middle class who were eager to benefit from the promise of racial equality. In this context, it became increasingly difficult for the colonial authorities to escape the fact that continued British political and economic exploitation of India depended on the maintenance of certain exclusive racial privileges for European British subjects in India. Even such benefits to India as supposedly accrued from the presence of British capital in India were seen as dependent upon the preservation of racial privileges for the British. Hence opponents of the Bill argued that the empowerment of native officials would hinder the smooth operation of British capital in India, leading to a flight of British capital from India.[23]

The gendered politics of colonial masculinity provided the vehicle for the crucial rearticulation of the 'fundamental principles of British policy in India' necessitated by the changes of the second half of the century. For only a few prominent Anglo-Indians like Fitzjames Stephen, a former Law Member of the Viceroy's Council and a Judge of Judicature in England, were willing to disavow unambiguously the liberal principle of racial equality and to celebrate colonial conquest for what it was. In his opposition to Ripon's policies, Stephen 'formulated a doctrine which others had not the ability to put in words or the cynicism to avow'.[24] He argued that the liberal spirit of the Queen's proclamation, known as the Indian 'Magna Carta', was a 'mere expression of sentiment and opinion' and had no legal force in India. The Government of India, he argued, must be guided by a more realistic set of principles. His clear-headed assessment of the nature and purpose of the colonial government in India bears quoting at some length:

> [The Government of India] is essentially an absolute Government founded not on consent, but on conquest. It does not represent the native principles of life or government, and it can never do so until it represents heathenism

and barbarism. It represents a belligerent civilization, and no anomaly can be so striking and dangerous as its administration by men who, being at the Head of a Government founded on conquest, implying at every point the superiority of the conquering race, of their ideas, their institutions, their opinions and their principles, and having no justification for its existence except that superiority, shrink from the open, uncompromising straight forward assertion of it, seek to apologize for their own position and refuse from whatever cause, to uphold and support it.[25]

While most Anglo-Indians in the Ilbert Bill controversy demurred from Stephen's frank and cynical position against the Bill, the politics of colonial masculinity served precisely to rearticulate the fundamental principles of British policy in line with Stephen's position.

The strategy of deploying the politics of colonial masculinity against the Ilbert Bill was disingenuous at best: its main purpose was to shift the onus of the debate from a straightforward defence of racial privileges to a question of the fitness of native civil servants. In the popular Anglo-Indian imagination, therefore, the effeminate Bengali *babu* was represented as the chief instigator and the chief beneficiary of the Ilbert Bill. The Ilbert Bill, it was argued, had originated at the instigation of a Bengali *babu*, B. L. Gupta; it was further held that the Bill would benefit disproportionately other Bengali *babus*, like S. N. Tagore and R. C. Dutt. Anglo-Indians singled out middle-class Bengali Hindus in their diatribes against the Bill. Opponents of the Bill suggested frequently that had the provisions of the Bill been limited to natives of provinces other than Bengal or to classes other than the Western-educated middle class there would be little ground for Anglo-Indian opposition to the Bill. One Anglo-Indian writer in the *Pioneer*, a semi-official Anglo-Indian newspaper, was convinced that 'were none but Hindustanis and Punjabis of good birth and education' likely to obtain power under the Ilbert Bill, there would be little to fear from natives abusing their power in trying European British subjects.[26] According to another Anglo-Indian who wrote to the *Englishman*, 'if Bengalis had the finesse of Parsi gentlemen it would be difficult to refuse them the privilege'.[27] Similarly, another writer in the *Englishman* gave the following rationale for the Anglo-Indian opposition to the Bill: 'I fancy most of us would not object to being taken before a fine old Sikh *Hakim* for instance. Is it the Sikhs who are clamouring for our loss of liberty? or is it any one of the warlike races of India?'[28] Yet the Anglo-Indian suspicion that 'none but a few Bengali *babus*' would benefit by the Bill had little basis in the actual proportion of Bengali Hindus who would be empowered by the Bill. W. W. Hunter, a supporter of the Ilbert Bill, presented a breakdown by province and religion of the thirty-three natives in the covenanted and uncovenanted branches of the civil service who would be affected immediately by the provisions of the Bill. Of the thirty-three native civilians, six were Rajputs, eight were Muslims, four were Parsis, five were Hindus from southern India, and only ten were Hindus from Bengal. Bengali Hindus made up less than one-third of those who would benefit from the Bill, practically the same ratio they bore to the general population of India.[29] Hunter's argument, however, failed to allay the suspicion of his Anglo-Indian colleagues. Hunter had taken the 'effeminate *babu*' to refer quite narrowly to middle-class Hindus of Bengal, whereas for the opponents of the Bill the term covered more loosely the entire Western-educated Indian middle class.

The opprobrium in the charge of native effeminacy, moreover, was not based simply on likening the unfitness of native civilians to the unfitness of women; rather, it was based on emphasising the very 'unnaturalness' of the disqualifications of the native civilians. Anglo-Indian opponents claimed that because native officers in the civil service were devoid of both 'manly physique' and 'manly character' they ought not to be placed in a position of authority over a more manly people. The 'constitutional timidity of the race', they argued, made the Bengali civilian unfit to exercise authority over the 'manly Englishman' or even over the other manly native races of India. Anglo-Indian officials declared that the inherent physical weakness or cowardice of the Bengali civilian rendered him incapable of performing his duties as a District Officer. Lord H. Ulick Brown, the Commissioner of Rajshaye and Cooch Behar, claimed that the Bengali officer would cower in fear at the prospect of trying 'burly European loafers' in the *mofussils*, and would only too readily make the case over to his subordinate, a European Joint Magistrate.[30] The Corinthean Theatre in Calcutta staged an updated version of Dave Carson's *Bengali Babu*, replete with contemporary allusions to the Ilbert Bill and the physical incompetence of the Bengali civilians. Contemporary Anglo-Indian satires, such as the immensely popular *A Glance in Advance or What's in Store for '84*, claimed that the Ilbert Bill's policy of placing a weakling race over manlier ones would lead to a total collapse of law and order in India. In such anti-Ilbert Bill pamphlets as *The Conflict of Caste*, moreover, dire consequences were predicted if the Ilbert Bill were passed; it warned that manly European British subjects could not be expected to take their subordination to an effeminate class of Indians lightly when even other native peoples chafed under the authority of such poor specimens of maleness.[31]

The alleged physical incompetence of the Bengali civilian was not just a matter of irrational sentiment or prejudice; it was perceived to have a direct bearing on the Bengali magistrate's ability to sympathise with the more 'sporting' public-school-trained Anglo-Indian who might be brought before him in a criminal case. When C. E. Buckland, a former member of the Board of Revenue in India, alleged at a public meeting in London that no further proof of the unfitness of the Bengali officer was needed than his failure as a 'sportsman', he was drawing attention to what was perceived as a crucial difference between the effeminate native officer and his sport-loving Anglo-Indian colleagues. Buckland reserved his greatest ridicule for Gupta, at whose initiative the Ilbert Bill had been proposed, by citing an incident in which the Bengali civilian had requested to be posted out of a station with 'excellent snipe shooting and a great opportunity for pig sticking'.[32] Although Indian newspapers caustically inquired 'how a proficiency in shooting wild animals can produce an efficiency in trying an offender', Buckland's Anglo-Indian contemporaries would have had no difficulty in recognising the connection betweeen sporting proclivities and the ability to exercise jurisdiction in the *mofussils*.[33] H. H. Risley, Officiating Deputy Commissioner of Manbhoom, for example, expressed concern that since Bengali officers 'do not hunt, shoot, (and) play games', they would not show proper leniency in evaluating criminal charges brought against Anglo-Indians in the *mofussils*.[34] Risley probably had in mind the criminal cases frequently brought against Anglo-Indians by natives in the *mofussils*. A great many of these cases involved accusations against Anglo-Indian hunters and sportsmen, who were frequently responsible for 'accidental' shooting deaths of unwary native peasants, or against Anglo-Indian planters, who were accused of using excessive physical force in 'disciplining' their native employees.[35] In most of these cases, it was impossible to get a conviction against the Anglo-Indian offender from an Anglo-Indian-dominated judicial system. Risley, alluding to the shared interest in 'manly' sports among Anglo-Indians, feared that the more effeminate Bengali Magistrate would be incapable of understanding the 'thoughtless schoolboy spirit in which the injury complained of has been done'.

The further point about the 'unnatural' disqualification of native civilians had to do with the fact that, as many Anglo-Indians believed, races that were 'physically cowardly' were 'rarely morally brave'. In assessing the fitness of native officers, therefore, Anglo-Indians alluded frequently to the various moral deficiencies of character among the 'unmanly' natives. Bengali officers were believed to lack moral courage and to be more prone to falsehood, perjury, sedition, sycophancy, and the blind adherence to social and religious prejudices than any other native race.[36] Even native 'competition' civilians, who had undergone a brief sojourn in England for the purpose of taking the competitive examination and had been exposed to an 'Anglicised' education, were found unfit by English standards of probity, independence, and objectivity. The records of individual Indian 'competition' civilians were thoroughly scrutinised during the Ilbert Bill controversy and examples of their alleged moral shortcomings were publicly aired as proofs of the unfitness of even the most elite of Indian civil servants. The new Lt.-Governor of Bengal, Sir Rivers Thompson, was perhaps the most critical in his official evaluation of the performance of native civilians in the Indian civil service. In concluding his survey of opinions on the Bill, he observed that native civilians suffered from a 'want of nerve' which made it difficult for them to perform their job successfully.[37] In an earlier speech on the question of native jurisdiction, Thompson made a pointed reference to a scandal which had led some years previously to the dismissal of Surendranath Banerjea from the Indian civil service. Banerjea, who later went on to become a prominent Bengali political leader, had been discharged from service on a charge of dishonesty that would most likely have been overlooked had he been a British officer.[38] Allegations against other Indian officers currently serving in the Indian civil service were also repeated in the speeches and writings against the Bill, without much foundation. Henry Sullivan Thomas, in his speech to the Viceroy's Legislative Council, cited a report written by an Anglo-Indian officer on Satyendranath Tagore, the first Indian to join the Indian civil service once entry had been opened through an open competitive examination. Sullivan's purpose was to illustrate that even exceptional Indians who had undergone the rigours of an examination in England that catered primarily for British candidates could not be expected to display the high standards of objectivity expected from officers of the elite service. The report by A. S. Borraidale, District Magistrate of Broach, had suggested that Tagore, because of his own religious prejudices, had been unable to convict a Hindu zealot for murder in a trial that had come before him.[39]

The most telling example of the moral failure attributed to the native civilian, however, was the Anglo-Indian charge that native civilians displayed an 'irrational' or 'emotional' support for the Ilbert Bill. There was a circular logic to this argument; the proof of the unmanly character of the native civil servant alternated between the charge of sycophancy and irrational dislike of Europeans. John Beames, the Commissioner of the Burdwan Division in Bengal and a staunch opponent of the Ilbert Bill, detected in his native subordinate Brajendranath De's advocacy of the Bill a 'tone of dislike to Europeans and almost disrespect towards Government'.[40] For Beames and several like-minded Anglo-Indian colleagues, this was the strongest argument against giving Western-educated Bengalis a larger share in the administration of the country. The various implications of effeminacy on the physique and character of the native officers were calculated to portray them as uniquely disqualified among all the native classes of India for the privileges of the Ilbert Bill. In so far as the logic of colonial masculinity identified the efforts to grant native civil servants equality as 'unnatural', it reinforced not only the racial hierarchies of colonial rule in India but also the gender hierarchies in both Britain and India.

At a second, and perhaps more important level, the politics of colonial masculinity reconstituted Anglo-Indian racial privileges as the benevolent protection of native and white women. The figure of the woman, therefore, was at the very heart of the definition of Anglo-Indian masculinity and Indian effeminacy in the Ilbert Bill controversy. The effeminacy of Indian men was in proportion to the subordination of Indian women; Indian men were to be disqualified from the privileges of the Ilbert Bill because of the manner in which they treated Indian women. British officials and missionaries in India were sanguine about their own role in 'uplifting' the position of Indian women; the colonial state was thus identified with the civilising role of the 'manly' protector of Indian women. Various scholars, however, have demonstrated that the colonial discourse about the subordination of Indian women served a variety of different functions for the justification of colonial rule. On the one hand, out of considerations of political expediency, the colonial state was often more than willing to compromise with, and even reinforce, orthodox indigenous patriarchal practices. On the other hand, the reforming zeal of the colonial state was directed typically against only select indigenous patriarchal practices; colonial officials and missionaries remained singularly uninterested in the impact of the collaboration between different forms of British and indigenous patriarchal practices.[41] The further point, as Lata Mani has argued, is that women were seldom either the subjects or even the objects of the colonial discourse on the 'woman question'; but, rather, women were merely the grounds on which the ideological struggle was waged between the colonial and the indigenous male elites.[42]

Certain specific manifestations of the subordination of women in orthodox elite and upper-caste Indian practices became the ground for the effeminacy of native men. Opponents of the Ilbert Bill, for example, associated native effeminacy only with particular forms of the subordination of women, such as the seclusion of women in *zenanas* (the female quarters in a native home) or the practice of *purdah* (veiling), found mainly among the elite and upper castes of the north and north-east parts of the country. In the words of one Anglo-Indian woman, 'in Bengal the men are notoriously destitute of manliness' because they 'are most harsh and cowardly in their treatment of the weaker sex'.[43] It was the patriarchal practices of the Bengalis, according to Mr J. Munro, Officiating Commissioner of the Presidency Division in Bengal, that 'hinder[ed] the development in Bengalis of those manly and straightforward qualities which under other conditions are found in Englishmen'.[44]

The opponents of the Bill used the protection of Indian women from such oppressive social practices as a litmus test for granting political concessions to Indians. The Anglo-Indian strategy of using women's subordination in India as a handy stick with which to beat back Indian demands for political equality had converted the 'woman question' into a battleground over the political rights of Indians. Expressing what was a common Anglo-Indian disdain for *zenana*-bred civilians', a British Deputy Commissioner in Assam wrote: 'Is it seriously meant that natives who practice polygamy treat their wives as caged birds, kept in the dark chiefly for the creation of sons ... who immolate infants of tender age to marriage, who compel infant widows to remain widows till death – are as such competent to try European men and women?'[45] British officials, non-officials, and missionaries argued that until native men learned to respect the rights of women they were not fit to be granted any political rights. This strategy of deferral was exemplified most famously in the argument of Mr J. J. J. Keswick, a senior partner in the British firm of Jardine, Skinner & Co. At the infamous anti-Ilbert Bill meeting held in the Calcutta Town Hall, Keswick defended the Anglo-Indian position on the Bill on the following grounds:

> when natives have so far advanced that the wives and sisters, daughters and mothers of those of the ranks from which our native civilians are drawn can come openly into Court and give evidence, and can mix with us and with our wives in society, then there will be so much of each other's innate nature known, that Government may seriously consider about giving natives the power they now ask.[46]

Keswick's speech, which echoed a dominant theme in the Anglo-Indian opposition, illustrates a further point about the implication of women in the politics of masculinity and effeminacy: knowledge of women became, in effect, synonymous with knowledge of the 'innate nature' of the British and the Indian people.

Supporters of the Ilbert Bill easily parodied such arguments as in the following verse from a poem entitled 'The Miller and his Men':

> And as we don't know his wife or daughter
> He can't know us as well as he ough'ter
> ... His principles too are sure to be shady
> As his mother's not trained like an English lady.[47]

When opponents of the Bill brought up the subordination of native women as the cause for their opposition to the Ilbert Bill, they held up, by way of contrast, the norms of the 'English lady' as the qualification for trying European British subjects. If the norms of the 'English lady' were to serve as the standard for granting Indian civil servants privileges under the Ilbert Bill, then, as supporters of the Bill pointed out, it was precisely the female relatives of the class of Western-educated Indians, from which native civil servants were drawn, who were most likely to approximate these norms. For as Hunter, in a speech to the Legislative Council, pointed out, native officials in the elite Indian civil service were perhaps even 'more English in thought and feeling than the Englishmen themselves'.[48] The female relatives of the Westernised Indian middle class, more than any other class of Indians, were more likely to be exposed to the kind of training expected of an 'English lady'. For, in order to become fit companions to Western-educated husbands, the middle-class Bengali woman or *bhadramahila* was encouraged to conform to at least some of the norms of Victorian bourgeois domesticity.[49] Indeed, the wives of many of the 'competition' Indian civilians were admiringly held up as examples of the modern or new Indian woman. Jnanadanandini Debi, the wife of Tagore, had not only given up *purdah*, but had for long charmed Anglo-Indian circles by her 'great self-possession'. Mohini Debi, the wife of R. C. Dutt, and Suadamini, the wife of B. L. Gupta, had both attended the Native Ladies' Adult and Normal School in Calcutta and had received votes of confidence from their husband's Anglo-Indian colleagues.[50]

Indians were thus struck by the peculiar irony in the Anglo-Indian case against the Bill: opponents who held up the norms of the 'English lady', nevertheless, favoured the orthodox over the more 'Westernised' *babus* for the privileges of the Ilbert Bill. C. E. Gladstone, Deputy Commisioner of Muzuffarnagar, for example, claimed that the orthodox Punjabi had a better understanding of the status of the English lady than the more Westernised Bengali.[51] The contradictions in the Anglo-Indian position drew bitter comment from Bengalis: 'What matter if our women pass F. A. and B. A. exams? They do not know how to clasp the waist and arm of any male and dance in European fashion. Therefore how is it possible to sanction Ilbert's Bill?'[52] In so far, therefore, as the status of Indian women was made the site for competing political agendas, none of the opposing sides were interested in going beyond a narrow and self-serving model of female emancipation.

The construct of white womanhood was similarly deployed as the basis for the elaboration of British or Anglo-Indian masculinity as the benevolent protection of women. The white woman had traditionally occupied a unique, yet contradictory, position in the masculinist colonial mythology. On the one hand, the white woman was a special object of reverence for white men. Any real or imagined threat to white women was perceived as a threat to the prestige of the entire British race. The political appeal of such a construct of white womanhood was perhaps never more evident than in the immediate aftermath of the rebellion of 1857. Perceptions of real and imaginary assaults by native men on white women became the pretext for the terrible vengeance that Anglo-Indians wreaked on the native population after the defeat of the rebellion.[53] On the other hand, however, ever since white women began arriving in considerable numbers in India from the late eighteenth and early nineteenth centuries, Anglo-Indian society had held white women uniquely responsible for the increase in racial tension in India. Lord Stanley, while presiding over a meeting of the East India Association on racial harmony, noted the sinister role that white women had played in India. He blamed the racial tension in India on white women because, as he argued, 'in all countries, national and race prejudices were more accentuated and more strongly felt and shown by the women then by the men'.[54] Yet, as a senior Anglo-Indian civilian from Madras noted with surprising candour, it was white men who had to make white women aware of their special responsibility for upholding the prestige of the white race in India. He wrote, 'we are in India and we belong to . . . the ruling race, ruling, too, principally by prestige and it is up to us and to our women to do nothing to lower that prestige. The women may not understand but their men ought to.'[55] The masculinist colonial mythology, therefore, required special obligations of, and restrictions on, white women in India. White women in India, for example, were held to an even narrower definition of the appropriate spheres of female activity than their counterparts in Britain.[56] For most of the nineteenth century, even such 'female' pastimes in Britain as philanthropic activities were never entirely acceptable for white women living in India: the primary object of the white woman in India was to reproduce the norms of Victorian British domesticity within the safely circumscribed limits of Anglo-Indian society. The following ironic comment on the lives of white women in India was made by Lady Wilson, the wife of a senior Anglo-Indian civilian, in the early twentieth century:

> You must understand that most Europeans of the old school would not allow a [European] lady to accept an Indian gentleman's proferred hospitality. They, would not permit her to drive through an Indian town, be a spectator of tent-pegging, or receive an Indian as a visitor, far less dine with him. They would, in short, prefer her to be as wholly absent from every kind of society as are the inmates of a *zenana*.[57]

It was in connecting white men's control over white women to their control over native men and women that the colonial construct of white womanhood was integral, as Ann Stoler has argued, to the social hierarchies that sustained colonial rule.[58]

It is not surprising, therefore, that the defence of white womanhood became an especially powerful symbol in the Anglo-Indian agitation against the Ilbert Bill. The prospect of a white woman appearing in public before a native judge in a *mofussil* court triggered the perennial Anglo-Indian anxiety that natives did not hold white women in the esteem which they deserved by virtue of their position in colonial society. Since, as many Anglo-Indians suspected, native men were not suitably impressed by 'the European woman's purity' and engaged in 'revolting and suggestive' parodies of European women and their dances to the applause and appreciation of native audiences, the prospect of a white woman appearing before a native court would demean further the status of all white women in native eyes.[59] Native civil servants, it was argued, were surrounded by 'childish and ignorantly superstitious women' from birth to manhood and, therefore, could have no regard for the 'free' and 'unfettered' white woman. If native judges, moreover, were allowed to handle cases involving such 'delicate' subjects as rape, marriage, or divorce among Europeans, the damage to the prestige of the white race would be unimaginable. Many Anglo-Indians claimed that a growing disrespect towards white women was already evident in the arguments of the native supporters of the Ilbert Bill. The *Ananda Bazar Patrika*, a vernacular newspaper in Bengal, had dared to suggest that white women were so vociferous in their opposition to the Bill because they feared that the presence of native magistrates would embolden their native servants to bring up charges of physical abuse that they had suffered at the hands of the *memsahibs*. Even the faint suggestion that white women might have something other than the noblest of motives in their opposition to the Bill caused a great stir in the Anglo-Indian community. Under the threats of libel and prosecution for sedition, the vernacular paper was forced to issue an apology for casting aspersions on the sacrosanct image of white women.[60] For the tarnishing of the image of white women in India was perceived as a blow to the prestige of the entire race. As was argued by a group of white women petitioners, moreover, the loss of prestige for white women went beyond merely the interests of the ruling race; it also had a harmful effect on white women's considerable 'influence for good on which the enlightenment and amelioration of the condition of ... Native sisters so largely depend'.[61]

So powerful was the appeal of white womanhood in the Anglo-Indian rhetoric against the Bill that even a strong defender of the Bill, like Henry Beveridge, proposed a compromise that would safeguard the prestige of white women. Beveridge anonymously presented a proposal in the columns of the Calcutta *Statesman* that would excuse white women from appearing in court before a native judge.[62] He urged that special concessions ought to be provided for white women in the Ilbert Bill, similar to the concessions already provided to record testimony in cases involving *purdanashin* women (native women who could not appear unveiled in public). Beveridge recommended the exclusion of non-Asiatic women in the extension of the jurisdiction of native magistrates over European British subjects so as to meet the objections of a large majority of Anglo-Indian men and women. While the popular Anglo-Indian press was quick to dismiss Beveridge's proposal as 'absurd', the proposal itself was an important indication of the importance of the figure of the white woman in the agitation against the Bill.[63]

The construct of white womanhood deployed by the opponents of the Bill, moreover, nicely brought together the various racial, gender, and class hierarchies in the self-image of the ruling race. Only the wives and female relatives of the more wealthy Anglo-Indians could actually afford the seclusion from native society to sustain the ideology of white womanhood. White women who did not belong to the requisite class background, therefore, posed a special problem to the self-image of whiteness upheld by the colonial elite. The 'common' European woman, like the 'poor white' who was either deported to England or incarcerated in workhouses in India, had an ambiguous status in Anglo-India.[64] Anglo-Indians feared that such women lowered the prestige of all white women in the eyes of native society. H. Holmswood, the Assistant Magistrate of Meherpore, for example, argued that by fraternising with a common European 'shop-girl' a native civil servant had demonstrated his disrespect of white womanhood: 'I have seen a native gentleman of the Service bring a European female of inferior rank – in fact a shop girl – into the English law courts when he came to report cases, and show surprise that his English companions objected to be associated with her on terms of equality'.[65] For Holmswood, therefore, native men who were not repelled by the coarseness of the 'common' European woman showed no understanding of the status of white womanhood.

The liminal status of the relatively small number of single and unchaperoned white women, mainly missionaries and a handful of other social reformers in India, became a cause for particular concern among Anglo-Indians during the racial polarisation of the Ilbert Bill agitation.[66] The Anglo-Indian response to a much-publicised case involving a female European missionary and a native Christian, tried in the Calcutta High Court in the midst of the Ilbert Bill agitation, was symptomatic of the fear and denial with which Anglo-Indians responded to any possibility of intimacy between white women and native men. While some considered the possibility of such an intimacy as preposterous, others saw the case as underscoring the need for stricter patriarchal control over white women. Mary Pigot, who was in charge of the Church of Scotland's Orphanage and *Zenana* Mission in Calcutta and had close ties with Bengali social reformers, had filed a suit for defamation of character against Revd William Hastie who was in charge of the General Assembly's Institution in Calcutta.[67] Hastie, who had already made himself unpopular with native Christians, had accused Pigot of 'impropriety' with a Mr Wilson, a married man, and with Babu Kali Charan Bannerjee, a native Christian teacher in her school. The case was tried in the Calcutta High Court by Judge J. F. Norris, a staunch opponent of the Ilbert Bill. Perhaps fearing a lengthy public discussion of the alleged intimacy between a white woman and a native man in the midst of the Ilbert Bill controversy, Norris decided to conclude the case hastily. He arrived at a peculiar verdict that awarded Pigot only one *anna* in damages without vindicating her of the charge of impropriety. The Judge felt that Pigot's relations with Bannerjee had not been of a 'proper character'.[68] The following year, however, an Appellate Bench overturned Norris's verdict and vindicated Pigot of any impropriety. Hastie's efforts to take the case to the Privy Council in 1885 were also rejected.

Significantly, Anglo-Indian public opinion in 1883 showed considerable sympathy for Pigot even after Norris's verdict. The Anglo-Indian press questioned the verdict by challenging the very assumption that any white woman would have chosen to be familiar with a native man. The native press, despite substantial support for Pigot, was quick to mock the defence of Pigot adopted in the Anglo-Indian press. One native newspaper had the following to say on the Pigot case:

> The *Englishman* refuses to believe that the fair Miranda of the Tempest, recently enacted at the High Court, could possibly go wrong with Caliban .... We wonder that the revelation in the High Court of Babu Kali Charan Bannerjee having got a pair of slippers from Miss Pigot, and of his having had his dinners at her house, has not yet been utilized by our vigilant contemporaries ... as a damaging fact against Mr. Ilbert's Criminal Procedure Bill.[69]

At least one Anglo-Indian 'District Judge' in Bengal, however, did recognise the implications of the Pigot case for the Anglo-Indian case against the Ilbert Bill. In a letter to the Calcutta *Statesman*, he deplored the fact that young unmarried female missionaries visited the homes of native gentlemen to educate their wives without heed to the propriety of such contact. He claimed that Missionary Societies that allowed 'unmarried ladies' to 'visit alone at houses where they cannot but frequently meet with male members of the Hindoo household in outer apartments' encouraged 'scandals', the implications of which were especially harmful in the context of the Ilbert Bill controversy.[70]

Even though only the more irresponsible sections of the Anglo-Indian community believed that empowering native civil servants posed a real threat to the security of white women in India, the rumours about the potential danger to which white women would be exposed by the Bill had a tremendous impact on the popular perception of the Bill in Britain and in India. For the real test of British masculinity was in the 'chivalric' protection of white women from native men. Englishwomen thus ridiculed the faint-hearted 'chivalry' of Ripon, Ilbert, and their like who had abandoned their duty to their countrywomen in favour of placating effeminate *babus* through the Ilbert Bill. The celebrated Anglo-Indian writer Rudyard Kipling, who was in India during the Ilbert Bill controversy, considered the Bill even years later as a measure that had made white women more vulnerable to the dangers posed by native men.[71] Far-fetched notions of the dangers to white women thus assumed extraordinary importance in the propaganda against the Bill. In the more hysterical and sensational arguments advanced against the Ilbert Bill, it was hinted that effeminate *babus* would use this opportunity to 'wage war' against white women. The Calcutta correspondent of *The Times*, for example, suggested that the Ilbert Bill gave those Indians who lacked proper manly courage the opportunity to express their discontent against British rule by attacking the British in the 'tenderest place': through attacks on innocent white women.[72] The *Englishman* seriously entertained a proposal for setting up a Committee of Safety to protect the honour of white women in the event that the Bill was passed.[73]

The suggestion that Bengali Magistrates might deliberately misuse their powers over European women was made early in the fight against the Bill by an Anglo-Indian who signed himself as 'X'. The melodramatic letter from 'X', which appeared in the *Englishman*, warned as follows: 'One's wife may be walked off for an imaginary offence ... what would more please our fellow subjects than to bully and disgrace a wretched European woman? The higher her husband's station and the greater her respectabilities, the greater the delight of her torturer'.[74] Another letter in the *Englishman* signed by a 'Junior Official' claimed that a native magistrate would first trump up a case against the *burra memsahib* or senior white woman in the station, and then would try to get into the good books of her husband by 'affording material aid in compromising the case'.[75] A senior officer in the army wrote as follows:

> Many English officers have English servant girls attached to their families in the *mofussil*; a native magistrate, puffed up with importance might set eyes upon one of the girls and make overtures to her. If she refused, as she

probably would do, what would be easier than for this native, acting under the smart of disappointment to bring a case against the girl to be tried in his court? A few *annas* would bribe all the native servants of the household and we might guess the result.[76]

Wild rumours that native magistrates would abuse their jurisdiction to fill their harems with white women began to surface in letters to the Anglo-Indian press as well as in the speeches at various anti-Ilbert Bill meetings held all over the country.

Although these arguments were frequently dismissed as 'purely fictitious', they served as extremely effective propaganda against the Bill.[77] The threat that white women living in isolated white settlements faced from the Ilbert Bill was commonly invoked to drum up support for the Anglo-Indian case in Britain. Returning Anglo-Indian officials painted terrible scenarios of the plight of helpless white women in India for British audiences at home. A meeting held at the Limehouse Town Hall in the East End of London, for example, was advertised as an effort to save defenceless Englishwomen in India. A placard in front of the hall bore the words 'Appeal to the people of England from Englishwomen in India', and a second placard outside the building stated that the meeting was being held 'in opposition to Lord Ripon's policy of placing Englishwomen under the criminal jurisdiction of polygamists – Native Magistrates'.[78]

The vague apprehensions about the danger to white women were further compounded by the publicity surrounding a few cases of alleged assault by native servants on white women in Calcutta in the summer of 1883. The local government as well as the Anglo-Indian press in Bengal hinted at a connection between these cases and the Ilbert Bill. The Lt.-Governor of Bengal, Rivers Thompson, appeared to encourage the inflammatory reports about such cases filed by some of his subordinates, such as E. V. Westmacott, the Magistrate of Howrah.[79] In his role as Magistrate, Westmacott regularly dealt with cases involving disputes between white women and native *dhobies* (washermen), *mehters* (sweepers), and *khansamahs* (cooks). He was convinced that there was an increase in the 'insubordination' of native servants in recent months, fuelled by the prospect of the Ilbert Bill. To quote from his official report to the Lt.-Governor: 'I do not suppose the *Baboos* who are agitating and leading the anti-European tendencies of Government are likely to indulge in rape or murder of Europeans, but I see very clearly what is the outcome of the *Baboo* agitation, when translated into language, intelligible to themselves by natives of the lower classes.'[80] Following through on his dubious political interpretation of these cases, Westmacott justified handing down harsh sentences to native servants to teach them a lesson.

The most widely publicised case was one involving the wife of James Hume.[81] A native *mehter* (sweeper), a former employee in the Hume household, was accused of attempted sexual assault on Mrs Hume. The *Englishman*, commenting on the case, hinted that the accused native was not acting alone but had been urged to commit his 'heinous crime' by the 'superior instigation' of native politicians.[82] Hume was the Public Prosecutor in a case against some Bengali students who had been arrested for protesting against Judge Norris's verdict in a contempt of court case involving the popular native politician Surendranath Banerjea. The rumour that native politicians were deliberately instigating native servants to attack white women made the Hume case a *cause célèbre* for the Anglo-Indian opposition. The case against Hurro Mehter, alias Greedhare Mehter, was tried by a mixed jury of Europeans and natives who found him guilty and convicted him to eight years' rigorous imprisonment. The *mehter* remained undefended and refused to admit his guilt to the end. Senior Anglo-Indian officials who feared that 'natives (might) subscribe to provide counsel for the man and make him another victim of English justice' were relieved that native politicians had displayed considerable restraint despite provocation from the irresponsible comments of some of the Anglo-Indian press.[83] Two years later, Mr A. O. Hume, a cousin of James Hume, informed the then Viceroy Lord Dufferin in a private communication that both James Hume and his wife had deliberately perjured themselves in court; Mrs Hume and Greedhare Mehter had been involved in an intimate relationship for some six months prior to the case. Mr Hume's discovery of this liason had led to the charge against the native of attempted sexual assault.[84] The climate during the Ilbert Bill controversy, however, had precluded a fuller investigation of the case.

Following the Hume case, the Anglo-Indian press reported rumours of other copy-cat cases of native assaults on white women. A female guest at Judge Norris's residence alleged that a native intruder had entered her bedroom while she was asleep one night. However, a thorough examination of the complaint by Mr H. G. Wilkins, the Under-Deputy Commissioner of Police, revealed that the 'failed villainy' was only a delusion in the mind of the young girl.[85] In another case, pursued with characteristic zeal by Westmacott, it was discovered that Mary Watkins, the wife of a railway guard, had charged her native sweeper of assault to get back at him for filing a suit against her husband in the Small Claims Court for the payment of his wages.[86] As the *Statesman*, one of the more liberal Anglo-Indian newspapers, wrote: 'The time is out of joint ... incidents which, in ordinary times, would have no political significance, are now being seized upon on all hands, and a political significance is attributed to them which, whether it rightly belongs to them or not, has the same effect upon the public mind as if it did.'[87] These cases came to have an important bearing on Anglo-Indian perceptions of the Ilbert Bill: it was alleged that the cases of assaults or attempted assaults by native servants on their white female employers were either instigated by native politicians or else by the native interpretation of the Ilbert Bill as the first step in the reversal of the racial hierarchy of colonial society.

The imminence of a threat to white women created the deepest impression against the Ilbert Bill among Anglo-Indians in India and Britain. At a protest meeting in London, a public telegram received from India on the Hume case had the desired impact. Sir Alexander Arbuthnot, a former high-ranking official in India, led a deputation to the then Secretary of State, Lord Kimberley, in which he alluded to the case as an argument against the Bill.[88] Although Kimberley rebuked Arbuthnot for suggesting a connection between the Hume case and the Ilbert Bill, Arbuthnot's speech met with the approval of several die-hard opponents of the Bill in England. Lord Lytton, a former Viceroy of India and a staunch opponent of the Ilbert Bill in the House of Lords, wrote to Arbuthnot approving his deputation to Kimberley; Lytton added 'I thought your speech perfect.'[89] Edward Stanhope, a former Conservative Under-Secretary of State for India, also tried in the House of Commons to raise a question about the 'horrible outrages upon English ladies in Calcutta and Howrah'. Stanhope's efforts, however, were defeated when another member interjected by asking him to 'obtain a statement of annual number of outrages on English women by English men'.[90] Nevertheless, rumours about the dangers to which white women were exposed by the Ilbert Bill did much to weaken support for the Bill in England and in India. Even Queen Victoria was reportedly so shaken by accounts of the outrages on Englishwomen in India that she was led to question in private the appointment of a liberal Viceroy like Ripon as her representative in India.[91] The formidable popularity of the Anglo-Indian case against the Ilbert Bill had to do, at least in part, with the picture of British masculinity as the benevolent protector of both white and native women in India.

Finally, and somewhat paradoxically, the politics of colonial masculinity also licensed a new public role for women, albeit only within the confines of a reconfigured imperial patriarchy. In Britain, feminist demands for greater involvement of women in education, professional employment, and in the public domain, as well as broader late nineteenth-century economic and political changes that brought more middle-class women into the market-place had created a new public visibility for middle-class women. Anglo-India was far slower in being affected by these changes. Although the politics of colonial masculinity did open up an opportunity for the mobilisation of female public opinion, the public participation of white women in the agitation against the Ilbert Bill was symptomatic of another process that Rosemary Hennessy identifies as inseparable from the changes occurring at the turn of the century in Britain: the recuperation of the challenges posed by the 'New Woman' in the racial politics of empire.[92]

The reorientation of racial politics in gendered terms in the Ilbert Bill controversy did open up a space, however limited, for the involvement of women. The involvement of white women in the Ilbert Bill controversy took various forms: white women flooded the Anglo-Indian press with letters against the Bill; they conducted a successful social boycott of the supporters of the Bill in Calcutta; and they took active part in the organisations and associations formed to fight the Bill. The activities of white women contributed substantially to the spread of the Anglo-Indian opposition. Beveridge, one of the few Anglo-Indian civilians who supported the Bill, recalled that 'English ladies appeared to him often to be drawing their skirts away from him as he passed'.[93] The boycott of all the Government House entertainments in Calcutta by the wives of the non-official community proved a great success. The female relatives of elite Anglo-Indian non-officials in India boycotted two full seasons of official entertainments during Ripon's Viceroyalty. Between ninety to a hundred women undertook to absent themselves formally from the Government House Levee and Drawing-Room held in December 1883. According to a report in the *Pioneer*, only 136 women attended the Drawing Room by Public Entry, of whom 69 were new presentations; more than 50 women were noted as being unavoidably absent.[94] The social life of the colonial elite suffered until the arrival of a new Viceroy whose parties white women could attend without compromising their position on the Bill.

Yet the public role assumed by white women in the Ilbert Bill controversy provoked some uneasiness from many an Anglo-Indian male. The public participation of white women threatened the colonial construct of white womanhood. The men were caught in a double bind: they feared that the public participation of women would expose them as more intemperate in their hostility towards natives than white men, thus jeopardising the more sanitised public image of white womanhood. The Home Member of the Viceroy's Council, James Gibbs, suspected that white women were 'far more unreasonable and active in opposition than the male'. The Viceroy, in a note to the Secretary of State, also acknowledged, that 'the ladies are, as is often the case, hotter than the men'.[95] Despite the bad faith in white men's assessment of the 'intemperate' role of white women in the agitation, the public role of white women during the controversy exposed the unrealistic aspirations of the construct of white womanhood. The letters of Flora MacDonald, one of the most intrepid letter-writers against the Bill, is worth quoting at some length:

> Englishmen, try to picture to yourselves a mofussil court, hundreds of miles away from Calcutta – in that Court a Native Magistrate is presiding with the supercilious assurance that a native assumes when he has an Englishman in his power. Before that man stands an English girl in all her maidenly dignity; she has been accused by her ayah (female house-servant) for revenge of a loathsome crime, a crime that is common among native women; the Court is crowded with natives of all castes who have flocked to hear an English girl being tried for an offence; this motley crowd laugh and jeer, and stare that English girl in the face, and spit on the ground to show her the contempt they have for the female sex; scores of witness are present to give evidence; a native Doctor has also been hired for that occasion; witnesses are cross-examined by a native pleader; the most irrelevant questions are asked, questions that only a native dare to ask. Picture to yourself that girl's agony of shame! By her stands her only protector, a widowed mother, who has not the means wherewith to secure the protection and counsel of her countrymen. That innocent girl, so kind, so affectionate, so loving, the stay of her widowhood, must go from the Court with shame, and with a blighted name .... It cannot be that Englishmen renowned for chivalry are willing to subject even the humblest of their countrywomen to dishonour.[96]

While Flora Macdonald never spells out the 'loathsome crime' that she claims is common among native women, her letter reveals a prurient imagination that was not entirely befitting an 'English lady'.

The white male anxiety about the new public role of white women came to focus on the Ladies' Committee in Calcutta. Although the wives and female relatives of prominent Anglo-Indian opponents of the Bill had been conspicuous at various public meetings held to protest the measure, the formation of an independent Ladies' Commitee to draft a separate women's petition against the Bill was seen as particularly controversial. The European and Anglo-Indian Defence Association, formed during the Ilbert Bill controversy for the purpose of safeguarding Anglo-Indian privileges, had gone as far as appointing a few white women to its organising committee. The Association had also received generous financial support from white women, including a donation for ten rupees diverted from *zenana* work in India.[97] Yet the formation of a separate Ladies' Committee, albeit under the auspices of the Defence Association, was received with a mixture of patriarchal condescension and open hostility in the Anglo-Indian community.

At the third meeting of the Defence Association on 22 March 1883, Mr James Furrell, the vitriolic editor of the *Englishman*, proposed drafting a separate women's petition against the Bill to be sent to the Queen. The petition was to be drafted with the co-operation of the Defence Association, which would provide women with organisational aid in obtaining signatures for the petition and in defraying all the expenses incurred. Furrell's proposal was followed by an inaugural meeting of nine leading Calcutta *memsahibs*. A separate Ladies' Committee was formed with Mrs L. R. Tottenham, the wife of a Judge of the Calcutta High Court, as the Honorary Secretary. Two other meetings of the Ladies' Committee were held on 31 March 1883 and 7 April 1883. There were at least twenty-seven women listed as members, including wives of High Court judges, senior civilians and military men, doctors, barristers, and merchants from Calcutta. All the members were urged to submit draft proposals to serve as models for the petition to be submitted to the Queen.[98]

While Anglo-Indian detractors of the Ladies' Committee emphasised its challenge to traditional gender roles, more sympathetic Anglo-Indian observers attempted to trivialise its implications with bemusement at the 'ladies' happy occupation to fill monotonous hours'. The *Civil and Military Gazette* commented tongue-in-cheek about the women's political skills; the paper observed:

> [the] lady who writes most powerfully – as a lady, a woman, and most womanly yet strongly withal – has probably the best chance of posing before the public as the petitioner in propria persona; the intrepid defender – on paper – of her countrywomen's rights.... who knows or can guess how many mute, inglorious politicians, how many Chathams, Pitts, Beaconsfields, Gladstones in petticoats may have been hidden away, lost to fame and the gratitude of posterity.[99]

Others, however, were more openly sceptical of the 'fashionable contagion' that had infected white women in India who wrote political letters to the press and met at each other's homes to form a separate committee. The *Pioneer*, for one, reminded the Anglo-Indian public that 'there are special reasons in India which emphasize the soundness of the Athenean proverb that she is the best woman who is least observed'.[100] Even the *Englishman*, a staunch defender of the Ladies' Committee, assured its critics that the Committee was not a permanent association, but had met only twice with the sole purpose of drafting a petition to the Queen. The members of the Ladies' Committee also tried to allay the suspicion of their white male critics by pointing out that 'no desire for publicity nor any ambition to enter the arena of political strife, had prompted (their) movement'.[101]

Whatever challenge the Ladies' Committee could have posed to the existing Anglo-Indian social order was safely circumscribed by the racial and gender politics of colonial masculinity. The petition of the Ladies' Commitee was prepared with the help of Mr J. G. Apcar, an Armenian barrister in Calcutta and a prominent member of the Defence Association. The list of signatures was headed by the wife of Judge Norris, and included 5,757 other women; many of the signatures were from Eurasian women and, therefore, not, in the strict sense of the word, European British subjects.[102] The form in which the women had signed their names on the petition – using their appropriate titles 'Miss' or 'Mrs' – further emphasised their dependence on their male relatives. The *Englishman* gently reminded the 'ladies' of their folly in signing their names with their titles: 'Mrs Smith or Miss Smith, as we should have thought every educated person knew, is not a signature but a description.'[103] The petitioners complained of the 'cruel wound' to the self-respect of white women if they were brought under the jurisdiction of men who did not allow their women to appear in public. At the same time, the petitioners also stressed the 'helplessness' of white women if they were left without the watchful eye of their own 'natural protectors': white men.[104] The challenge of white women's political participation was thus safely circumscribed within a traditional gender politics.

Even efforts to mobilise women specifically on the basis of a 'pride of womanhood', as was tried by Annette Ackroyd-Beveridge, were recuperated by and for the racial politics of Anglo-India. Beveridge, who had started a college for working women in London in 1854, had come to India on the invitation of Indian social reformers to promote native female education. Following her disputes with Indian social reformers, however, she abandoned her work for female education to marry Henry Beveridge of the Indian civil service.[105] Annette Ackroyd-Beveridge saw herself as a liberal critic of traditional British and Indian patriarchy as well as of blatant Anglo-Indian racism. Together the Beveridges earned a reputation for their hospitality to elite and middle-class Indians. Unlike her husband, however, Beveridge had always been a staunch opponent of political reforms that would empower the educated *babus* of India.[106] Her well-publicised opposition to the Ilbert Bill was expressed in a strong letter to the *Englishman* published on 6 March 1883. Beveridge clarified that her position on the Bill was not based on the 'pride of race', but on something deeper: the 'pride of womanhood'. According to Beveridge, the 'ignorant and neglected' women of India testified to the 'justice of the resentment which English women feel at Mr. Ilbert's proposal to subject civilised women to the jurisdiction of men who have done little or nothing to redeem the women of their race, whose social ideas are still on the outer verge of civilisation'. For Beveridge, this 'pride of womanhood' emanated from the 'form of respect' to which white women were accustomed; and which respect they were not willing 'to abrogate in order to give such advantages to others as are offered by Mr. Ilbert's bill to its beneficiaries'.[107]

In pitting the 'pride of [white] womanhood' against the extension of legal equality to native men, Beveridge evoked what had become a popular strategy in the Anglo-Indian agitation: she both invited white men to serve as the benevolent protectors of white women from native men and excluded native women from the logic of her argument about the 'pride of womanhood'. The limits of Beveridge's alternative politics of womanhood are best illustrated in her allusions to the alleged atrocities committed by native men against white women during the rebellion of 1857:

> Six and twenty years have not elapsed since no inconsiderable portion of the most active classes of North India proved they did not understand what is meant by justice and mercy to the innocent and helpless. Six and twenty years do not suffice to change national characteristics or to educe from savages the qualities at once strong and delicate which make good judges.

As Beveridge's Indian critics pointed out, by the same logic Indian women could also 'claim the privilege of not being tried by the race to which belonged the brutal [British] soldiers', who were accused on numerous occasions of sexual assault on native women.[108] Beveridge's alternative politics of womanhood, no less than the politics of colonial masculinity, was imbricated in what Ania Loomba has called the patriarchal racism of colonial rule.[109]

A gender politics that ignored the ways in which gender relations were imbricated in other social arrangements fell prey to the recruitment of the 'New Woman' for the politics of class domination at home and of racial domination abroad.[110] Hence Beveridge's politics of womanhood became much too easily an unabashed celebration of a 'civilised' British patriarchy over an 'uncivilised' Indian patriarchy. The Bihar Ladies' Petition to the Viceroy, for which Beveridge had campaigned tirelessly among wives of Anglo-Indian officials and planters in Bihar, presented the following case against the Bill: 'we see that in the social systems of India women are ignorant and enslaved . . . we see the men of their races insensible to their degradation, if not contented with it. Therefore, we assert that men born or bred on such a system are unfitted to become the judges of women of a totally different type of society.'[111] Even criticism from liberal public opinion in Britain did not make Beveridge waver from her position. In a letter to her husband defending her position on the Ilbert Bill, she wrote as follows:

> I cannot regret having written the letter to the *Englishman* . . . of a people

uncivilized who care about stone idols, enjoy child marriage and seclude their women, and where, at every point the fact of sex is present to the mind – I call it uncivilized in any nation when I see two people together and the notion of their being a man and a woman is the fact suggested by their manner, and not the more commonplace one (as in England) of two people.[112]

Although Beveridge and other white women in India often claimed to have only the interests of native women at heart and no 'unwomanly animosity' against their fellow subjects, they contributed to upholding the social hierarchies of the politics of colonial masculinity.

While some white women, especially in Britain, did express solidarity with Indians over the Ilbert Bill, white feminists during the Ilbert Bill controversy by and large ignored the impact of colonial masculinity on the status of white women. The *Englishwoman's Review*, which devoted space regularly to contributions on the Empire, largely ignored the Ilbert Bill except for noting the opportunity it had provided white women for participating in politics.[113] It is only recently that this moment of Victorian feminism is beginning to be studied in the context of the history of imperialism. As various scholars have noted, not only did the relations between British and Indian women often replicate the hierarchies of imperial and colonial relations, but the stereotype of the 'downtrodden Indian woman' provided an opportunity for British women to exert their influence in India through what Barbara Ramusack characterises as 'maternal imperialism'. Indeed, as Antoinette Burton has demonstrated, the 'Indian woman' was the foil against which imperial Victorian feminism defined its own self-image.[114] The further point, however, is that the impact of imperialism on Victorian feminism went beyond this legacy of racism. For, as the history of white women's involvement in the Ilbert Bill agitation illustrates, it was the racial politics of imperialism that made possible the conservative recuperation of feminist challenges to the existing social order at the turn of the century in Britain.

Although Indian women were less directly involved than white women in the public controversy over the Ilbert Bill, it also had important implications for the construct of modern Indian womanhood. The politics of colonial masculinity in the Ilbert Bill agitation had highlighted the symbolic value of Indian women in the reconstitution of colonial racial politics; for the definition of British masculinity in the controversy rested on the formula that Gayatri Chakravorty Spivak has characterised as 'white men saving brown women from brown men'.[115] Thus the first step in reclaiming Indian masculinity was to substitute Indian men for white men as the benevolent protectors of native women. In the Ilbert Bill agitation, Indian men began by defending

Indian women from the disparagement of white men who, in their zeal to condemn native men, often also condemned native women. The 'insulting' references to Indian womanhood in the speeches and writings of Anglo-Indian opponents of the Bill prompted many a 'chivalrous' Indian male to champion the honour of the Indian woman against her Anglo-Indian detractors. Lalmohun Ghose, a Bengali political leader, presented a strong defence of the character of Indian women in castigating the speech of Mr H. H. H. Branson, one of the most vitriolic Anglo-Indian speakers at the infamous Calcutta Town Hall meeting.[116]

Indian public opinion betrayed the same ambivalence towards women's public participation that characterised Anglo-Indian responses to the role of white women in the Ilbert Bill agitation. For even though Indian public opinion was most critical of the role of white women in the Ilbert Bill controversy, it, nevertheless, also recognised the value of an effective response from Indian women to white women. By singling out white women – 'white in complexion . . . [but] black at heart' – as the worst offenders in the Anglo-Indian agitation against the Ilbert Bill, Indian men shared with Anglo-Indian men the hostility towards the new public roles of women. The *Reis and Reyyat* satirised white women's contributions and attributed the defeat of the Ilbert Bill to white women's refusal 'to submit to the jurisdiction of the Calibans lusting after the Mirandas of Anglo-India'.[117] The *Dacca Prakash* referred disparagingly to the 7,000-odd European women who had participated in the agitation as 'white *kalis*'; the *Amrita Bazar Patrika* likened them to 'Lady Macbeths' who had a 'hardening effect upon their husband's hearts'.[118]

At the same time, however, many Indians also invoked the achievements of the modern Indian woman to neutralise the Anglo-Indian case against the Bill. The male editors of the *Amrita Bazar Patrika*, for example, had both Indian and Anglo-Indian society fooled for several months by a native female memorial, allegedly signed by members of the Bengali *bhadramahila*, in response to the white women's petition to the Queen.[119] Even though the native female memorial was exposed as a hoax, the attempt of Indian men to ventriloquise the voice of Indian women reflected a new admission of the significance of the public mobilisation of Indian women. The memorial turned the arguments of the white women petitioners on its head: it argued that native men were qualified to try European British subjects because the modern Indian woman was better educated than the white women who were agitating against the Bill. The memorialists asserted that 'we Indian women are not ignorant and enslaved'. They argued that while there were thousands of ignorant women in India, 'as a like number exists in

England', it was unfair to generalise from this and to use it as a disqualification against native men for trying European British subjects. The memorial, unlike the white women's petition, was also signed in the proper manner: 'Binodini, Bhafini, Sundari, Sulochona, Manorama, Thakomani, Chapala, Horu, and others'.[120] The memorial reversed the arguments of the white women by claiming superiority for the native women memorialists against the white women petitioners. The memorial presented the argument thus:

> we are not inferior in intelligence or education to the Englishwoman who have come forward to protest against the Bill . . . some of us have obtained University degrees – among the lady agitators against the Bill there is not a single graduate, Mrs. Tottenham and Mrs. Norris are not B. A.'s; but among us there are B. A.'s who have received first class education at Bethune College. . . . Sir Richard Garth [Chief Justice] and Mr. Croft [Director Public Instruction] may be appointed to bring us and the English ladies who have remonstrated, under severe tests, and see if we are not intellectually superior to them. If our superiority is produced the Bill should become law at once.[121]

The reference to the superiority of the educational qualifications of native women alluded to the fact that the University of Calcutta had admitted female graduates to its degree programme in 1878, before any of the English universities.

There was, moreover, further evidence of the Bengali *bhadramahila's* public involvement in support of the Ilbert Bill. The native female teachers at the Bethune School for women in Calcutta rallied their students to support the Bill. Kamini Sen, a teacher at the school and the wife of a 'statutory' native civilian, organised her female students to wear badges and attend meetings in support of the Bill.[122] The *Bengalee* also commented on the 'unique feature' that encouraged some of the native women's organisations to become involved in politics. The Bengali Ladies' Association, which was not in any way a political organisation, convened a special meeting with about seventy women present to express sympathy with the wife of the Bengali political leader Surendranath Banerjea, who was imprisoned for contempt of court in the midst of the Ilbert Bill controversy. There were several reports of Bengali women publicly protesting Banerjea's imprisonment.[123] But native public opinion, like Anglo-Indian opinion, was not entirely sanguine about women's involvement in the controversy; the *New Dispensation*, for example, deplored the fact that the political conflict over the Ilbert Bill had dragged 'harmless and helpless ladies through the dirt of all this Billingsgate'.[124] Others like the editors of the *Amrita*

Bazar Patrika had recognised, somewhat cynically perhaps, the symbolic value of native women's contributions. At a meeting of the Indian Association in 1883, Banerjea urged that the services of Indian women be used 'in the political elevation of the country'. The male-sponsored nature of native women's involvement in the Ilbert Bill controversy prefigured later more successful accommodations of the modern Indian woman within a new and reconstituted nationalist Indian patriarchy.[125]

The politics of colonial masculinity in the Ilbert Bill controversy thus did more than just reproduce a traditional social order. Rather, it was part of a broader process of political, economic, and ideological realignments in the imperial social formation. The politics of colonial masculinity gave a new lease of life to the racial exclusivity of Anglo-Indians in India: the charge of 'effeminacy' to isolate certain native groups checkmated the demand to extend political rights to Indians; and the 'unnaturalness' in the claims for political and legal equality of these groups extended the rationale for continued Anglo-Indian racial domination. In so far, moreover, as the politics of colonial masculinity allowed for an expansion in the public role of women, it also made the new role of women vulnerable to recuperation in the racial politics of empire. Indeed, the politics of colonial masculinity in the Ilbert Bill controversy links the 'New Woman' in Britain no less than the 'effeminate *babu*' in India to the changing imperatives of the late nineteenth-century imperial social formation.

Notes

1 For the full text of Ilbert's proposal and of Act 3 of 1884, see *Great Britain Parliamentary Papers 1884*, vol. 60, c. 3952 (Hereafter: *Parliamentary Papers*). The definition of European British subjects given in Section 4 of the Criminal Procedure Code was rather arbitrary. It included persons who were neither European nor British, and excluded persons who may in all respects have been European and British but not of legitimate descent. See *Abstract of the Proceedings of the Council of the Governor General of India Assembled for the Purpose of Making Laws and Resolutions 1883*, vol. 22, p. 13 (Hereafter: *Council Proceedings*), National Archives of India (NAI), New Delhi.

2 See Edwin Hirschmann, *White Mutiny: The Ilbert Bill Crisis in India and the Genesis of the Indian National Congress* (Delhi: Heritage Publishers, 1980). I have drawn largely from Hirschmann's account of the details of the controversy.

3 See Hirschmann, *White Mutiny*; S. Gopal, *The Viceroyalty of Lord Ripon 1880–1884* (London: Oxford University Press, 1953); Christine Dobbin, 'The Ilbert Bill: A Study of Anglo Indian Opinion in India, 1883', *Historical Studies Australia and New Zealand*, 13: 45 (Oct. 1965), 149–66. For an earlier attempt to examine the politics of gender and race in the Ilbert Bill controversy, see Mrinalini Sinha, ' "Chathams, Pitts, and Gladstones in Petticoats": The Politics of Gender and Race in the Ilbert Bill Controversy, 1883–84', in Nupur Chaudhuri and Margaret Strobel (eds.), *Western Women and Imperialism: Complicity and Resistance* (Bloomington: Indiana University Press, 1992), pp. 98–116.

4 Quoted in Hirschmann, *White Mutiny*, p. 105.

5 See speech of Major-General Hopkinson, former Chief Commissioner of Assam, in

W. S. Seton-Karr, *The Ilbert Bill: A Collection of Letters, Speeches, Memorials, Articles etc. Stating the Objections to the Bill* (London: W.H. Allen & Co., n.d.), p. 120 (Hereafter: *Ilbert Bill*).
6 *Ilbert Bill*, p. 120.
7 Quoted in Janaki Nair, 'Uncovering the Zenana: Visions of Indian Womanhood in Englishwomen's Writings, 1813–1940', *Journal of Women's History*, 2:1 (Spring 1990), p. 22.
8 Lepel Griffin, 'The Place of Bengalis in Politics', *Fortnightly Review*, 57 (Jan.–June 1892), p. 811.
9 For a discussion of the bourgeois ideology of separate spheres as formative of middle-class life in nineteenth-century Britain, see Leonore Davidoff and Catherine Hall, *Family Fortunes: Men and Women of the English Middle Class, 1780–1850* (Chicago: University of Chicago Press, 1987); and Mary Poovey, *Uneven Developments: The Ideological Work of Gender in Mid-Victorian England* (Chicago: University of Chicago Press, 1988). Although Amanda Vickery challenges the usefulness of the notion of separate spheres for understanding nineteenth-century British women's history, her argument nevertheless does not deny the existence of 'separate spheres' ideology in mid-Victorian Britain. See Amanda Vickery, 'Golden Age to Separate Spheres? A Review of the Categories and Chronology of English Women's History', *Historical Journal*, 36:2 (1993), 383–414.
10 Griffin, 'The Place of Bengalis in Politics', p. 811.
11 For the background to the Ilbert Bill, see Hirschmann, *White Mutiny*, pp. 5–23; and *Council Proceedings*, 2 Feb. 1883, p. 37. For a history of the legal privileges enjoyed by the European British subjects in India, see Nemai Sadhan Bose, *Racism, Struggle for Equality and Indian Nationalism* (Calcutta: Firma KLM Pvt. Ltd, 1981).
12 'Gupta in consequence of his position and his station in Calcutta, was simply selected by some of his countrymen to represent their wishes to the Head of the Government', *Bengalee* (Calcutta), 17 Feb. 1884, p. 77. The biographer of R. C. Dutt claims that it was Dutt who had initiated the proposal and prompted Gupta to take it up with the Government. See J. N. Gupta, *Life and Work of R. C. Dutt, C. I. E.* (Delhi: Gian Publishing House, 1986), p. 93.
13 See H. A. Cockerell, Secretary of Government of Bengal to Secretary Government of India, Home Department, *Legislative Department Papers of Act I-3 of 1884*, 30 Mar. 1882, Paper No. 1 (Hereafter: *Leg. Dept Papers*), NAI. See also *India, Home Department, Establishment Proceedings*, Aug. 1880, Pros. Nos. 43–44 A, NAI.
14 See *Government of India, Legislative Department Proceedings*, May 1884, Nos. 1–401, Pros. No. 2 (Hereafter: *Leg. Dept Pros.*), NAI.
15 See Gopal, *The Viceroyalty of Lord Ripon*, pp. 131–3.
16 For a history of the creation of the 'statutory' appointments, see S. K. Bajaj, 'Indianization of ICS – The Formation of the Statutory Civil Service, 1879', *The Punjab Past and Present*, 5:9 (Apr. 1971), 211–26.
17 See Note from Calcutta High Court, *Leg. Dept Papers*, Paper No. 4.
18 See S. Gopal, *The Viceroyalty of Lord Ripon*, p. 135. Also Hirschmann, *White Mutiny*, p. 25; and *Council Proceedings*, p. 153.
19 *Englishman* (Calcutta), 24 Feb. 1883, p. 1.
20 See S. Gopal, *The Viceroyalty of Lord Ripon*.
21 *Civil and Military Gazette* (Lahore), 22 Jan. 1883, p. 5.
22 Government of India to Secretary of State, 10 Aug. 1883, *Leg. Dept Pros.*, Pros. No. 369.
23 For a summary of the various arguments against the Ilbert Bill, see Hirschmann, *White Mutiny*, pp. 116–40.
24 Ilbert to Justice Markby, 12 Sept. 1884, *Ilbert Papers*, vol. 12, 1882–85, India Office Library and Records (IOLR), London.
25 Letter to *The Times* (London), 1 Mar. 1883, in *Ilbert Bill*, p. 13.
26 *Pioneer* (Allahabad), 26 Mar. 1883, p. 1; 12 Mar. 1883, p. 5; and 20 Mar. 1883, p. 6.
27 *Englishman*, 14 Mar. 1883, p. 2; also 17 Mar. 1883, p. 2.
28 *Englishman*, 2 Mar. 1883, p. 2.

29 Letter to *The Times*, 10 Dec. 1883, in *Opinions in Favour of the Ilbert Bill: Being A Collection of the Recorded Opinions of Some of the Most Eminent Men in Support of That Measure* (Calcutta: Doorga Das Chatterjee, 1885), pp. 65–6 (Hereafter: *Opinions*).
30 *Leg. Dept Papers*, Paper No. 55.
31 APW, *The Conflict of Caste* (Allahabad: Pioneer Press, 1883), pp. 5–6, 27. Also see Hirshmann, *White Mutiny*, p. 232; and Raymond K. Renford, *The Non-Official British in India to 1920* (Delhi: Oxford University Press, 1987), p. 262.
32 Quoted in *Bengalee* (Calcutta), 21 July 1883, p. 341. For the importance of *shikar* or hunting for Anglo-Indians, see Scott Bennett, 'Shikar and the Raj', *South Asia*, 7:2 (Dec. 1984), 72–88; and John M. MacKenzie, *The Empire of Nature*, (Manchester: Manchester University Press, 1988).
33 See *Navavibhakar*, 30 July 1883, in *Report on Native Newspapers of Bengal Presidency*, 1883, No. 32, p. 4645, NAI (Hereafter: *RNBP*). Also *Bengalee*, 4 Aug. 1883, p. 351.
34 *Leg. Dept Papers*, Paper No. 55.
35 Ram Gopal Sanyal (ed.), *Record of Criminal Cases as Between Europeans and Natives for the Last Sixty Years* (Calcutta: Bengali Press, 1893). Also W. Stobie, 'An Incident of Real Life in Bengal – Injustice in an Indigo Planter's Field', *Fortnightly Review*, 42 (July-Dec. 1888), 329–41.
36 See the arguments of Anglo-Indian officials in *Leg. Dept Papers*, especially Papers Nos. 31, 55 and 70.
37 *Leg. Dept Papers*, Paper No. 55. For Rivers Thompson's speech, see *Council Proceedings*, 9 Mar. 1883, pp. 220–1.
38 See *India, Home Department Establishment Proceedings*, Aug. 1880, Pros. Nos. 43–44 A, NAI. For a discussion of Banerjea's dismissal, see Bose, *Racism*, p. 157.
39 *Leg. Dept Pros.*, Pros. No. 374; and Appendix 5, Pros. No. 441.
40 *Leg. Dept Papers*, Paper No. 55. Also see Brajendranath De, 'Reminiscences of an Indian Member of the Indian Civil Service', *Calcutta Review*, 132:2 (Aug. 1954), 85–98. For a discussion of the hostility between Beames and De, see Barun De, 'Brajendrananth De and John Beames – A Study in the Reactions of Patriotism and Paternalism in the ICS at the Time of the Ilbert Bill', *Bengal Past and Present*, 81:151 (Jan.-June 1962), 1–31.
41 See Joanna Liddle and Rama Joshi, 'Gender and Imperialism in British India', *South Asia Research*, 5:2 (1985), 147–65.
42 Lata Mani, 'Contentious Traditions: The Debate on Sati in Colonial India', *Cultural Critique*, 7 (1989), 119–56.
43 *Englishman*, 26 Apr. 1883, p. 2.
44 *Leg. Dept Papers*, Paper No. 55.
45 *Leg. Dept Papers*, Paper No. 51.
46 For the full text of speeches made at the Calcutta Town Hall meeting, see *The Friend of India and Statesman* (Calcutta), 1 Mar. 1883, Supplement (Hereafter: *Statesman*). The argument in Keswick's speech was put to verse in the poem 'Our Peers', quoted in *Bengalee*, 3 Mar. 1883, p. 102.
47 Quoted in *Reis and Reyyet* (Calcutta), 7 Apr. 1883, p. 160.
48 *Council Proceedings*, pp. 193–7.
49 See Meredith Borthwick, *The Changing Role of Women in Bengal, 1849–1905* (Princeton: Princeton University Press, 1984) and Ghulam Murshid, *Reluctant Debutante: Response of Bengali Women to Modernization, 1849–1905* (Rajshahi: Rajshahi University Press, 1983). For changes in the Muslim community, see B. Metcalf, 'Islam and Custom in 19th-century India', *Contributions to Asian Studies*, 17 (1978), 62–78.
50 See Borthwick, *The Changing Role of Women*, pp. 240–60; Also Sushama Sen, *Memoirs of an Octogenarian* (Simla: Anjali, 1971), p. 10. H. M. Kisch, a colleague of Gupta's in the ICS, had words of praise for Mrs Gupta. See Ethel A. Waley Cohen (ed.), *A Young Victorian in India: Letters of H. M. Kisch* (London: Jonathan Cape, 1957), pp. 171–2.

51 *Leg. Dept Papers*, Paper No. 64.
52 *Samaya*, 28 May 1883, *RNBP*, No. 23, pp. 262–3.
53 Lady Canning, the wife of the then Viceroy of India, had assured Queen Victoria that there was no 'credible evidence' that the mutineers had sexually assaulted white women in 1857, quoted in Margaret Macmillan, *Women of the Raj* (New York: Thames & Hudson, 1988) p. 102. Also see Nancy L. Paxton, 'Mobilizing Chivalry: Rape in British Novels About the Indian Uprising of 1857', *Victorian Studies*, 36:1 (Fall 1992), 5–30.
54 See Lord Stanley, *East India Association Pamphlet*, p. 14, in *India Office Tracts*, vol. 658, IOLR. For an Englishwoman's protest against such charges, see 'English Women in India', *Calcutta Review*, 80:159 (Jan. 1885), 137–52.
55 W. O. Horne, *Work and Sport in the Old Indian Civil Service* (London: William Blackwood & Sons Ltd, 1928), p. 23.
56 See MacMillan, *Women of the Raj*. Also Maud Diver, *The Englishwoman in India* (London: William Blackwood & Sons Ltd, 1909).
57 Lady Wilson (Anne Campbell Macleod), *Letters from India* (London: William Blackwood & Sons Ltd, 1911), p. 33.
58 Ann Stoler, 'Making Empire Respectable: The Politics of Race and Sexuality in Twentieth-Century Colonial Cultures', *American Ethnologist*, 16:4 (Nov. 1989), 634–60.
59 APW, *Conflict of Caste*, p. 48.
60 *Ananda Bazar Patrika*, 27 Aug. 1883, *RNBP*, No. 36, pp. 549–51. Also see *Englishman*, 4 May 1883, p. 2.
61 Petition of Englishwomen in India to the Queen in *Ilbert Bill*, p. 92.
62 *Statesman*, 27 Mar. 1883, p. 2; and 29 Mar. 1883, p. 2.
63 For the rejection of Beveridge's proposal, see *Englishman*, 28 Mar. 1883, p. 2; 30 Mar. 1883, p. 2; 2 April 1883, p. 2; and 7 Apr. 1883, p. 2.
64 See David Arnold, 'European Orphans and Vagrants in India in the Nineteenth Century', *Journal of Imperial and Commonwealth History*, 7:2 (1979), 104–27.
65 *Leg. Dept Papers*, Paper No. 55.
66 For foreign women missionaries in India, see Geraldine Forbes, 'In Search of the "Pure Heathen": Women Missionaries in Nineteenth-Century India', *Economic and Political Weekly*, 21:17 (26 Apr. 1986), WS2-WS8.
67 For a discussion of the Pigot case, see Kenneth Ballhatchet, *Race, Sex and Class Under the Raj: Imperial Attitudes and Policies and their Critics 1793–1905* (New York: St. Martin's Press, 1980), pp. 112–16.
68 For a full text of the verdict, see *Statesman*, 24 Nov. 1883, Supplement.
69 See *Reis and Reyyet*, 29 Sept. 1883, p. 459; and 15 Sept. 1883, p. 434.
70 *Statesman*, 3 Oct. 1883, p. 2.
71 See Rudyard Kipling, *Something Of Myself For My Friends, Known and Unknown* (New York: Doubleday, Doran & Co., Inc., 1937), pp. 55–6.
72 Quoted in *Reis and Reyyet*, 28 Apr. 1883, p. 195.
73 *Englishman*, 26 June 1883, p. 2.
74 *Englishman*, 10 Feb. 1883, p. 4.
75 *Englishman*, 7 May 1883, p. 2.
76 Quoted in *Reis and Reyyet*, 21 Apr. 1883, p. 182.
77 There were, of course, some Anglo-Indians who were critical of such arguments. See the letters of 'Gamin de Bon Accord' in the *Statesman*, 7 Mar. 1883, p. 2; and W. S. Blunt, *India Under Ripon* (London: T. Fisher Unwin, 1901), p. 272.
78 Cited in *Bengalee*, 1 Sept. 1883, p. 409.
79 Rivers Thompson to Ripon, *Ripon Papers: Letters of Rivers Thompson*, vol. 54, 17 June 1883, British Museum (BM), London.
80 Ibid. Also see Steuart Bayley to Ripon, enclosing Westmacott to Barnes, *Ripon Papers: Letters of Bayley 1881–84*, 26 June 1883, BM.
81 See Calcutta Town Police Report for 1883 in *India, Home Department Police Proceedings*, Aug. 1884, B, No. 1, NAI. For details of the case, see *Englishman*, 31 July 1883, p. 3. For a discussion of 'rape' in post-1857 colonial fiction, see Jenny Sharpe,

Allegories of Empire: The Figure of Woman in the Colonial Text (Minneapolis: University of Minnesota Press, 1993), esp. ch. 4.

82 *Englishman*, 26 June 1883, p. 2. Rivers Thompson was to repeat this charge in his communication to the Viceroy; *Ripon Papers*, vol. 54, 17 June 1883; senior officials were concerned that this view was being repeated by several Anglo-Indians at the time, see Bayley to Ripon, *Ripon Papers: Letters of Bayley*, 25 June 1883.
83 See Bayley to Ripon, *Ripon Papers: Letters of Bayley*, 26 June 1883.
84 Hume to Dufferin, *Dufferin Papers: Correspondence in India*, vol. 78, *July-Sept. 1885*, 4 July 1885, IOLR.
85 Cited in *Bengalee*, 28 July 1883, p. 351.
86 *Bengalee*, 21 July 1883, p. 338.
87 *Statesman*, 25 June 1883, p. 2.
88 The telegram was read by Sir Roper Lethbridge at a meeting held at the St James Hall in London. See *Ilbert Bill*, p. 19; for Arbuthnot's deputation, see p. 126.
89 Quoted in Lady Constance Arbuthnot (ed.), *Sir Alexander Arbuthnot: Memories of Rugby and India* (London: T. Fisher Unwin, 1910), p. 246.
90 Cited in Hirschmann, *White Mutiny*, p. 189.
91 Blunt, *India Under Ripon*, p. 6.
92 See Rosemary Hennessy, 'New Woman, New History', in *Materialist Feminism and the Politics of Discourse* (New York: Routledge, 1993), pp. 100–38.
93 Quoted in Lord William Beveridge, *India Called Them* (London: George Allen & Unwin Ltd, 1947), p. 39.
94 *Pioneer*, 11 Dec. 1883, p. 1; *Englishman*, 12 Oct. 1883, p. 2; *Bengalee*, 8 Dec. 1885, p. 555. At least one Anglo-Indian memsahib, the wife of a pro-Ilbert Bill Anglo-Indian member of the Viceroy's Council, recorded her extreme displeasure at the social boycott conducted by white women. See Mrs Herbert Reynolds, *At Home in India or Taza be Taza* (London: Henry J. Drane, 1903), p. 185.
95 Gibbs to Ripon, *Ripon Papers: India Miscellaneous Public Documents*, BP 7/6, 18 Nov. 1883, BM (Hereafter: *IMBP*). Also Ripon to Kimberley, *IMBP*, BP 7/3/, 2 Dec. 1883.
96 *Englishman*, 13 Mar. 1883, p. 2. See also her letter on 26 Apr. 1883, p. 2.
97 *Englishman*, 23 July 1883, p. 2.
98 See reports in the *Englishman*, 23 Mar. 1883, p. 2; 2 Apr. 1883, p. 3; 3 Apr. 1883, p. 2; and 7 Apr. 1883, p. 1.
99 *Civil and Military Gazette*, 13 Apr. 1883, p. 3.
100 *Pioneer*, 13 Apr. 1883, p. 2.
101 See letter from a Lady on the Committee to the *Englishman*, 3 Apr. 1883, p. 2; also see *Englishman*, 16 Apr. 1883, p. 2.
102 See *Statesman*, 16 June 1883, p. 2.
103 *Englishman*, 25 Apr. 1883, p. 2.
104 For the text of the petition, see *Ilbert Bill*, pp. 90–3.
105 See Pat Barr, *The Memsahibs: The Women of Victorian India* (London: Secker & Warburg, 1976), pp. 161–8, 186–9. For Ackroyd-Beveridge's role in the social reform movement, see Borthwick, *The Changing Role of Women*, pp. 88–92; and Barbara Ramusack, 'Cultural Missionaries, Maternal Imperialists, Feminist Allies: British Women Activists in India, 1865–1945', *Women's Studies International Forum*, 13:4 (Winter 1990), 309–21.
106 For Ackroyd-Beveridge's antipathy towards the *babu*, see Beveridge, *India Called Them*, pp. 166–7; also Barr, *Memsahibs*, pp. 163–4.
107 *Englishman*, 6 Mar. 1883, p. 2.
108 *Bengalee*, 31 Mar. 1883, p. 152. For other comments that singled out Ackroyd-Beveridge's letter for criticism, see *Hindoo Patriot* (Calcutta), 12 Mar. 1883, p. 128 and 26 Mar., 1883, p. 146; *Reis and Reyyet*, 17 Mar. 1883, p. 124 and 14 Apr. 1883, p. 171.
109 Ania Loomba, *Gender, Race, Renaissance Drama* (Delhi: Oxford University Press, 1992).
110 Rosemary Hennessy argues for locating the reconfiguration of the feminine subject

in Britain in changing imperial and colonial policy in the late nineteenth century. See Hennessey, 'New Woman, New History'.
111 *Leg. Dept Papers*, Paper No. 28.
112 Quoted in Beveridge, *India Called Them*, p. 248.
113 Cited in Janaki Nair, 'Uncovering the Zenana'. Although the *Bengalee*, 26 May 1883, p. 241 referred to support for the Ilbert Bill from liberal-minded women in London, there was little evidence of interest in the Bill among feminist groups in Britain.
114 See Vron Ware, *Beyond the Pale* (London: Verso 1992); Antoinette Burton, 'The White Woman's Burden: British Feminists and the "Indian Woman", 1865–1915', *Women's Studies International Forum*, 13:4 (Winter 1990), 245–308. Due to the timing of its publication, I was unable to consult Burton's more recent work *Burdens of History: British Feminists, Indian Women and Imperial Culture, 1865–1915* (Chapel Hill: University of North Carolina Press, 1994).
115 Gayatri Chakravorty Spivak, 'Can the Subaltern Speak? Speculations on Widow Sacrifice', *Wedge*, 7/8 (Winter/Spring 1985), p. 121.
116 See *Lal Mohun Ghose* (Madras: G. A. Natesan, 1906), pp. 11–18. For Branson's aspersions on the character of Indian women, see his speech quoted in *Hindoo Patriot*, 5 Mar. 1883, p. 112.
117 *Reis and Reyyet*, 28 Apr. 1883, p. 196.
118 *Amrita Bazar Patrika* (Calcutta), 27 May 1886, p. 4; and *Dacca Prakash*, 24 June 1883, RNBP, No. 26, p. 353.
119 The hoax was first reported in the *Bengalee*, 30 June 1883, p. 301; in the meantime the memorial had been widely reproduced in Indian and Anglo-Indian newspapers.
120 Cited in *Civil and Military Gazette*, 7 May 1883, p. 2.
121 *Ibid.*
122 See Usha Chakraborty, *Condition of Bengali Women Around the Second Half of the Nineteenth Century* (Calcutta: Burdhan Press, 1963), p. 134. Also see the recollections of Sarala Debi, *Jibaner Jharpatra*, cited in Borthwick, *Changing Role of Women*, p. 339.
123 See *Bengalee*, 19 May 1883, p. 230; and *Statesman*, 14 May 1883, p. 3.
124 See *New Dispensation* (Calcutta), 22 July 1883, quoted in Borthwick, *Changing Role of Women*, p. 339.
125 For a discussion of the reconstitution of Indian patriarchy under colonial rule, see Kumkum Sangari and Sudesh Vaid, 'Recasting Women: An Introduction', in Sangari and Vaid (eds.), *Recasting Women: Essays in Indian Colonial History* (New Brunswick: Rutgers University Press, 1990), pp. 1–26.

CHAPTER TWO

Containing crisis: the native volunteer movement, 1885–86

In March 1885, in the wake of a Russian war scare, the Viceroy Lord Dufferin called for an increase in the strength of the Volunteer Force in India by authorising the creation of a Volunteer Reserve Force. Following the call to raise more volunteers, the Anglo-Indian recruiting officer in Madras accepted the offers of service from four 'native gentlemen'; shortly afterwards, however, the invitation to the Indian volunteers was rescinded in compliance with a telegram from the Military Department of the Government of India.[1] The rebuff to the native volunteers in Madras was followed by demands all over India for the creation of separate native volunteer corps. The Government of India received eighteen petitions on native volunteering from Bengal, ten from Madras, seven from Oudh, three from the Punjab, and one each from Assam and Bombay.[2] By 1 June 1885, the Bengal Government alone had received twenty-seven such petitions totalling over 1,800 signatures.[3] The call for native volunteering was led by the Indian press in urban centres such as Calcutta, Bombay, Madras, Poona, Allahabad, Meerut, Benares, Lahore, and in numerous *mofussil* centres, especially in Bengal. Throughout the year, both the Indian and the Anglo-Indian press hotly debated the merits of native volunteering. In March 1886, almost a year after the government had received volunteer petitions from all over India, Dufferin formally rejected the demands for native volunteering at a public gathering in Madras.[4]

The native volunteer controversy, as Briton Martin Jr. has pointed out, was a 'lost opportunity' to mobilise native elites behind Dufferin's administration.[5] For although colonial rule was based on the subordination of the interests of the Indian people as a whole to British imperial interests, it required for its survival the collaboration of a substantial portion of the indigenous elites.[6] The strategies of colonial rule were forced to negotiate between the short-term goal of maximising British over Indian interests and the more long-term goal of ensuring the continued investment of indigenous elites in the colonial structure. By the late nineteenth century, however, the delicate balance that helped sustain elite collaboration in India was under pressure. The capacity of the colonial authorities to manoeuvre between short-term and long-term interests for the stability of the colonial regime was affected by such changes as these in the imperial social formation of the last quarter of the nineteenth century: the challenge to Britain's world economic status from rivals such as Germany and the United States, the impact of feminist and working-class challenges at home, and the growing pressure from the crisis of Irish nationalism. The impact of Britain's increasingly beleaguered position on its strategies of colonial rule also gave rise to, and was shaped by, changes in elite politics within India: above all, the growing shift from collaboration to criticism of colonial policies by a section of the Westernised intellectuals and the vernacular literati among the Indian elites.[7] The native volunteer movement was followed by the creation of an all-India nationalist platform for elite Indian public opinion. By the end of the year, three major political conferences were held in Madras, Calcutta, and Bombay respectively, of which the most significant was the Indian National Congress, convened in Bombay in December 1885.

One colonial official, in a surprisingly candid admission of the reason for rejecting the native volunteer movement, suggested that native volunteering would promote union between native elites when 'on the principle of *Divide et Impera* it cannot surely be our province to give unnecessary encouragement to any means of amalgamation'.[8] Native volunteering, he argued, would be

> training to arms a body of men over whom, when not actually undergoing instruction, [British] control would be of the slightest, and should thus be facilitating the spread throughout the country of a martial spirit and a familiarity with the use of arms which all recent policy (as evidenced by the Arms Act) has tended to discourage.

The colonial fear of 'amalgamation' applied quite specifically to the political and social distinctions within elite groups; for the demand for native volunteering was confined only to the elites – there was never any question of extending the privilege of volunteering to anyone below the educated community in India. Even though the elaborate colonial classification of 'martial' and 'non-martial' Indian castes was not fully developed until the end of the century, and then mainly as a means for justifying the selective recruitment of soldiers for the post-1857 Indian army, the distinction itself had a long history in the colonial preference for certain sections of the native elites.[9] Kumkum Sangari reminds us that, out of economic, political, and ideological considerations, which were connected as much to the political economy of colonialism in India as to the hegemony of gentrified and aristocratic social values in Britain, colonial rule in India was for long partial to the ' "martial", aristocratic, land-owning, and non-commercial groups'.[10] Colonial policies in fact provided special recognition for the martial traditions of select native groups: mainly, in the words of Dufferin, for the 'landowners, the leading Mahomeddan families, and the aristocracy'.[11] The native aristocracy and wealthy landowning families were given some limited opportunities for advancement in the regular army, from which particular communities and the professional and service groups were excluded altogether. The Arms Act of 1878, which exempted Europeans and Eurasians and compelled Indians to pay a licence fee for the possession of arms, provided special concessions for wealthy Indian landholders. The demand for native volunteering, therefore, constituted a challenge to both the racial and class dimensions of the strategies of colonial rule. Indeed, in so far as the politics of colonial masculinity rearticulated simultaneously the racial and class dimensions of martial traditions, it ultimately recuperated the challenge to colonial rule represented by the native volunteer movement.

The history of an intersecting racial and class dimension in the colonial ideology of martial traditions can be traced to the development of the Volunteer Force as an institution of social control in India. The bivalent racial and class dimension that underpinned the history of volunteering in India was shaped not simply by grafting the strategies of domestic class politics in Britain on to the racial politics of colonial rule.[12] Rather, it was shaped by the particular imperative of colonial strategies of rule: the co-optation of native elites in the perpetuation of a racist social order. The ideology of martial traditions, therefore, developed asymmetrically in metropolitan Britain and colonial India. For whereas volunteering in India reinforced a specific racial and class definition of martial traditions, volunteering in nineteenth-century Britain encouraged a national racial ideology of martial traditions. After an early period of instability in the late eighteenth and early nineteenth centuries when the volunteer movement in Britain was identified both as an 'anti-revolutionary force' and as a force with subversive democratic implications, the reinstitution of volunteer service and the creation of a permanent Volunteer Force in 1859 brought a new social stability to the institution of volunteering in Britain.[13] Volunteering thus became a truly 'national' institution in Britain. Although the enthusiasm for volunteering in nineteenth-century Britain was in part a middle-class response to the aristocratic monopoly in the regular army and the militia, the fact that noblemen continued to be sought after as commanding officers for the newly created Volunteer Corps, as Hugh

Cunningham points out, 'makes it exceedingly difficult to see the Force (simply) as an expression of middle class anti-aristocratic feeling'.[14] Official support for volunteering in Britain, as Cunningham demonstrates, was not forthcoming until after the Reform Acts had made it politically and socially safe to put arms into the hands of the middle classes. The spread of arms, first to the middle class, and, within the first decade of the existence of a permanent Volunteer Force in Britain, to the working class, reflected the successful construction of hegemony after the political and social crisis of the 1830s and 1840s. Working-class enthusiasm for the 'recreational' dimension of volunteering, moreover, coincided with the increasingly conservative character of the new working-class culture that was emerging in Britain from the 1870s onwards: the era which Gareth Stedman Jones has characterised aptly as the period of the 'remaking of the working class' in Britain.[15] Furthermore, the role of the Volunteer Force was redirected – primarily for purposes of national defence rather than for the preservation of internal law and order – in order to inoculate it from overt class politics at home. Even the Irish and the Indians in England were admitted into volunteer corps as further testimony of the new-found confidence in volunteering in the second half of the nineteenth century.[16]

In sharp contrast, volunteering in India was deliberately promoted as an exclusive privilege. The fragmentation of the colonial ideology of martial traditions in India along racial and class lines was produced out of the dual constraints on the history of volunteering: the balance between the racial privileges of the colonial elite and the class privileges of the indigenous elites. For although volunteering in India was always identified as an exclusive Anglo-Indian and Eurasian privilege, the importance of elite Indian support to maintain law and order could never be ignored by the volunteer movement. Despite the fact that the militia as well as volunteer companies had played a role in the history of the East India Company in India, the volunteer movement took hold only after the 1857 Indian rebellion.[17] The Volunteer Force in India had its roots in the feeling of insecurity generated by the small British presence in the midst of what seemed, especially in the aftermath of the 1857 rebellion, a hostile native population. The Volunteer Act (Act Twenty-Three of 1857) recognised that the function of the Volunteer Force in India was primarily for 'the suppression of internal disorder and not [for] defence against external danger'.[18]

Even at the height of the racial polarisation of 1857, however, the volunteer movement could not afford to ignore the crucial support of native elites for the reproduction of the colonial social order. During the 1857 Indian rebellion, the Government of India had accepted the offers of Anglo-Indians and Eurasians to protect European lives and property in

India. The volunteers were called upon to maintain law and order for the Anglo-Indian community so that British troops could be relieved from garrison duty and be redeployed for the suppression of the rebels. Indians of the landed and propertied classes, especially in Bengal, offered their services in 1857 to help the colonial authorities maintain law and order; in a few cases the offers of assistance from Indians were cordially accepted by Anglo-Indian volunteers.[19]

The Volunteer Act of 1857 was deliberately vague about the bivalent racial and class dimension of volunteering in India. On the one hand, because the volunteers were called upon to aid in the suppression of internal as opposed to external danger, it was taken for granted that the Volunteer Force would have to remain an essentially European force; but, on the other hand, because native elites also had a stake in the suppression of internal disorder, the possibility of non-Europeans contributing to the volunteer movement in India was left open. Hence, even though the Volunteer Act had clearly designated the Volunteer Force as a European force, there was nothing in the Act that expressly called for the exclusion of 'pure Asiatics' from the volunteer movement. Section One of the Volunteer Act provided that members of the volunteer corps should be subject for certain military offences to 'the Articles of War for the European officers and soldiers of the East India Company'. In 1869 the Volunteer Act was amended and the obsolete Articles of War of the East India Company were replaced by 'Articles of War for the time being in force for the better government of Her Majesty's Army', by which was usually meant the Articles of War for British rather than for Indian troops. In Paragraph Thirty-Five of the new Act, moreover, the Volunteer Force was expressly described as a European force to be given precedence over native troops of the regular army on the parade ground. The provisions for court martial under Section Nine of the Act and the powers for repressing disorder under Sections Twenty-Three and Twenty-Four also assumed a European rather than a native force.[20] Yet Eurasians, who for technical purposes were not defined as 'European British subjects', had always formed part of the Volunteer Force in India. The large presence of Eurasians in the Volunteer Force did not compromise the precedence given to the Volunteer Corps as a European force on the parade ground. Similarly, there was no reason to believe that the Volunteer Act itself placed any obstacles on 'pure Asiatics' participating in the volunteer movement in India.

The deliberate ambiguities in the Volunteer Act paved the way for efforts to reconcile the racial exclusivity of volunteering with the necessity of securing the support of indigenous elites. It allowed the colonial authorities to espouse a policy of official neutrality on native volunteering even as they did everything to discourage the admission of natives as volunteers. The official position on native volunteering was first articulated by Lord Canning in 1861 in his response to petitions from Parsi and Bengali 'gentlemen' to form a separate native Volunteer Corps in connection with the Presidency Corps in Bombay and Calcutta respectively. Canning argued that while the existence of European corps were justified as short-term reinforcements for British troops at a time of internal crisis, there was no basis for separate native volunteer corps since it was very unlikely that there would ever be a shortage of native recruits for the native part of the army.[21] At the same time, the Governor-General offered the following concession to native elites:

> if any natives, whether Parsees or others, should desire to take their place amongst the European members of the Volunteer Corps, understanding sufficiently the English language, adopting the uniform of the Corps, and being willing and able to share in its duties, the Governor General in Council would be glad to see them enrolled in it.

Canning's policy had guided successive administrations in responding to petitions for native volunteering. While in a few instances, local officials and commandants of individual corps were able to overcome Anglo-Indian and Eurasian prejudices and avail themselves of the opportunity of enrolling natives in existing corps, the official policy of leaving the question of native volunteering up to the whims of individual European corps and its members effectively negated the prospects of native volunteering. The admission of natives had been most successful in Burma, where the Chief Commissioner overrode the local opposition from die-hard Anglo-Indian exclusionists and succeeded in enrolling Burmese youths in the Cadet or College Companies attached to the Regular Corps.[22] There were other isolated examples, such as in the Railway Corps of the Bombay Presidency and the local companies in Berar and Baluchistan, where a few Parsis had been admitted as volunteers.[23] In so far as the Government could rely upon Anglo-Indian and Eurasian volunteers to block the inclusion of natives, it could safely maintain a stance of official neutrality on native volunteering without fearing any alteration in the essentially European character of the force.

Although the expedient policy of official neutrality held together the colonial ideology of martial traditions for awhile, very soon the asymmetry in racial and class politics began to expose the contradictions of volunteering in India. For to the extent to which volunteering promoted a primarily racial definition of martial character in India, it ultimately undermined the usefulness of volunteering as an instrument of social stability. The 'positive' side of the racial definition was that by encouraging every able-bodied Anglo-Indian male in India to cultivate a martial spirit, it overwhelmed the otherwise rigid class-distinctions within the Anglo-Indian community. Commenting on the significance of volunteering for the British in India, Sir Richard Temple, Governor of Bombay, wrote

> The value of the volunteer movement is to be estimated not only by the numbers it may produce in time of peace, but by the moral effect it has upon the European civil community in India, teaching them to be self reliant in respect of armed defence, and imparting to them the confident bearing which arises from discipline and training, and which tends to overawe the evil disposed when troubles threaten.[24]

Apart from its advantages from the 'military point of view', volunteering was commended for cementing social ties within the Anglo-Indian community. For, in the words of one Anglo-Indian volunteer, 'volunteering had a great merit in, like hunting, bringing all classes [of Anglo-Indians] together'; it was through volunteering, he argued, that an 'officer by degrees got to know the character of every man in the place'.[25] Indeed, the bulk of the Volunteer Force in India was comprised not of the class of elite Anglo-Indian officials and non-officials in India but of railway employees, the largest single group of working-class Britons in India apart from the British troops in the Indian Army.[26] The European labourers and artisans employed in the railways, who were otherwise marginalised from the main centres of Anglo-Indian social life in India, were obliged to join railway units of the Volunteer Force. Similarly, pressure was put on Anglo-Indians employed in less prestigious posts as government clerks and factory staff to enrol in local volunteer companies. In fact, for the 'lower-class' European in India, as one British soldier rightly observed, 'life (was) generally military'; for 'nearly every European one meets is a soldier, or at least hopes to be one some day, either as a volunteer, or as belonging to the regular army'.[27] Whereas working-class Britons were pressed into becoming 'useful' as volunteers, enthusiasm for volunteering among the elite Anglo-Indian population usually peaked only at times when there were rumours of some new threat from the native population. For the Anglo-Indian elites, continued interest in volunteering was sustained mainly by the 'club-like' atmosphere associated with the volunteer corps; the headquarters of the Corps were often the centre of Anglo-Indian social activities. From the 1880s onwards there was even a separate corps of Light Horse Volunteers meant for 'men of means', like the Anglo-Indian planters, who either detested or did not have the time for infantry work.[28] The racial definition of 'martial' character had made it possible to mobilise the services of the majority of Anglo-Indians and Eurasians in India for a social order that disproportionately benefited a much smaller Anglo-Indian elite.

The other side of the racial definition, however, was that it allowed the volunteer movement to be identified with strictly sectarian Anglo-Indian interests. This became especially apparent during the anti-Ilbert Bill agitation, when a mob of armed and unruly Anglo-Indian volunteers threatened to hold the colonial government hostage to defend the racial privileges of the Anglo-Indian community. There were rumours that the Volunteer Corps in Bengal would boycott the Annual Prize Day presided over by Lord Ripon and refuse to form the Guard of Honour for the Viceroy on his return to Calcutta in the winter. The boycott was finally called off, but the *Englishman* boasted that out of approximately 900 volunteers only 343, most of whom were government employees and student cadets, reported to form the honour guard for the Viceroy.[29] There were also rumours that the Behar Volunteers – who were invited to Calcutta at the height of the controversy for inspection and military exercises by the anti-Ilbert Bill Lt.-Governor Sir Rivers Thompson – had hatched a conspiracy to kidnap the Viceroy from Government House and deport him secretly to England via the Cape.[30] As Dufferin later wrote, the volunteers in the Ilbert Bill controversy had shown themselves 'only too ready to respond to popular influences, and to add a dangerous element to [the] violence of political agitation'.[31] The behaviour of the volunteers temporarily dampened even official enthusiasm for the volunteer movement in India.

If further indication were needed of the growing crisis in the colonial ideology of martial traditions, then it could also be found in the changing attitude of Indian elites towards the volunteer movement. Those sections of the native elites who were hitherto excluded from a military role in colonial society transformed the demand for native volunteering: the demand was no longer restricted to a few isolated petitions to the Viceroy, but was taken up by political organisations like the Indian Association that had spearheaded the movement for native volunteering during Ripon's viceroyalty.[32] Indians had offered their services as volunteers during the Ilbert Bill controversy in response to Anglo-Indian volunteers who threatened to resign in opposition to Ripon's policies. Approximately 200 native clerks of the Punjab Northern State Railway were inspired by the news of an *en masse* resignation of Anglo-Indian volunteers to petition the Viceroy to allow native volunteering. As in the past, however, the Viceroy simply directed the petitioners to try and enrol in the existing Punjab Volunteer Rifle Corps. The response from the Commanding Officer of the Corps was predictable: he regretted that the constitution of the first Punjab Volunteer Rifles did not permit 'pure Asiatics' as members of the Corps.[33] A. O. Hume, a retired British civil servant, took up the cause of the native petitioners in a letter entitled 'Volunteers vs. Mr. Ilbert's Bill' published in the *Pioneer*.[34] Hume's support for native volunteering was dismissed in the Anglo-Indian press, which was deluged by letters attacking his 'preposterous suggestion'. An orgy of ridicule followed, directed mainly at the prospect of effeminate Bengali volunteers: Anglo-Indian critics suggested that 'Ram Jam Tunga Ghose and Company could (not) be induced to fire at a target much less at an enemy.'[35] Yet there was some optimism among Indians that Ripon, on the eve of his departure from India, might sanction the formation of native volunteer corps. While pressure from the Indian side was kept up by Surendranath Banerjea's Indian Association in Bengal, sympathetic colonial officials added the weight of official opinion in favour of native volunteering. Dr Cowie, the Deputy Surgeon-General of Bengal, forwarded a petition of about 150 native students from Campbell Medical School, along with a strong recommendation in support of the petition, to the Government of India. Ripon, however, was unwilling to start a fresh controversy by pressing for native admission to the Volunteer Corps.[36]

The challenge to the colonial ideology of martial traditions, moreover, coincided with a new politics of sectional self-assertion among the Indian elites. The shift in the attitude towards volunteering reflected the broader changes that were taking place in elite Indian politics in the last quarter of the nineteenth century. A new generation of native politicians were emerging who defined themselves against the more traditional landed elites represented in such organisations as the British Indian Association of Bengal. In Bengal, the reorganisation of the Calcutta Corporation in 1876 had provided the institutional base for the influence of new political leaders.[37] The Indian Association, founded by Banerjea, was the most prominent new political organisation of Bengal. In the 1870s the Banerjea-led agitation for civil service reforms had quickly acquired a Pan-Indian character, reflecting similar changes in elite Indian politics in other parts of the country as well. The Ilbert Bill controversy of 1883 had provided the most important catalyst for the consolidation of this new all-India elite public opinion. In Bengal, the Ilbert Bill controversy had accentuated the differences between the older British Indian Association and the younger Indian Association. While the organs of the wealthy landed interests in Bengal were relatively silent over the Ilbert Bill in protest against the proposed Bengal Tenancy Bill that would have checked the arbitrary exercise of the landlord's power over tenants, the Indian Association took the first step in establishing an all-India nationalist forum by convening the first Indian National Conference in Calcutta.[38] A rejuvenation of elite Indian public opinion was also represented in such organisations as the Madras Mahasabha in Madras, the Bombay Presidency Association in Bombay, and the Poona Sarvajanik Sabha in Poona. These changes raised anew questions about the exclusion of certain sections of the Indian elites from the colonial ideology of martial traditions.

It was the native volunteer movement of 1885–86 that finally brought to a head the developing crisis in the colonial mix of the racial and the class dimensions of martial traditions in India. The politics of colonial masculinity provided the vehicle for rearticulating the intersection of the racial and the class assumptions in the ideology of martial traditions. This rearticulation not only rejected the native volunteer demand without relying on an exclusively racial definition of martial traditions, but also recuperated the challenge posed by the new developments in elite Indian politics.

First, the politics of colonial masculinity rearticulated the ideology of martial traditions to make possible a satisfactory colonial response to the native volunteer movement – one that simultaneously sympathised with the loyalty of Indian elites and rejected their demands to volunteer. This strategy was disingenuous at best: in the name of continuity with official policy, it, in fact, facilitated a new institutionalisation of the racial exclusion of Indians from the volunteer movement in India. In so far as the native demand to volunteer was an outpouring of loyalty from indigenous elites towards colonial rule, an outright rejection of the native demands by the colonial authorities would have been counterproductive to the strategies of colonial rule. The Russian war scare of 1885 had prompted generous offers of financial and military assistance from independent princely states as well as offers to volunteer from wealthy landowners, members of the mercantile community and of professional and service groups in British India. Just as Banerjea in the pages of the *Bengalee* was urging the educated community to volunteer because of their special obligation to the colonial regime, so also the representatives of the wealthy *zamindari* (landlord) community, like Raja Rajendra Lal Mitra, were urging the formation of independent native volunteer corps in the pages of the *Hindoo Patriot*.[39] According to Banerjea, Indians wished to volunteer 'to testify their sense of duty to the country and their devout loyalty to the Queen Empress'.[40] The show of loyalty from Indian elites at a time when the threat of 'Russian hordes' swarming across the north-west frontier was still alive was no doubt gratifying to the colonial authorities so soon after the racial bitterness of the Ilbert Bill controversy.

The entire premise of the native volunteer movement, moreover, was based on the recognition that native elites had a special stake in the preservation of the colonial social order. Indeed, in recognition of the special responsibility of native elites, the Bombay politician Dadabhai Naoroji, among others, recommended the use of the 'property and education test' as the criterion for the selection of native volunteers.[41]

THE NATIVE VOLUNTEER MOVEMENT

Just such a proposal for native volunteering was presented to the Viceroy by Hume, acting on behalf of native political leaders. The proposal clearly restricted the selection of native volunteers to candidates with a 'good education, adequate knowledge of English, an unblemished character, and a respectable family'. It also recognised the importance of maintaining European control over native volunteering: the selection of native volunteers was to be left to a recruiting committee part European and part native; those recommended could be admitted either to the existing corps or to separate native corps; the commissioned officers of the Corps would be all Europeans, chosen from either the regular army or from the existing officers of the Volunteer Corps (later an opening could be provided for natives to become commissioned officers in the Volunteer Corps).[42] The native volunteer movement was a powerful testimony to the continued investment of Indian elites, despite the criticism of specific colonial policies, in the colonial social structure.

The nature of the native volunteer movement made any outright defence of the racial exclusivity of volunteering in India by the colonial authorities unwise; instead, the logic of colonial masculinity was deployed to provide a more ingenious response to the native demands. It permitted the continued expression of special favour to Indian elites whose worthiness to volunteer could be recognised in terms of the rights of manly or martial races. At the same time, however, the dynamics of colonial masculinity could block actual and concrete demands for native volunteering by conjuring up the spectre of the 'effeminate *babu*'.

The impending threat from Russia temporarily silenced the more overt Anglo-Indian opposition to the native volunteer movement. The *Bengalee* remarked on the surprising restraint shown by the Anglo-Indian press on the native volunteer movement:

> Even the *Englishman* newspaper – the organ of the extreme section of the Anglo-Indian party – the advocate of monopoly and of exclusion, of special right and special privileges – is inclined to view with satisfaction the growth of a movement, which is capable of illimitable expansion and which may be turned into a source of infinite strength to the Empire.

In early April, the *Bengalee* was still reporting that the 'bulk of the Anglo-Indian press is in sympathy with the native volunteer movement'.[43] Even the Calcutta correspondent of *The Times* of London, who had earlier been instrumental in spreading disinformation about the Ilbert Bill in Britain, found it 'hard not to sympathize with the loyal aspirations of the petitioners' who had offered their services as volunteers.[44] A visiting British politician, who was not known for his sympathies for the political demands of Indians, nevertheless found it 'ridiculous that in such cities as Bombay, Calcutta, Madras and many others, volunteers are recruited solely among Europeans'.[45]

At the same time, however, ridicule of the dubious value of effeminate native volunteers was also the most popular defence against the extension of volunteering privileges to Indians. Expressing a fairly common Anglo-Indian opinion, especially after the immediate threat from Russia had abated, the *Civil and Military Gazette* of Lahore wrote that 'none but fighting classes should be enrolled [in the Volunteer Corps]. The clerkly element should be as conspicuous by its absence, as it is in the regular army ... the *babu* although a valiant wielder of the pen, is not so handy with the sword.'[46] The premise that the demand for native volunteering came primarily from natives from 'non-warlike provinces' and from communities without a strong martial tradition, therefore, went a long way towards discrediting the entire native volunteer movement. Anglo-Indian officials argued that native volunteers would consist primarily of effeminate *babus* who alone would have either the time or the motivation to serve as *'mufti sepais'* (literally: unpaid soldiers).[47] The *Englishman* expressed scepticism of the military value of volunteering from the educated community of Bengal: 'should native loyalty ever be put to that crucial test, it is needless to ask where, during the fierce struggle that must ensue, will be found the race, who in the language of Macaulay "would see his country over-run, his house laid in ashes, his children murdered or dishonoured without having the spirit to strike one blow".'[48] 'Not a single Bengali *Babu* from Assam to the Sunderbunds', Sir Lepel Griffin argued in the *Asiatic Quarterly Review*, 'would fire a shot for the English if they were engaged in a war *l'outrance* with Russia.'[49] In an ingenious variation to the standard ridicule of 'effeminate *babu*' volunteers, one colonial official suggested that *babu* volunteers endangered the entire basis of volunteering in India. For weak and cowardly volunteers, who could not be relied upon to ensure the safe custody of their rifles and ammunition, would make it possible for the arms of the volunteers to fall into the hands of the *badmashes* or the dangerous 'criminal elements' in native society.[50] It also became common among Anglo-Indians to interpret the native demand for volunteering not as an assertion of the 'manly' right to self-defence, but as the 'nervousness' of an effete class of Indians.[51]

Nothing, however, more thoroughly exposed the agenda of colonial masculinity in the native volunteer movement than the special antipathy it invoked towards the alleged 'effeminacy' of educated Indian volunteers. Although it was the 'effeminacy' of the educated Indians that was cited most often as the reason for not extending the volunteer movement to natives, the argument supporting educated Indian volunteers, made by a very small handful of Anglo-Indians, was most instructive. These men saw some value to colonial rule in securing the political gratitude of the educated community in India. They offered an interesting twist to the arguments about the dubious value of 'effeminate *babu*' volunteers: the non-martial character of the educated community, they suggested, was, in fact, a compelling argument for extending the privilege of volunteering to the educated community. Since 'for direct military purposes', the educated community posed no threat to the colonial government, it was both militarily safe and politically expedient to gratify the desire of the educated community to volunteer. Robert Knight, the liberal editor of the *Statesman*, argued that the 'educated natives may not be warlike', but 'the same reason makes them less of a menace'.[52] Henry Harrison, Chairman of the Corporation of Calcutta, who was in all probability the author of one of the most celebrated pamphlets on native volunteering, *Ought Natives to be Welcomed as Volunteers* by 'Trust and Fear Not', made a similar case in favour of the demands of the native volunteer movement. He argued that because the educated community in India was 'too unwarlike and too weak in numbers to be of much importance', they did not 'constitute any serious menace from the military point of view'.[53] Since there was little threat to the security of the Empire from extending the privilege of volunteering to the educated community, both Harrison and Knight suggested that it would be politically beneficial to encourage the educated community to invest in the martial values that were lauded so highly by the colonial rulers themselves. Knight argued that it was the special responsibility of the colonial Government to encourage in India the cultivation of martial values that had proved so beneficial in Britain:

> We know from our own public schools at home, how much improvement and healthy enjoyment, the boys get from the regular training they receive in drill ... what is it that we ourselves complain chiefly about in native character, but that it is wanting in the courageous and manly behaviour to which we justly attach so high an importance in the culture of our own youth. And now that a strong desire for this same culture has taken the possession of the minds of our native students and teachers alike, it would surely be unwise to check or suppress it ... we do wrong to [the educated classes] by excluding them from the army as a profession, and might with equal wisdom and safety, gratify their strong desire for permission to form Volunteer Corps amongst themselves.[54]

Similarly, Harrison considered the emulation of 'British' values by the educated community in India a healthy development that would have a politically and socially stabilising influence for colonial rule:

> many educated natives, in Bengal specially, have for years past, felt the

reproach which attaches to their want of courage and corporeal activity, and have earnestly set themselves to remedy these defects: hence on all sides we find efforts to follow the example of Europeans among native students. Football and cricket are becoming popular and gymnasia introduced. The volunteer movement is connected with the same feeling; it is honorable to have a *'corpus sanum'* as the vehicle of a *'mens sana'*, and drill and discipline are not to be despised as aids to this.[55]

In calling for colonial rule to be consistent with its professed ideals, however, the Anglo-Indian advocates of native volunteering naively believed in the good faith of the colonial ideology of martial traditions. The point of the colonial ideology of martial traditions, however, was never to encourage the cultivation of a martial spirit among Indians – merely to justify the racial exclusivity of volunteering in India.

The real achievement of the rearticulation of the colonial ideology of martial traditions by colonial masculinity was thus its impact on the racial exclusivity of volunteering in India: for it made possible an even more explicit acknowledgement of the racial exclusivity of volunteering than before. The appearance of continuity in the official policy towards volunteering masked the crucial fact that the circumstances for volunteering in India had changed. Both as a result of the anxieties aroused by 'a mob of armed unruly Europeans' reminiscent of 1883 and of the external threat from Russia there had been a subtle shift in the definition of volunteering in India; from its role primarily for the suppression of internal trouble it was assigned a new role in freeing up British troops in India for combat duty abroad. This subtle shift in the role of volunteering was noted by Dufferin: 'recent events have brought into prominence that aspect of the Volunteer movement amongst Europeans in India in which that force may be regarded rather as an addition to our military garrison than as a body constituted for purposes of self defence'.[56] To mark this shift, the Volunteer Force in India was brought under the more centralised control of the Military Department in India.[57] At the annual Calcutta Trades Association Dinner in January 1885, leading Anglo-Indian officials and non-officials in the city noted with satisfaction that the duty to volunteer 'is being taken up in such a spirited manner in the *mofussil*, and that a body of volunteers is now to be found in every centre of European population'. In raising a toast to the volunteers, Brig.-General H. C. Wilkinson predicted that before the year was out there would be 'nearly double the number of armed Europeans in India'.[58] The annual returns in February 1885 already showed an increase of 5,000 men from the previous year. Commenting on the increase, the *Englishman* observed: 'Volunteering is a much more serious affair in this country than in England where the holiday element enters largely into it. A national sentiment that will convert 5,000 busy civilians into volunteers in the hot season, must be genuine.'[59] The changes in the role of volunteering had brought with it a renewal of official enthusiasm for armed Anglo-Indians and Eurasians in India.

Because the renewed interest in volunteering also brought to the fore the need for a more explicit clarification of the role of natives in the volunteer movement, it put the policy of official neutrality on native volunteering to its severest test. In early 1885, despite offers from the native population to aid in the war effort against Russia, the Government approved a proposal for setting up a Volunteer Reserve Force that was directed only to the Anglo-Indian and Eurasian population. The proposal for the creation of a Reserve Force had been made by Lt.-Col. J. H. Rivett-Carnac and forwarded the previous year to the Military Department of the Government of India by Sir Alfred Lyall, Lt.-Governor of the North-West Provinces and Oudh. Rivett-Carnac's proposal was to raise an additional 60,000 volunteers in India. The Reserves were not regulars, but constituted a second line of volunteers. The members would not be enlisted, but would only be required to give their names for registration. The Government would then undertake to provide them with a Martini Henri Rifle with fifty rounds of ammunition yearly, a capitation grant of ten rupees, and a uniform allowance of five rupees. The only concession to native volunteering in Rivett-Carnac's original proposal, but not repeated in the Military Department's draft, was mention of an explicit encouragement to 'native Christians' to volunteer.[60]

Ironically, the new changes in the volunteer movement made the exclusion of Indians from the movement even more rigidly institutionalised. The circulars issued by the Military Department to local officials on the composition of the Reserve Force, as Briton Martin has shown, were often quite explicit about the exclusion of natives.[61] When Anglo-Indian and Eurasian volunteers in Madras threatened a revolt at the decision of Major Spring Branson, a ranking officer of the Volunteer Corps, to allow 'native gentlemen' to join the Madras Volunteer Artillery, the Military Department at Calcutta hastily instructed the Madras Government to prohibit volunteering by the 'native' classes. With the backing of the Government of India, the Chief Secretary of the Madras Government informed the prospective native volunteers that 'the Volunteer Corps, as at present constituted, are regarded as an auxiliary force in India, and are, therefore, only open to Europeans and Eurasians'.[62] Elsewhere, Martin notes, officials were more careful about the wording of the announcement for the Reserve Corps; no ambiguity was left about the racial composition of the Force. The die-hard Anglo-Indian exclusionists, with the additional weight of official opinion behind them, were thus able to scuttle any efforts to allow native entry in any of the newly created volunteer corps. Furthermore, following the incident at Madras, there were rumours that natives serving in existing volunteer corps in Burma, Ceylon, Quetta, and in some parts of India had been asked to resign in pursuance of a new interpretation of official policy on native volunteering.[63]

It was a mark of the success of the politics of colonial masculinity that, despite the more explicit exclusion of natives from the volunteer movement, there was no departure in public from the existing policy of official neutrality on native volunteering, first articulated by Canning in the 1860s. Yet Dufferin's government in 1885 had been under tremendous pressure to clarify its position on native volunteering. A petition dated 27 March 1885 signed by Maulvi Khuda Baksh, a leading Muslim pleader of the Patna Bar, and thirty-six other pleaders had opened the floodgates for similar petitions from all over the country on the volunteer question.[64] The Indian press was also clamouring for the Government to state its position on native volunteering. Public meetings on the question were held all over India; in Bengal alone meetings were held in Calcutta, Chinsurah, Krishnanagur, Nuddea, Mymensingh, and several of the *mofussil* towns.[65] The majority view, especially in the wake of the Madras affair, was for the creation of separate native volunteer corps. A memorial from Calcutta, signed by approximately 400 natives in Calcutta and its suburbs, was taken by the colonial authorities as the prototype of the numerous petitions received on the question. The Calcutta Memorial was signed by *zamindars*, barristers, *vakils* (lawyers), government officers, professors, students, doctors, newspaper editors, merchants, traders, and clerks in and around Calcutta. The petitioners urged the Government to accept their services as volunteers; the rejection of the native demand, they suggested, would 'cast an unmerited slur' upon native loyalty.[66]

The official response to the native demands was modeled on the argument first articulated by A. P. MacDonnell, the Secretary of the Government of Bengal, in a note that he appended to the Calcutta memorial and forwarded to the Military Department of the Government of India. MacDonnell began by denying the charge made in the Calcutta memorial that there was any discrimination on the basis of race or religion in the composition of the Volunteer Force in India; he also denied that there had been any change in official policy on the admission of natives in the Volunteer Corps. He therefore recommended that there was no need for departure from the existing policy on native volunteering.[67] This line of argument was later adopted in the Official Despatch on the subject of native volunteering prepared by the Military Department of the Government of India. The Despatch, dated 21 September 1885, recommended that the Secretary of State in London reject the native volunteer petitions on grounds that it was neither advisable nor necessary to depart from the policy on native volunteering set by Canning in 1861.[68]

Whereas the colonial authorities could rely legitimately on the legal precedent established in the Volunteer Act to reject the creation of separate native volunteer corps, they were on shakier ground on the question of the admission of natives to existing European corps. The Official Despatch on the native volunteer movement, therefore, chose to focus primarily on the legal difficulties involved in sanctioning separate native volunteer corps. The Viceroy had asked the Law Member C. P. Ilbert to explore the legal aspect of the demands of the native volunteer movement. Ilbert was the only member of the Viceroy's Council who supported the native demands, and failing that, he had recommended concessions on some other demands of the educated community in India. Clearly outvoted by the majority opinion, however, he informed Dufferin that since the Volunteers came under the Articles of War for European troops serving in India, 'the incorporation of Natives into independent Volunteer companies would be illegal' unless sanctioned by the 'Secretary of State [and] in all probability an Act of Parliament'.[69] On the question of the admission of natives in existing corps the Despatch of the Government of India was deliberately vague: it merely confessed that it was helpless in dealing with this matter in the face of the opposition of Anglo-Indian and Eurasian volunteers. Dufferin informed the Secretary of State that 'we may regret the spirit which underlies' the exclusion of natives from existing corps, but 'it is impossible for us to ignore or minimise it'.[70] Yet contrary to these professions of helplessness, the official position, most notably in its encouragement to the expansion of the volunteer movement in 1885, had compromised any semblance of official neutrality on native volunteering.

The lack of clarity on the position of natives in the volunteer movement only sought to mask the fact that volunteering had already hardened into an exclusive racial privilege in India. For, unlike in the past, the official position on native volunteering was now more explicitly involved in the preservation of the racial exclusivity of volunteering. The Calcutta correspondent of *The Times* reported that the Government was unable to accept the demands for native volunteering purely on 'legal grounds'.[71] Extending the legal arguments against the creation of separate native corps to the admission of natives even in existing corps, the *Englishman* claimed that 'volunteers are considered a European group and hence on parade they occupy a place immediately after the European troops on the extreme right (but) if natives were admitted into the corps they would lose this privilege and be placed on the left of the native regulars in the brigade'.[72] The rejection of the native volunteer movement provided further ammunition to the most die-hard Anglo-Indian and Eurasian exclusionists against the admission of Indians in the volunteer movement.

The official response to the native volunteer movement did not resolve once and for all the question of native volunteering; its real value, indeed, lay in successfully eliding the hardening of the racial politics of volunteering in India. In 1890–91, not long after the fiasco of the native volunteer demand of 1885, natives once again offered to volunteer in large numbers in Bengal, partly in response to rumours that a few Parsis and Madrasis had been allowed to volunteer by military order, and partly in response to the call of the Lt.-Governor of Bengal for increasing the strength of Anglo-Indian and Eurasian volunteers in the province. The petition went up to the Viceroy, Lord Lansdowne, who rejected it. This time, however, the Viceroy's response raised a question in the House of Commons in Britain; the Government of India was asked to clarify its position on the right of natives in India to bear arms. The Under-Secretary of State for India, John Gorst, assured the House that there had been no change in official policy on native volunteering, and that anyone in India could become a volunteer provided his European colleagues agreed.[73] An anecdote from the 1920s recounted by an Anglo-Indian official, Sir Henry Sharp, however, reveals more accurately the rigid principle of racial exclusion that had become inseparable from the history of volunteering in India. A Bengali employee of the Bengal Assam Railway was sent as a station master to a small place which abounded with tigers. The man was a keen sportsman, but since he could not afford to buy a rifle he decided to join the Volunteers so that he would be able to use his service rifle for sport. He gave his name as Sydney Kenneth Mackenzie, instead of his real name Satish Chandra Mukherji, in order to pass as a dark-complexioned Eurasian. He was duly enrolled and given his rifle. On being found out as a 'pure Asiatic', he was ejected from the Volunteer Corps and had his rifle taken from him.[74] So even though the logic of colonial masculinity retained the double valence of the racial and class dimension of martial traditions in India, its real achievement was to mask the fact that the volunteer movement itself had become more firmly a symbol of exclusive racial privilege.

A second contribution of colonial masculinity to the native volunteer controversy was to serve as a criterion for distributing the rewards of loyalty to different sections of the Indian elites. The distinction between 'martial' and 'non-martial' Indian elites became the basis for separating the so-called positive from the negative constituents of the native volunteer movement. Colonial officials were at pains to distinguish between the 'bonafide eagerness of the warlike races ... to share in the burdens of the country and the risks of defensive war' and the 'utter sham' of the 'landless, comparatively poor, and socially inferior' group who were merely using the question of volunteering 'to strip away any apparent distinction which belongs to their fellow subject'.[75] On the one hand, with mainly native politicians and intellectuals in mind, the majority of the Anglo-Indian officials raised the fear that the volunteer corps would be converted into political societies 'entirely wanting in the practical sense which has enabled Volunteer Corps in England to steer clear of political views of any kind'.[76] Native volunteer corps, it was argued, would make native politicians 'formidable politically' and would give them the service of an armed body of men for demanding the extension of political reforms.[77] The association of the native volunteer movement with the new developments in elite politics in India, moreover, allowed the colonial authorities to dismiss the entire volunteer movement as a mainly 'Bengali agitation', associated with the 'advanced political parties' and 'artificially stimulated by the press and wire pullers'.[78] In fact, the conviction that native politicians were trying to make 'political capital' out of the volunteering issue convinced many Anglo-Indians against native volunteering.

On the other hand, with mainly the landed aristocracy in mind, there were some officials who were willing to consider such limited schemes for native volunteers as the creation of a yeoman cavalry, the admission of natives in mixed volunteer corps, or the formation of separate native volunteer corps, and some advancement of native elites in the regular army.[79] The admission of wealthy landowners and scions of aristocratic families with a martial tradition in existing European volunteer corps received the support of several senior Anglo-Indian officials consulted on the volunteer question. Sir Charles Aitchison, Lt.-Governor of the Punjab, recommended some concession to native volunteering because, he argued,

> the movement in favour of native volunteering is by no means confined to young and advanced politicians or to those who have received an English education. It began with men like Baba Khem Singh and others, and is strongly supported by many of the older members of the community ... men of mature years and tried loyalty, who have, on more than one critical occasion, identified themselves in our battles.[80]

The willingness of colonial officials to entertain some limited proposal for native volunteering depended on the extent to which they associated the demand for volunteering with the landed elites and other more reliable allies of the colonial government.

Yet the distinction between the 'martial' and 'non-martial' constituents of the native volunteer movement did not translate into any concessions, however limited, towards native volunteering; rather, it only rationalised the decision not to make any changes in the volunteer movement. For, on the one hand, the 'martial' and 'non-martial' distinction had secured a consensus against any scheme of native volunteering that would include the native politicians and intellectuals of the educated community in India. Both those who were against all concessions to the native volunteer movement as well as those who were willing to offer some concessions like allowing natives of 'high birth' and 'warlike character' to enrol as volunteers could agree on this. But, on the other hand, the lack of consensus on an alternative scheme for native volunteering that could exclude the 'undesirable' sections of the native elites doomed any prospect of extending the volunteer movement to natives. As Dufferin put it, it was not possible to devise a satisfactory scheme for native volunteering restricted to 'particular classes' without invoking 'arbitrary distinctions', which would not only be perceived as 'obnoxious', but would also prove 'difficult to maintain'.[81] The further point, as J. W. Edgar of the Bengal Government recognised, was that there could be no guarantee that the so-called 'martial' natives would indeed remain more loyal to colonial rule than the 'non-martial' natives:

> The mere statement that such corps might, and probably would, include the sons and grandsons of the Brahmins and Rajpoots who fought against us under Kooer Singh [ref. to 1857 rebellion], as well as Wahabis in Patna and Ferazies in East Bengal [ref. to anti-British orthodox Muslim sects] seems sufficient to dispose of the question. If, on the other hand, it be said that these classes would, as a rule, be excluded if permission to volunteer were confined to men who had received an English education, I would point out that the distinction which in this way would be made between manly, high spirited, brave men like the high caste Hindoos of Shahbad, or the Mahomeddans of Behar and Bengal, and the weaker and more effeminate race who form the majority of the educated class, would create a danger little less grave than the one guarded against.[82]

Nothing, therefore, came of any of the suggestions to allow some limited form of native volunteering.

If no concessions were made to native elites in the native volunteer controversy, despite the willingness of many colonial officials to placate at least the so-called martial natives, it was because the authorities in Britain and in India placed different emphasis on the racial and class dimension of the colonial ideology of martial traditions. Although the majority of the officials consulted in India by Dufferin between June and July 1885 advised him to reject the native volunteer demand and to 'act as if Great Britain were to govern India for all time, doing nothing to undermine its foundations', the Viceroy himself was acutely aware that it was 'desirable to show' some 'confidence in the loyalty of natives'.[83] In the wake of the alliance between the landed aristocracy and the educated community on the issue of volunteering, the Viceroy recognised the need to pursue some alternative to the demand for native volunteering so as to placate the so-called 'martial' over the 'non-martial' native elites. He, therefore, turned to a proposal that he had been working on even before dealing with the demands of the native volunteer movement; the proposal suggested a minor reorganisation of the army to give 'higher class native gentlemen' appointments to the commissioned ranks of the army in a separate native infantry and cavalry regiment. With the agitation over native volunteering exciting the attention of native elites in India, Dufferin hoped that his proposal for the promotion of a 'certain proportion of natives to responsible commands in the Regular Army' would placate the leading aristocratic families and the landed magnates in India. Anglo-Indian officials had assured the Viceroy that 'if military service were made more attractive to native gentlemen' it would conciliate 'the sympathy of the manly races of Hindustan and the Deccan' and allow the Government to 'regard with more equanimity the disappointment which the advanced Bengali might express at an adverse decision' on native volunteering.[84] Dufferin wrote to the Secretary of State that while native volunteering would put arms indiscriminately into the hands of 'excitable university graduates' and thus encourage their spurious demands for political and social equality, reforms in the army would be restricted to traditional native elites and would not challenge the 'absolute preponderance of material power' in the hands of the British.[85] Dufferin's recommendations for the army were leaked to the press well before he had issued any public response on the native volunteer movement.[86] But the India Office and the new Secretary of State in London, relatively isolated from the pressures of domestic politics in India, found concessions to Indians in the army even more dangerous than allowing select natives to volunteer.[87] The authorities in Britain considered the army, which was one of the largest employers of working-class Britons in India, hardly the place to experiment with relaxing the privileges of race. But notwithstanding the ultimate failure of Dufferin's plan to 'please old families' at the expense of the 'claims of the educated community', his proposal for Indians in the regular army, no less than his response to the native volunteer movement, laid the the framework for responding to the growing constraints on rewarding elite collaboration in the last quarter of the century.[88]

The third, and perhaps most important, impact of the politics of colonial masculinity on the native volunteer controversy stemmed from its intersection with the class interests of Indian elites. For, above all, colonial masculinity recuperated the radical edge in the demand of the native volunteer movement. If at one end of the social scale the demand for native volunteering posed a challenge to the social distinction between the landed aristocracy and the educated community, at the other end, as a critique of expensive colonial financial and military policies, it also contained the potential for bringing the demands of elite Indian politicians in closer harmony with the interests of the uneducated and impoverished millions. One prescient Anglo-Indian editor recognised the potential of such a development; he warned of the advent of 'a new era in the history of political agitation in India'.[89] For in the midst of the volunteer controversy public meetings were being held in Bengal where peasants, landed elites, and the educated community made common cause in criticising the expensive financial policies of the colonial Government. However, because the primary concern of the native volunteer demand was the emasculation of the elite Indian male, its radical potential was contained by the reassertion of native masculinity. In so far, therefore, as colonial masculinity coincided with the self-perception of effeminacy among native elites, it limited the native volunteer movement to a narrower critique of colonial policies for 'demilitarising' the indigenous elites.

The question of native volunteering did provide an opportunity to Indian political leaders for bridging the gap between elite politics and the mass protests of tribal revolts and the post-1870 agrarian unrests in Bengal. For the colonial administration under Dufferin had embarked on an aggressive and expensive foreign policy with important implications for all Indians. The Viceroy had sent a small force comprising mainly British troops to Afghanistan in the event of a war with Russia. To make up for the subsequent decline in the number of British troops left in India, the Viceroy called for a temporary reinforcement of British troops from Britain for garrison duty in India. This, as Indian political leaders pointed out, was a far more expensive solution than that of accepting the offers of 'loyal' natives who were willing to serve as volunteers to preserve law and order in the country.[90] Adding to the financial burdens, moreover, the Viceroy proposed to increase the army by some 30,000 additional troops. But any increase in the native portion of the army required a corresponding proportionate increase in the more expensive British component of the army; the Army Commission of 1879 had recommended for the 'safety' of the army not only to 'counterpoise native against native' in the native portion of the army, but also to 'counterpoise' the native army with a sufficient European force equipped with superior weapons and placed in complete control of the artillery and arsenals.[91] The large financial outlay entailed by the troop increases at a time when Indian finances were already very shaky could be met only by increased taxation or by a retrenchment in public expenditure in India. Indian politicians, increasingly sensitive to the impact that these unnecessary and expensive imperial adventures had on the overburdened Indian finances, were beginning to connect the demand for native volunteering to the stunning 'indifference' of the colonial authorities to the 'welfare' of the people.[92] But the potential for such a critique of colonial rule was quickly lost in the inordinate emphasis that native political leaders placed on the demilitarisation of the elite Indian male.

The fact that colonial masculinity could also be appropriated to represent the interests of the indigenous elite and their hegemonic aspirations was ultimately the most telling testimony to its success in rearticulating the ideology of martial traditions. The elite Bengali male's self-perception of effeminacy was itself a dimension of the struggle for hegemony of the indigenous elites under the conditions of nineteenth-century colonialism: for, in Tanika Sarkar's provocative suggestion, at a time when the Bengali elite still eschewed direct criticism of colonial rule, it expressed its hegemonic aspirations not so much by assuming economic and political leadership of colonial society, but by attributing to itself – specifically to the elite male physique – all the ravages and despair of colonial rule.[93] Hence when Indian politicians made grandiose claims, which tied the issue of native volunteering to 'the highest hopes and aspirations of the people' and the failure to accede to their demands as a 'humiliation of the people', they were elevating the elite project of redeeming Indian, and especially Bengali, masculinity as the inaugural moment in the awakening of all of India to the contradictions of colonial rule.[94] The *Bengalee*, which was one of the leading advocates of the native volunteer movement, commented on the implications of native volunteering for the Bengalis, proverbially the most non-martial of the native elites in India:

> Every one remembers the celebrated passage in Macaulay's *Life of Warren Hastings*, where he speaks of the people of these provinces not furnishing a single *sepoy* to the armies of the East India Company. What estimate would Macaulay form of our national progress, if he found that in less then half-a-century from the time when he thus wrote, the youth and the manhood of the people, whom he described in such terms, were ready to enlist themselves as citizen soldiers in the service of their Queen and their country.[95]

For the Bengalis, the interest in volunteering, like that in 'manly sports' and 'gymnastic exercises', was part of a new awakening to the emasculation of the Bengali male under colonial rule. The volunteering question thus provoked special indignation among Bengalis who were already acutely aware of the humiliation of their non-martial status. The Bengali press pointed to the anomaly of Bengalis being allowed to serve as volunteers in Britain, but denied the same privilege on their return to India. Four Bengalis – J. C. Bose, N. L. Haldar, M. Mullick, and P. L. Roy – who had signed the Calcutta memorial on native volunteering had served as volunteers in England.[96] In 1885, moreover, two Bengali civil surgeons were among eight army surgeons chosen for frontier service. If Bengali doctors could perform frontier service, the vernacular press in Bengal argued, it was difficult to understand why Bengalis were discriminated against in military duty.[97]

It was the desire of native elites for a greater martial role, hitherto reserved only for the native aristocracy and landed magnates, that was behind the demand for political and social equality in the native volunteer movement. The most popular complaint of the native volunteer movement, therefore, was directed at the unjustness of colonial policy that allowed sundry 'foreigners' living in India to join volunteer corps but prevented the high caste/class Indian from sharing in the defence of the country. As one complaint in the *Bengalee*, betraying the author's own racist assumptions, noted:

> Here are Africans, West Indians, Armenians and Jews in short all races and all creeds who find ready admittance into the army of Her Majesty's citizen soldiers. Are we alone to be excluded from this right? . . . Does our Aryan blood carry with it so great a stigma that the dusky sons of Africa and the mixed race of America and of our own city are to be trusted and honored in preference to ourselves?[98]

Native editors also compared the British distrust of placing arms in the hands of the natives in India with the policies followed by other European powers: the Russians, they pointed out, had Asians in senior positions in the army, and the French had recently urged natives in the French possessions in India to enrol as volunteers.[99] On a more ominous note, Indian political leaders warned of the consequences of thwarting the legitimate demands of the Indians. Banerjea, for example, cited the recent developments in Ireland as a lesson to heed for the colonial authorities in India. The *Bengalee* warned 'let not the words "too late" be marked upon every privilege and upon every concession' lest the delay will 'fail to conciliate or to awaken gratitude' but will only provoke the natives.

But just as elite nationalist politics in 1885 was still a demand for the liberalisation of colonial policies rather than for the replacement of British rule, so also the criticism against the 'demartialising' of the natives in the native volunteer movement was still very much within

THE NATIVE VOLUNTEER MOVEMENT

the framework of colonial masculinity. The rejection of the native volunteer demand by the colonial authorities had injected a powerful new dimension in the self-perception of 'effeminacy' among elite Bengali males: it was the colonial authorities who were now held chiefly responsible for 'emasculating' the Bengalis. The Bengalis were believed to have redeemed their 'manliness' by their willingness to volunteer. Since the demand for native volunteering was seen as part of a broader movement for the physical regeneration of the Bengalis, the colonial authorities were held responsible for deliberately squashing the development of a martial spirit among the Bengalis. The official hostility towards native volunteering was thus seen as a deliberate plot 'for weakening and emasculating the Indians, and for crushing out their manliness'.[100] The *Bengalee* raised the distinct possibility that the colonial authorities might have a stake in keeping the natives emasculated: 'are we to be debarred from cultivating the manlier qualities because, forsooth the possession of them by a subject race might be a source of embarrassment to the Government?'[101] Similarly, the *Praja Bandhu*, a Bengali weekly published from the French possession at Chandernagore, wrote: 'are the English afraid of Bengalis, or do they not trust them? Are Bengalis quite unable to bear arms, or is this the result of the one-sidedness so conspicuous in English character?'[102] Indian political leaders tried to recover some political meaning out of the failure of the native volunteer movement. Banerjea, making a case for the redemption of Bengali 'manliness', argued that the enthusiasm for volunteering in Bengal had 'by the solid and irresistible logic of facts' succeeded in refuting 'once [and] for all the imputation of unmanliness which our critics took a delight in bringing against us'.[103] The *Amrita Bazar Patrika* also took comfort, some years later, in the explanation that it was the fear of the Bengalis rather than their weakness that had led the colonial authorities to reject the native volunteer demand:

> the Bengalees [had] offered to be volunteers, but their offer was not accepted. This did not however show any cowardice on the part of the Bengalees as it did on the part of those who declined the offer. The disarmament of the Bengalees again does not show that the Bengalees are regarded as cowards by the responsible people of the land. [104]

The editor of the *Indian Mirror* in Bengal commented that the native volunteer movement and the subsequent native critique of colonial policies for 'demilitarising' the Indians had sown the 'germs of a new national life' in India; but in so far as the native critique was itself deeply invested in the politics of colonial masculinity, it failed to develop the full potential of the challenge represented by the native volunteer movement.[105]

It was precisely because the redemption of Indian masculinity was undertaken within the colonial ideology of martial traditions that even the most strident Indian critique of the 'demilitarisation' of the Indian not only failed to impress the colonial authorities, but also reflected a more ambivalent attitude towards colonial rule. At the same time as Indian politicians blamed colonial policies for 'systematically crushing out of us all martial spirit', they defended their right to cultivate a martial spirit on the grounds of their special investment in the structures of colonial rule. This contradiction was played out in the various all-India political conferences held at the end of 1885. At these conferences, Indian political leaders criticised colonial policies such as the Arms Act, the rejection of the native volunteer movement, and the absence of natives in senior ranks in the army for 'demilitarising' the native population. The second meeting of the Indian National Conference held in Calcutta in December 1885, and jointly sponsored by the Indian Association, the British Indian Association, and the Central National Mahomedan Association of Bengal, paid by far the greatest attention to this issue in its proceedings. Ashutosh Biswas was one of the most prominent speakers at the meeting to denounce the colonial strategy of 'demilitarising' the native elites: 'The people have been "de-militarised" by being disarmed. They have not the same taste for warlike pursuits as before; and how is it possible to retain such a taste, when their arms are taken away from them?'[106] The Indian National Congress, at its second annual meeting held in Calcutta the following year, also devoted more attention to the specific critique of colonial policy for emasculating the Indian male. Raja Rampal Singh chastised the colonial Government for 'degrading our nature' and 'for converting a race of soldiers and heroes into a timid flock of quill-driving sheep'; but, in keeping with the nature of such complaints, he also assured the colonial authorities that if Indians were given the opportunity to bear arms, they would willingly give their lives 'for the support and maintenance of that Government to which we owe so much'.[107] The critique of colonial policies simply for 'demartialising' the Indian elites could not sustain a more radical challenge to colonial rule.

It was thus not just the racial but, rather, the combined racial and class dimension of colonial masculinity that served to contain the crisis posed by the native volunteer movement to the strategies of colonial rule. The intersection of racial and class politics, moreover, suggests that the colonial ideology of martial traditions had at least as much to do with the construction of hegemony in Britain as in India. In India the politics of colonial masculinity served not only to reconcile racial exclusivity with the interests of indigenous elites, but also to recuperate the critiques of colonial rule in the elite opposition to the demartialising of Indians. Indeed, the logic of colonial masculinity set the limits of the challenge posed by the native volunteer movement precisely because its racial and class politics were both intersecting and asymmetrical: unifying across class lines to create white solidarity even as it coopted elites, across racial lines, for the strategies of colonial rule.

Notes

1 See Briton Martin Jr, *New India, 1885* (Berkeley: University of California Press, 1969), pp. 102–33.
2 Letter to Lord Randolph Churchill (Military Department), 21 Sept. 1885, *India: Letters Military and Marine, July-Dec. 1885*, Letter No. 166 (Hereafter: *Letters Military*), India Office Library and Records (IOLR), London.
3 Pros. No. 1887, *Military Proceedings B October 1885 nos. 1874 – 1900* (Hereafter: *Military Proceedings B*), National Archives of India (NAI), New Delhi.
4 Dufferin's rejection of the native volunteer petitions is quoted in *The Times* (London), 8 Mar. 1886. For the reasons for the delay in Dufferin's response to the native volunteer movement, see *Military Collection 108 Volunteer Corps in India Files 1–10*, File No. 3 (Hereafter: *Military Collection*), NAI.
5 See Martin, *New India*, ch. 5, 'Lord Dufferin's Lost Opportunity: The Indian Volunteer Question and the Indian National Union'. I am indebted to Martin's account of the volunteer movement in India.
6 This point has been made in Michelguglielmo Torri, ' "Westernized Middle Class", Intellectuals and Society in Late Colonial India', *Economic and Political Weekly*, 25:4 (27 Jan. 1990), PE-2 – PE-11. For a more general discussion of the role of elite collaboration in the strategies of colonial rule, see Ronald Robinson, 'Non-European Foundations of Imperial Rule: Sketch for a Theory of Collaboration', in Roger Owen and Bob Sutcliffe (eds.), *Studies in the Theory of Imperialism* (London: Longman, 1972), pp. 117–42.
7 See Torri, ' "Westernized Middle Class"'. Also B. R. Tomlinson, 'India and the British Empire, 1880–1935', *Indian Economic and Social History Review*, 12 (1975), 337–80. For the challenges to Britain's world economic position, see M. W. Kirby, *The Decline of British Economic Power Since 1870* (London: Allen & Unwin, 1981); and Paul Warwick, 'Did Britain Change? An Inquiry into the Causes of National Decline', *Journal of Contemporary History*, 20 (1985), 99–133.
8 Letter from Col. Sir E. R. C. Bradford, Agent at Rajputana, 4 July 1885, *Dufferin Manuscripts, Letters to Viceroy from Persons in India, May–Oct. 1885*, Letter No. 10 (Hereafter: *Viceroy India*), IOLR.
9 For a discussion of the 'martial' race theory for recruitment in the post-1857 army in India, see David Omissi, '"Martial Races": Ethnicity and Security in Colonial India 1858–1939', *War and Society*, 9:1 (May 1991), 1–27.
10 See Kumkum Sangari, 'Relating Histories: Definitions of Literacy, Literature, Gender in Early Nineteenth-Century Calcutta and England', in Svati Joshi (ed.), *Rethinking English: Essays in Literature, Language, History* (New Delhi: Trianka, 1991), p. 36. For the hegemony of aristocratic social values in Britain, see Martin Wiener, *English Culture and the Decline of the Industrial Spirit 1850–1980* (Cambridge: Cambridge University Press, 1981). The meaning of the hegemony of aristocratic social and cultural values for locating the politically hegemonic 'fraction' of the ruling classes in nineteenth-century Britain has been more contentious; for the classic statement of two opposing points of view, see Perry Anderson, 'Origins of the Present Crisis', *New Left Review*, 23 (1964), 26–53; and E. P. Thompson, 'The Peculiarities of the English', *Socialist Register*, 2 (1965), reprinted in *The Poverty of Theory and Other Essays* (London: Merlin Press, 1978), pp. 35–91.
11 Quoted in letter from Lord Dufferin, 7 August 1885, *Dufferin and Ava Collection*,

vol. 2, Correspondence to Secretary of State Nov. 1884-Dec. 1889, Letter No. 50 (Hereafter: *Dufferin and Ava vol. 2*), IOLR. For the Indian Army, see P. Mason, *A Matter of Honour: An Account of the Indian Army, Its Officers and Men* (New York: Holt, Rinehart & Winston, 1974); and S. P. Cohen, *The Indian Army: Its Contributions to the Development of the Indian Nation* (Berkeley: University of California Press, 1971).

12 For a similar argument on the asymmetry of racial and class politics in the strategies of colonial rule, see Gauri Viswanathan, *Masks of Conquest: Literary Study and British Rule in India* (New York: Columbia University Press, 1989).

13 For two different points of view on the volunteer movement, see J. R. Western, 'The Volunteer Movement as an Anti-Revolutionary Force, 1793–1801', *English Historical Review*, 71 (1956), 603–14; and Linda Colley, 'Whose Nation? Class and National Consciousness in Britain 1750–1830', *Past and Present*, 113 (Nov. 1986), 97–117.

14 Hugh Cunningham, *The Volunteer Force, A Social and Political History 1859–1908* (London: Croom Helm, 1975), p. 55. I am indebted to Cunningham's study of the volunteer movement in Britain.

15 Gareth Stedman Jones, 'Working-Class Culture and Working-Class Politics in London, 1870–1900: Notes on the Remaking of A Working Class', in *Languages of Class: Studies in English Working-Class History 1832–1982* (Cambridge: Cambridge University Press, 1983), pp. 179–238.

16 There was no separate Volunteer Act for Ireland, however, for fear that the knowledge of drill and the spread of arms would contribute to sectarian conflict. See Cunningham, *The Volunteer Force*, Appendix, pp. 156–7.

17 For a history of the volunteer movement in India, see Major E. H. H. Collen, 'The Volunteer Force of India', *Journal of the United Services Institution of India*, 12:58 (1883) cited in Martin, *New India*, ch. 5; also see Col. J. F. F. Cologan, 'History of Volunteering in India', *Journal of the Royal United Services Institution*, 35: 164 (Oct. 1891), 1091–1100; Capt. E. Dawson, 'The Volunteer Force of India', *Journal of the Royal United Services Institution*, 46:288 (Feb. 1902), 206–15; Capt. B. Duff, 'Strangers in a Strange Land', *Journal of the United Services Institution of India*, 18:77 (1889), 308–39; and Capt. A. H. Mason, 'Vicinus vrit Ucalegon', *Journal of the United Services Institution of India*, 18:77 (1889), 340–83.

18 See Preamble of Act Twenty-Three of 1857, quoted in *Letters Military*, Letter No. 166.

19 According to Collen, between 1857 and 1860 there were only European and Eurasian volunteers in the Volunteer Force in India; but for evidence of Bengalis assisting the Volunteer Corps in 1857, see *Sadharani*, 26 Apr. 1885, *Report on Native Papers Bengal Presidency, Jan.-June 1885*, No. 18, p. 623 (Hereafter: *RNBP*), NAI. For a sample of elite Bengali response to the disturbances of 1857, see Sambhu Chunder Mukherjee, *The Mutinies and the People; or Statements of Native Fidelity Exhibited During the Outbreak of 1857–58* (Calcutta: I.C. Bose & Co., 1859).

20 See *Letters Military*, Letter No. 166.

21 *Ibid.*

22 'At present [there is] only one company in the whole Indian Empire that permits natives i.e. cadet company of the St. John's College, Rangoon', *Pioneer* (Allahabad), 22 Mar. 1885, p. 1. Also *Bengalee* (Calcutta), 11 July 1885, p. 328. For the resignation of Anglo-Indian volunteers in protest against native admission in the cadet corps in Burma, see *Letters Military*, Letter No. 166.

23 See *Bengalee*, 4 Apr. 1885, p. 163; and *Hindoo Patriot* (Calcutta), 13 Apr. 1885. In the 1870s the Viceroy Lord Lytton had, in response to native demands, reiterated official support for the admission of native volunteers in existing European corps. Jahangir B. Wacha had set up his own Parsi Volunteer Corps for Parsis in 1861; see S. M. Edwardes, *Kharshedji Rustomji Cama 1831–1909* (London: Oxford University Press, 1923), p. 18.

24 Sir Richard Temple, *India in 1880* (London: John Murray, 1880), p. 391.

25 See J. H. Rivett-Carnac, *Many Memories of Life in India: At Home and Abroad* (London: William Blackwood & Sons Ltd, 1910), p. 372.

26 See Collen, 'Volunteer Force'; and David Arnold, 'European Orphans and Vagrants in India in the Nineteenth Century', *Journal of Imperial and Commonwealth History* 7:2 (Jan. 1979), 104–27.
27 H. S., *The Young Soldier in India, His Life and Prospects* (London: W. H. Allen & Co., 1889), p. 202.
28 Rivett-Carnac, *Many Memories*, pp. 364–6. For the 'club' life associated with volunteering, see the discussion of the Behar Light Horse Volunteers and their club at Bankipore, near Patna, in Lillian Luker Ashby with Roger Whately, *My India* (London: Michael Joseph Ltd, 1938), p. 98. Also *Englishman* (Calcutta), 23 Mar. 1885, p. 3.
29 *Englishman*, 3 Dec. 1883, p. 5. Also see *Pioneer*, 10 Mar. 1883, p. 2; and *Civil and Military Gazette* (Lahore), 10 Mar. 1883, p. 2.
30 See Edwin Hirschmann, *'White Mutiny': The Ilbert Bill Crisis in India and the Genesis of the Indian National Congress* (New Delhi: Heritage Publishers, 1980), pp. 239–40. Also *Bengalee*, 1 Dec. 1883, p. 541.
31 *Letters Military*, Letter No. 166.
32 For the role of the Indian Association in the native volunteer demand in 1884, see *Sanjivani*, 26 Apr. 1884, *RNBP Jan.-June 1884*, No. 18, p. 508. Even earlier native politicians had raised the issue at a public meeting in Bombay in 1877. See Martin, *New India*, p. 104. Although acting on Lytton's orders, Richard Temple, Governor of Bombay and Honorary Colonel of the volunteer corps, found that he risked resignation of Anglo-Indian members if the Parsis were admitted to the corps; see *Bengalee*, 4 April 1885, p. 163. Thus Lytton's order to admit natives as volunteers was not availed of freely; see *Military Proceedings B*, No. 1881.
33 Quoted in *Reis and Reyyat* (Calcutta), 31 Mar. 1884, p. 257. See also *Bengalee*, 7 Apr. 1883, p. 175.
34 *Pioneer*, 6 Mar. 1883, p. 5.
35 *Pioneer*, 19 Apr. 1883, p. 5; For similar letters to the *Pioneer*, see 12 Mar. 1883, p. 5; 16 Mar. 1883, p. 6; 23 Mar. 1883, p. 6; 26 Mar. 1883, p. 1.
36 See *Samaya*, 24 Nov. 1884, No. 48, p. 1444; *Bangabasi*, 29 Nov. 1884, No. 49, p. 1465; and *Sanjivani*, 12 Dec. 1884, No. 49, p. 1489, *RNBP July-Dec. 1884*.
37 See Rajat Ray, *Social Conflict and Political Unrest in Bengal, 1875–1927* (Delhi: Oxford University Press, 1984).
38 *Ibid.*, p. 100.
39 *Hindoo Patriot*, 6 Apr. 1885, cited in Martin, *New India*, p. 111.
40 *Bengalee*, 11 Apr. 1885, p. 175.
41 Naoroji to Ilbert, 4 May 1885, *Ilbert Papers*, IOLR, cited in Martin, *New India*, p. 114.
42 For Hume's scheme see *Pioneer*, 28 Sept. 1885, p. 5. Also Martin, *New India*, pp. 116–17.
43 *Bengalee*, 11 Apr. 1885, p. 175; and 18 Apr. 1885, pp. 183–184.
44 *The Times*, 16 Apr. 1885, p. 6.
45 Samuel W. Baker, 'Reflections in India 1880–1888', *Fortnightly Review*, 44 (July–Dec. 1888), p. 225.
46 Quoted in *Bengalee*, 19 June 1886, p. 291.
47 Letter from Lepel Griffin, Agent in Central India, 21 June 1885, *Viceroy India*, Letter No. 421.
48 *Englishman*, 24 Jan. 1885, p. 3.
49 Lepel Griffin, 'Indian Volunteers and Indian Loyalty', *Asiatic Quarterly Review* (Jan., 1889) quoted in *Englishman*, 11 Apr. 1887, p. 6.
50 Note from A. P. MacDonnell, Secretary Government of Bengal, 15 July 1885, *Viceroy India*, Letter No. 42.
51 See *Pioneer*, 21 May 1885, p. 4.
52 *Statesman* (Calcutta), 26 May 1885, p. 2.
53 'Trust and Fear Not', *Ought Natives to be Welcomed as Volunteers* (Calcutta: Thacker, Spink & Co., 1885), in *India Office Records Tract*, vol. 658, p. 3 (Hereafter: *IOR Tract*), IOLR.
54 *Statesman*, 9 Apr. 1885, p. 2 and 22 Apr. 1885, p. 3.

55 *IOR Tract*, pp. 18–19.
56 *Letters Military*, Letter No. 166. See also Dufferin's Minute of 8 Dec. 1888 cited in Hira Lal Singh, *Problems and Policies of the British in India 1885–1898* (New York: Asia Publishing House, 1963), p. 164.
57 Rivett-Carnac, *Many Memories*, p. 369.
58 Quoted in *Englishman*, 31 Jan. 1885, pp. 7–8.
59 *Englishman*, 26 June 1885, p. 4; 24 Feb. 1885, p. 7.
60 Martin, *New India*, p. 109–10. The Government of India later denied that any special encouragement was given to native Christians to volunteer. See note by A. P. MacDonnell, 24 Apr. 1885, *Military Collection*, File No. 3.
61 See instructions from the Military Department to local officials on the Reserve Force cited in Martin, *New India*, pp. 105–6.
62 See discussion of the Madras affair in Martin, *New India*, pp. 106–9.
63 See *Bengalee*, 12 June 1886, pp. 281–2.
64 See *Military Collection*, File No. 3.
65 For reports of some *mofussil* meetings in Bengal, see *Bengalee*, 25 Apr. 1885, p. 200; and 9 May 1885, p. 223.
66 See *Bengalee*, 11 Apr. 1885, pp. 175–76; also *Indian Mirror* (Calcutta), 11 Apr. 1885; and *The Times*, 13 Apr. 1885, p. 6.
67 24 Apr. 1885, *Military Collection*, File No. 3.
68 21 Sept. 1885, *Letters Military*, Letter No. 166. For the discussion on the despatch in the Viceroy's Executive Council, see Diary Entry, 7 Sept. 1885, *Ilbert Papers*, vols. 4 and 5, IOLR.
69 Quoted in Martin, *New India*, pp. 121, 169.
70 *Letters Military*, Letter No. 166.
71 *The Times*, 24 May 1885, p. 5.
72 *Englishman*, 27 July 1885, p. 3.
73 *Report of the Administration of Bengal*, 1891–92, NAI. See also *Bengalee*, 26 Dec. 1891, p. 593; and *Som Prakash*, 31 Mar. 1890, *RNBP Jan–Dec. 1890*, No. 14.
74 Sir Henry Sharp, *Goodbye India* (London: Oxford University Press, 1946), p. 129.
75 *Viceroy India*, Letters Nos. 421, 42.
76 *Viceroy India*, Letter No. 42.
77 From Sir Alfred Lyall, 13 May 1885, *Viceroy India*, Letter No. 308.
78 From Dufferin, 29 May 1885, *Dufferin and Ava vol. 2*, Letter No. 37.
79 C. H. T. Crossthwaite, Officiating Chief Commissioner Central Provinces, 2 July 1885, *Viceroy India*, Letter No. 1. For a discussion of the 'progressive' and 'imperialist' view on native volunteering, see Martin, *New India*, pp. 156–74.
80 17 June 1885, *Viceroy India*, Letter No. 406.
81 Dufferin to Lord Reay, Governor of Bombay, quoted in Martin, *New India*, p. 122.
82 *Viceroy India*, Letter No. 42.
83 *Dufferin and Ava vol. 2*, Letter No. 37.
84 MacDonnell, *Viceroy India*, Letter No. 42.
85 See 10 July 1885, *Dufferin and Ava vol. 2*, Letter No. 45 and 28 August 1885, Letter No. 53; also *Letters Military*, Letter No. 166.
86 See Martin, *New India*, pp. 125–6.
87 7 August 1885, *Dufferin Manuscripts: Letters to the Viceroy From the Secretary of State*, Letter No. 63 (Hereafter: *Secretary of State*). IOLR.
88 Hira Lal Singh, *Problems and Policies of the British*, p. 171. Also Martin, *New India*, pp. 170–2.
89 *Statesman*, 20 June 1885, quoted in Martin, *New India*, p. 141.
90 See Martin, *New India*, esp. pp. 140–1.
91 Hira Lal Singh, *Problems and Policies of the British*, p. 142.
92 This tension is present in the speech on native volunteering at the second annual conference of the Indian National Congress. See the Extract of Raja Rampal Singh's speech in John R. Mclane (ed.), *The Political Awakening in India* (Englewood Cliffs, NJ: Prentice-Hall, Inc., 1970), pp. 40–2.
93 Tanika Sarkar, 'The Hindu Wife and the Hindu Nation: Domesticity and

Nationalism in Nineteenth-Century Bengal', *Studies in History*, 8:2 (1992), 213–35.
94 *Bengalee*, 11 July 1885, p. 328; and 6 June 1885, p. 268.
95 *Bengalee*, 18 Apr. 1885, pp. 183–84.
96 *Bengalee*, 11 Apr. 1885, pp. 175–76. Also *Hindoo Patriot*, 13 Apr. 1885.
97 *Surabhi*, 5 May 1885, *RNBP Jan.–June 1885*, p. 641. Also *Bengalee*, 25 Apr. 1885, p. 199.
98 *Bengalee*, 11 July 1885, p. 328.
99 *Bengalee*, 11 July 1885, p. 316; *Prajabandhu*, 10 July 1885, *RNBP July-Dec. 1885*, No. 29, p. 907.
100 *Surabhi*, 5 May 1884, *RNBP Jan.-June 1884*, No. 19, p. 549.
101 *Bengalee*, 18 Apr. 1885, p. 188.
102 *Praja Bandhu*, 9 Oct. 1885, *RNBP July-Dec. 1885*, No. 42, pp. 1314–15.
103 *Bengalee*, 2 May 1885, pp. 207–8.
104 *Amrita Bazar Patrika* (Calcutta), 29 Mar. 1888, p. 6.
105 *Indian Mirror*, 25 Apr. 1885.
106 Quoted in *Bengalee*, 2 Jan. 1886, p. 4.
107 Quoted in Omissi, ' "Martial Races" ', p. 15.

CHAPTER THREE

Competing masculinities: the Public Service Commission, 1886–87

On 4 October 1886, the Government of India issued a Resolution appointing a Public Service Commission whose object was 'to devise a scheme which may reasonably be hoped to possess the necessary elements of finality, and do full justice to the claims of Natives of India to higher and more extensive employment in the public service'.[1] The Commission consisted of a main division of enquiry into the conditions for native employment in the civil service and a second division of enquiry conducted by a sub-committee into the employment of natives and Europeans in specific departments connected with the civil administration. It began the task of examining witnesses on 15 December 1886 and completed the examination by April 1887. The Commission held sittings at Lahore, Allahabad, Jubbalpore, Bombay, Madras, and Calcutta, examining a total of 849 witnesses orally; in addition, it received 113 written replies to questions that it posed. The Minutes of Evidence contained in twenty thick folios were the most extensive ever collected on any public subject in India up to that time. The recommendations of the Commission were embodied in a 153-page Report, completed on 23 December 1887, and presented on 18 January 1888.[2] Although the Report itself contained very few concessions to native employment in the higher echelons of the public administration in India, its recommendations were further watered down by the Government of India and the Secretary of State before being put into effect in 1892.

If there was one arena in which elite Indian politics had a long history of making demands on colonial rule, it was in the employment of Indians in the civil administration of India. The Public Service Commission, therefore, was both a response to the native civil service agitation and an attempt at containing it. Its major contribution was the reorganisation of the civil service, which previously consisted of an upper or 'covenanted' and a lower or 'uncovenanted' branch, into a three-tier system consisting of a smaller *corps d' élite* represented by a British-dominated, all-India Imperial Service, a larger native-dominated Provincial Service, to be recruited locally and appointed to serve exclusively in its own province, and an inferior Subordinate Service. The reorganisation had a negative impact on native employment: on the one hand, it made the top level of the administration more rigidly exclusive than before; and, on the other, it confined all increases in native employment at the senior levels of the administration to cadres that were fragmented along strictly 'provincial' lines. As Bradford Spangenberg reminds us, the Commission that was appointed to redress native grievances had the opposite result: it not only added little to the 'Indianisation' of the higher branches of the public administration in India, which had to wait until after the First World War, but also provided a more rigid basis for the exclusion of Indians from the senior levels of the civil administration in India.[3]

The full nature of the impact of the Public Service Commission was only partially grasped in the following comment on the Commission in a contemporary Indian newspaper:

> so many 'native' civilians, so many 'native' medical officers and so many 'native' Engineers clearly imply so many the less foreign importations of similar profession ... [consequently] a cabal has been formed in this country which delights in decrying the result of English education and English culture among the native population, and holding up its type, the Bengali to ridicule and derision.[4]

The 'Bengali phobia' that the *Bengalee* identified in the working of the Public Service Commission was not new; it represented a long and deeply held colonial prejudice against the encroachment of Western-educated Indians on British monopoly in senior branches of the civil administration in India. But what was new about the 'Bengali phobia' during the Public Service Commission was its resonance with the elaborate classification of various religious and provincial differences between natives. Indeed, the deliberations of the Public Service Commission coincided with the massive colonial offensive in the late nineteenth century aimed at the classification of natives by religion, caste, province, class, and so on, each with its own set of fixed and mutually antagonistic characteristics.[5] Such hoary colonial stereotypes as the 'passive' Hindu and the 'lawless' Muslim, or the 'manly' Punjabi and the 'effeminate' Bengali, which underpinned the recommendations of the Public Service Commission, had their counterparts in the proliferation of more formal ethnographic surveys, census reports, scholarly treatises, and Caste Handbooks that compiled detailed information on the characteristics of different native 'types'.

The elaborate classification of the colonial population by caste, religion, region, and so on, performed an important ideological service for colonial rule. For the amassing of detailed information on the colonial population in India, as Arjun Appadurai reminds us, was qualitatively different to the wealth of classificatory information also being collected by nineteenth-century social explorers and social investigators within Britain; for not only was the object of social investigation in India the entire colonial population instead of the social margins that were usually the principal objects of social investigation in Britain, but, even more importantly, the classification of colonial populations had a much more profoundly interventionary impact in redirecting and reorienting existing group identities in India.[6] The classification of various native 'types', moreover, was more directly assimilated in the elaborate mechanism for disciplining the colonial population and in the justification for colonial rule.[7] Hence Sir John Strachey, a former Lt.-Governor in India and a prominent advocate of Anglo-Indian interests, could say before a group of Cambridge undergraduates in Britain that 'there is not, and never was an India, or even any country of India . . . no Indian nation, no "people of India"', but only a conglomeration of different and mutually antagonistic native groups.[8] It was to discredit native claims to the representative status of 'Indians' that the 'Bengali phobia' was deployed most effectively in the deliberations of the Public Service Commission.

Nicely anticipating the divisive outcome of the Public Service Commission, the semi-official Anglo-Indian paper the *Pioneer* gave the following warning to natives testifying before the Commission in the Punjab and the North-West Provinces:

> If open competition is to be the sole gate of entrance to high office in India, it is perfectly clear that the natives of northern India must make up their minds to give place to the Bengali and Madrasi for an indefinitely long term of years. If, however, the natives of northern India want to have a share in the sweets of high office, they must . . . content themselves with the less perfect way of provincial appointments.[9]

By appealing to differences between natives, the *Pioneer* was laying the foundations for a new basis for the reorganisation of the civil service in India. The focus on provincial and religious differences between natives introduced a new dimension to civil service reform in India. Indeed, the Public Service Commission did more than simply ignore native claims to higher employment in the public administration in India. Rather, by reorganising the civil service along the lines of a specifically sectarian definition of colonial masculinity, which simultaneously provided a provincial and religious context for native masculinity and an imperial context for 'English' masculinity, it not only introduced a greater rigidity in the exclusion of Indians from the higher reaches of the public administration in India, but also formalised the inferiority of the native-dominated branch of the civil service *vis-à-vis* its British-dominated branch.

The context for introducing a specifically sectarian definition of colonial masculinity was provided by the need to bolster the aristocratic disdain that the colonial authorities had so far deployed to manage the challenge of native employment in the civil administration. Indeed, the focus on the irreconcilable provincial and religious differences between natives in the deliberations of the Public Service Commission provided a solution of sorts to the stalemate that had been reached on native employment in the higher levels of the civil administration. Out of financial considerations as much as out of the political pressure from the native civil service agitation, the colonial authorities were being forced gradually to accommodate not only to greater use of native agency in the public administration, but at higher levels of the administration than before. These pressures were being managed with the addition of sectarian politics in civil service reform; such a politics provided the rationale for a more exclusive British-dominated cadre to head the public administration in India – even beyond what had been accomplished through the aristocratic disdain that the colonial authorities always displayed towards Western-educated native civil servants.

The aristocratic disdain for native civil servants had shared much in common with the prejudice against the social and regional backgrounds of British civil servants; but this common aristocratic bias was at the same time also mediated by a racial politics that contrasted the 'manliness' of the British civil servant with the 'effeminacy' of the native civil servant. Nowhere, except perhaps in the army, has the aristocratic politics of colonial masculinity received as much attention from contemporaries and scholars alike as in the civil service of India, the senior branch of which represented the only permanent, official, British element in the colonial administration of India.[10] The model of masculinity in the colonial administration was that of the 'gentlemanly administrator'.[11] Yet doubts about the 'gentlemanly' and hence 'manly' qualifications of the British civil service recruit, especially after the introduction of the competitive examination system for the covenanted civil service in 1858, remained a constant preoccupation with all those connected with the selection of candidates for the civil service in India. These concerns, moreover, reflected a marked aristocratic as well as Anglocentric bias; the prejudice against the new generation of British competition civilians in India was directed mainly at the success of non-university men, of products of Scottish and Irish universities, and of those who had successfully 'crammed' for the examination outside such 'gentlemanly' institutions as the great English public schools and 'Oxbridge'. Throughout the nineteenth century, therefore, various changes were introduced, such as the lowering of the age limit for the examination, the addition of a *viva voce* component to the examination as a test of 'character', a period of compulsory probation at one of the approved universities in Britain, and the introduction of a riding test, to ensure proper 'gentlemanly qualifications' among the British civil service recruits.[12]

But if there were persistent doubts about the 'masculinity' of British candidates obtained through the competitive system, these were nothing as compared to the hypermasculinist condemnation of native candidates who succeeded at the competitive examination in London. For even the relatively minor inroad of native civilians in the senior or covenanted branch of the civil service through the competitive examination was cause for considerable alarm. The competitive examination – both because it was held only in London and geared towards subjects taught at British institutions and because the upper age limit for the examination was consistently lowered to attract the preferred kind of 'manly' British recruit – was never conducive to the success of native candidates. From the first introduction of the competitive examination up to 1886, a total of ninety-three native candidates had appeared at the examination in London and only fifteen had been successful. At the time of the Public Service Commission, there were only twelve natives in a total of approximately 900 covenanted civilians in India.[13] On the one hand, the prejudices against the native competition civilians were remarkably similar to those against British competition civilians: native candidates came from undistinguished social backgrounds and did not belong to the traditional ruling classes in India; the well-crammed native civilian did not display 'qualities of physical and intellectual manhood'; and, finally, the class of native competition civilians did not command the respect of the native population in India.[14] On the other hand, the stereotype of the 'clever Bengali' – nine out of the fifteen successful native candidates at the competitive examination in London were Bengalis – offered a much more pointed racial attack against the native candidates secured through the competitive examination in London. The stock figure of the 'weak-kneed, effeminate, effete Bengalee' became an important weapon in the colonial arsenal for keeping the competitive examination in London and hence the covenanted civil service more favourable to the British than the native candidate.[15]

THE PUBLIC SERVICE COMMISSION

The combination of the racial and class prejudices against native competition civilians was used to keep challenges to the monopoly of the British civil servant at bay: it allowed the colonial authorities to rely on alternative proposals to select the 'right sort' of natives for the civil service that gave the appearance of the willingness of the colonial authorities to appoint natives to senior levels of the administration but without in any way compromising the superior position of the predominantly British competition civilians. For native civilians were underrepresented not only in the covenanted civil service, but also in senior uncovenanted posts. Under pressure to expand employment opportunities for natives, the Government of India had issued a circular in 1879 that declared that, with some important exceptions, all appointments in the uncovenanted service – which employed the majority of native civilians – should be reserved for the 'natives of India'; and that any post carrying a salary of 200 rupees per month or above should not be given to non-natives without the sanction of the Governor-General. Yet in 1887, as H. M. L. Alexander demonstrates, Europeans and Eurasians still held 66 per cent of the higher appointments in the uncovenanted service compared to 34 per cent held by natives.[16] A Parliamentary Act of 1870 had gone even further in recommending the nomination of suitable natives whose merit and experience had been tested in the lower or uncovenanted service to the posts normally reserved for covenanted civilians.

Yet the legacy of the aristocratic disdain towards native civil servants ensured that proposals to increase native employment could be interpreted in a manner that guaranteed that any such increase did not place more natives on an equal footing with British civil servants. The subsequent interpretations of the 1870 Act, for example, sacrificed the test of merit and experience for nominating natives to covenanted posts; instead, it was mainly 'manly' recruits from 'good' families who were nominated in the hope that what aristocratic natives lacked by way education or training they would more than make up for by bringing their territorial or political influence to the support of the government. With this purpose expressly in mind, the Viceroy Lord Lytton in 1877 had proposed an ingenious scheme for utilising the provisions of the 1870 Parliamentary Act. Lytton's scheme was to prohibit natives altogether from appearing at the competitive examination in London and to compensate natives for the loss by setting up an 'upper native service', to which natives of the proper social class and influence would be nominated by the Government of India.[17] Although the Secretary of State did not accede to Lytton's proposal, the Statutory Rules formulated in 1879 for the nomination of natives to covenanted posts reflected some of Lytton's aristocratic bias. The nominations under these regulations went largely to natives with social and political influence over able uncovenanted civilians. The further point, moreover, was that even though the statutory rules assured natives one-sixth of the total number of covenanted posts in addition to the number of offices to which they were entitled on the basis of their performance at the competitive examination in London, it did not guarantee 'statutory' civilians equality with the covenanted civilians recruited through the regular process of the competitive examination.[18]

While the class-based statutory appointment of natives appeared to be a wonderful strategy for appointing more natives to senior administrative positions without challenging British monopoly, it was in practice found to have created as many problems as it was hoped it could resolve. Criticism of the statutory system came from Anglo-Indians and natives alike. Middle-class native politicians continued to focus their demands on the competitive examination in London, not only because of the aristocratic bias in the system of statutory nominations, but also because the 'statutory' civilians were not accorded full equality with the covenanted civilians. Even more biting was the criticism of the statutory civilians from Anglo-Indian officials. Colonial officials were forced to acknowledge the failure of a system that sought to appoint more 'manly' natives to senior government appointments on no other criterion but that of social background: the experiment had produced a cadre of senior civilians who were generally looked upon as inferior not only to the native competition civilian, but also to the experienced men of the junior uncovenanted service.[19]

The Public Service Commission, which was constituted specifically to respond to the failure in the system of statutory nominations and the subsequent impasse in the appointment of natives to senior administrative posts, offered a new basis for civil service reform: it tied the criteria of the 'right sort' of native civilian not only to social and educational backgrounds, but also to provincial and religious backgounds. In this reorientation of civil service reforms along sectarian lines, the colonial authorities were aided by the history of uneven success of various native groups in government employment. For not only were the majority of native covenanted civilians in 1886 Bengalis, but, even more importantly, Bengalis in the lower levels of the civil service had been among the most successful of the native groups that had also followed the expansion of the colonial administrative structure into other provinces in India. Furthermore, Muslims, who were slower to make the transition to English education, had reaped fewer of the benefits of government employment based solely on educational qualifications in proportion to their numbers in the general population. Of the twelve serving native covenanted civilians, recruited between 1864 and 1886, eight were Hindus, three Parsis, and one Christian. The first Muslim candidate passed the competitive examination in 1885 and entered the ranks of the covenanted civil service in 1888.[20]

When the colonial authorities raised the spectre of 'Bengali' and 'Hindu' domination, moreover, it struck a responsive chord in the native community. For by the time of the Public Service Commission, new forms of native political and social mobilisation had also emerged in India. These new forms of mobilisation, partly in response to the impact of colonial technologies of rule that were based on an elaborate classification and enumeration of the native population, and partly in response to the new opportunities for political representation under colonial rule, were themselves often mobilised along the lines of caste, religious, linguistic, and regional affiliations. Even the incipient political nationalism of the late nineteenth century, constituted largely in terms of the patriotic defence of an essentially 'upper-caste' and 'Hindu' way of life, was strongly implicated in these forms of social and political mobilisation.[21] The emerging politics of native self-assertion, therefore, itself made possible the addition of a sectarian dimension of colonial masculinity to the reorganisation of the civil service that ultimately limited native opportunities in the public administration in India.

It was, moreover, precisely because the sectarian definition of colonial masculinity provided different contexts for the representations of 'English' and native masculinity – imperial versus provincial and religious – that the Public Service Commission was able to secure British domination of top administrative positions on a firmer footing. The point of identifying 'unmanliness' as a specifically Bengali or Hindu characteristic was not only to encourage a sectarian politics of competing native masculinities, but also to preclude any embarrassing comparisons between British and native masculinity. For only shortly prior to the Public Service Commission, doubts had surfaced once again about the 'manliness' of the British civil servant in India. Upon receiving a report from the Government of Bombay, dated 31 September 1882, the Secretary of State had urged the Government of India to undertake an inquiry on the 'constitutional robustness' of the British civil servant.[22] The inquiry was prompted by the startling statistics of the physical and mental health of British civilians sent to Bombay in the last ten years; of a total of thirty-seven civilians, five had gone insane, seven had retired, and thirteen were in poor health. Commenting on what these statistics said about British civil servants in India, *The Times* in London lamented that 'aggravated eccentricity, intolerable manners, unmanliness and a sort of half and half imbecility' were met every day in the 'once proud Indian Civil Service'.[23] The Government of India, however, on the basis of the reports from other local governments, took the official position that the 'experience of Bombay is not repeated in other parts of India'; but the growing suspicion about the 'unmanliness' of the British civilians, especially those recruited under the lower age limit set in 1876, could not be dismissed so easily. Even the Home Member of the Government of India, Steuart Bayly, expressed scepticism about the assessment of some of the local governments that had categorically stated that the experience of Bombay was not repeated in their provinces. As Bayly concluded, 'the lists of the North West Provinces and Bengal do not quite bear out the general views taken by the Lt.-Governors of the Provinces – NWP list is a very depressing one and the Bengal list shows 4 cases of insanity among the men between 1870–1877'.[24] These doubts about the British civil servant did not surface in the deliberations of the Commission, except perhaps indirectly in the discussion about raising the age for the competitive examination. For the imperial representation of 'English' masculinity during the Public Service Commission, as compared to the specifically sectarian representation of Bengali or Hindu effeminacy, precluded any expression of doubt about the British civil servant.

If the objective of the civil administration was to uphold 'English principles and method of Government', then, the general consensus was that only British domination of the competitive examination could achieve this objective. That it was never the intention of the colonial authorities in the proposal for the Public Service Commission to allow more native civilians to compete on a par with British civilians at the competitive examination was apparent from the outset. The Commission itself was a poor substitute for the larger Parliamentary Committee initially promised to inquire into the administration in India. The purpose of appointing a Commission for the expansion of native employment was not meant to challenge British monopoly over key administrative posts, but only to determine the *minimum number* of such posts that must remain in British hands for the maintenance of imperial interests in India. This was clearly stated in the guidelines for the Commission provided by the Secretary of State to the Viceroy:

> many perplexing questions would become more easy of solution . . . if a conclusion could be arrived at as to the approximate number of European public servants who must necessarily, for the efficiency of the administration and the political security of the Empire, be maintained in each branch of the public service in India.[25]

The assumption that imperial interests rested on British monopoly of key administrative posts in India was thus taken as axiomatic at the time of the Public Service Commission.

The terms of the Government of India Resolution constituting the Commission, moreover, expressly limited the Commission to an inquiry into the means of enlarging native employment in the civil service and its related departments without going into the conditions suitable for British candidates at the competitive examination.[26] While the questions posed by the Commission, therefore, allowed witness after witness to expatiate on the fitness of native civil servants, the virtues of the British civil servant were celebrated only in the abstract. The scope of the Commission, therefore, allowed for a sectarian elaboration of colonial masculinity that, on the one hand, set up one rival native group against another in competing native masculinities, and, on the other, contributed to at least a public mythology of the unassailable superiority of an imperial 'English' masculinity.

The significance of sectarian native politics for cementing British exclusivity in the civil administration was underscored also in the composition of the Commission. There was little surprise in the selection of the Anglo-Indian members of the Commission: the Commission not only secured an Anglo-Indian majority, but the Anglo-Indian members were chosen carefully so as to allay whatever alarm there was in the Anglo-Indian community at the appointment of the Commission.[27] Apart from the President, Sir Charles Aitchison, who was then Lt.-Governor of Punjab, the representatives of Anglo-Indian interests in the Commission included the following: four covenanted civilians, nominated by each of the local governments; one covenanted civilian, C. H. T. Crossthwaite, to serve as the representative of the Government of India; one uncovenanted civilian; one member representing non-official Anglo-Indian opinion; one member to represent the Eurasian community; and a Judge of the Madras High Court, who provided judicial and legal expertise for the Commission. Not a single native covenanted civilian was included in the selection of the five covenanted civilians for the Commission. Similarly, Anglo-Indian civilians who had gained a reputation for being sympathetic to the demands of the native civil service agitation, like Henry Cotton, Henry Beveridge, and A. Cotterell Tupp, were excluded from the Commission.[28] A. O. Hume, a former civilian now active in native political circles, also offered his services to the Commission, but his offer was rejected.[29] Apart from Aitchison, not one of the Anglo-Indian members appointed to the Commission was known to even favour the principle of the appointment of natives to high administrative posts in the civil administration.

It was in the selection of the native members of the Commission, however, that the colonial appeal to sectarian native differences was most evident. The pressure for the inclusion of some native public opinion on the Commission came from the Liberal Party in Britain as well as from native political organisations in India. But the selection of the six native members for the Commission was calculated to exploit all the anomalies of the native civil service agitation for the benefit of colonial interests. The demand of the native civil service agitation coincided both with the desire for racial equality for Indian civilians and with the welfare of the country as a whole; for the demand for the extensive use of 'native agency' in the public administration in India was prompted at least in part by the recognition that the inordinate employment of 'foreign agency' had contributed to the wretchedness and poverty of the mass of the people in India. Yet at the same time, the most prominent cause taken up in the native civil service agitation – the removal of the unfair disabilities against natives at the competitive examination in London – also exposed the vulnerabilities of the movement: it catered predominantly to the interests of upper-class Hindus and of the Western-educated community in India who had the most to gain from expanded opportunities at the competitive examination.[30] No doubt aware of this anomaly, the Home Department of the Government of India issued a memorandum which urged that the only criterion that should be recognised in the appointment of natives to the Commission was the division between Hindus and Muslims.[31] The Hindu members were to be nominated by the local governments in consultation with the Hindu-dominated political associations in the province and the Muslim members were to be nominated directly by the Government of India. The Government of India also reserved the right to nominate a more reliable native ally from the nobility or from men of property and influence in India. Men with 'extreme' views on civil service reform like the Bombay politician Dadabhai Naoroji, whose nomination to the Commission was expressly recommended by Aitchison, were deliberately excluded.[32] Other prominent native political leaders associated with the civil service agitation were also avoided. The Hindu members of the Commission consisted of R. C. Mitter, Judge of the Calcutta High Court; K. L. Nulkar, President of the Poona Sarvajanik Sabha; S. Ramaswami Mudaliyar, a *vakil* (lawyer) of the High Court at Madras; and Raja Udhai Pertab Singh of Bhinga, a *taluqdar* (landlord) of Oudh. Apart from Mudaliyar, whose views on civil service reform were as yet 'unknown' to many Anglo-Indian officials, the first two Hindu members were appointed specifically for their 'moderate' views on civil service reform.[33] The Raja of Bhinga was appointed for his avowedly pro-British views and his hostility towards the Western-educated community.[34] The criterion for the selection of the Muslim members on the Commission was also aimed to minimise support for any direct challenge to British domination at the competitive examination. Although one of the two Muslim members, Sir Sayyid Ahmad Khan Bahadur, founder of the Muhammaden Anglo-Oriental College at Aligarh, had been active in the native civil service agitation up until 1884, he had since become an outspoken critic of the competitive examination as the primary mode for selecting native civil servants.[35] The colonial authorities were calculating that at least three of the six native members, Raja Bhinga and the two Muslim members who were nominated directly by the Government of India, would go along with the majority Anglo-Indian opinion on the Commission.

Thus constituted, the Commission was poised to exploit the differences between Hindus and Muslims for making the British-dominated covenanted service even more exclusive than before. On the important question of settling the primary mode of recruitment for native candidates to the civil service, therefore, the Public Service Commission played the evidence of Hindu witnesses against Muslim witnesses examined by the Commission: it made no recommendations to increase native opportunities at the competitive examination; and, at the same time, also discontinued the system of statutory nominations, which was the only other way for natives to serve in covenanted posts. While a majority of the Hindu witnesses, especially in Bengal, had expressed a preference for the competitive examination over the system of statutory nominations, the evidence from Muslims, who as a group had received a fair share of the statutory appointments, was more in favour of the statutory system.[36] The majority of the Anglo-Indian witnesses shared the criticism of the system of statutory nominations, but were equally critical of the application of competitive examinations for native recruitment.

The spectre of 'Bengali' and 'Hindu' domination at the competitive examination was thus disingenuously deployed by several of the Anglo-Indian witnesses to mask their own hostility towards allowing natives to compete at the competitive examination in London. The Public Service Commission was asked to consider whether there was reason to believe that 'the young natives obtained under the existing system of open competition in England for the public service in India are the best, as regards character and capacity, who could be got for it under any system'.[37] The line of enquiry pursued by the Commission thus gave Anglo-Indian witnesses ample opportunities to cast doubts not only about the statutory native civilians, but also about the quality of native candidates obtained through the competitive examination. In fact, several Anglo-Indian witnesses recommended discontinuing the competitive examination for native candidates who allegedly were devoid of the 'pluck' and 'character' of their British colleagues. Hence the competitive examination, they argued, was suited only for the

British candidate. W. Lee-Warner, Secretary to the Government of Bombay, told the Commission that no natives should be allowed in the covenanted civil service. The average native, he argued, compared very poorly to the average British candidate: 'the Indian boy, who only attends a day school, has no chance of acquiring the habits of mind which the public school boy of England acquires in his journey through the University and open competition to India'.[38] In perhaps one of the more intemperate testimonies before the Commission, John Beames, Commissioner of Burdwan in Bengal, made the argument that natives did not 'possess the qualities which fit them to be admitted into the covenanted civil service'; for, he argued, 'if you take a Native and teach him English, he does not thereby acquire the qualities of an Englishman'. Beames told the Commission that he would 'leave the Civil Service exactly as it was, and would introduce no innovation except such as would exclude natives more thoroughly than at present. He found natives wanting in pluck, tact, firmness, courage and decision and would like the covenanted service to be restricted to Europeans.'[39] Yet when asked by the Commission, in the presence of a native covenanted civilian Brajendranath De, to comment more specifically on the performance of native covenanted civilians, Beames refrained from elaborating his censure.[40] In reply to a question posed by Mitter, he simply stated, 'I prefer my countrymen as you may prefer yours.' Commenting in his diary on his testimony before the Commission, Beames wrote that he had 'cut (his) own throat without being aware of it'; but, as Beames's biographer points out, the Bengal Government, which promoted Beames to the Board of Revenue a month later, was obviously not perturbed by his outburst.[41] In London, *The Times* was also adding its weight to the dominant Anglo-Indian view on competitive examinations: 'Englishmen generally have the requisite [manly] qualities though examinations do not prove the fact, but the Bengali generally does not possess them though examinations do not bring out this deficiency.'[42]

Although the Report of the Public Service Commission itself refrained from declaring outright that the competitive examination was unsuitable for native recruitment, it did little more than simply keep the competitive examination technically open for native recruitment. In fact, the Report provided only a half-hearted vindication of the performance of native competition civilians: 'although, on the one hand, there may not have been any instances of exceptional success in the official careers of the Native gentlemen who have entered the service through the English competition, on the other hand they have not fallen short of the positions which civil servants with the same length of service ordinarily attain'.[43] Since the Commission itself was just as sceptical of the competitive examination as of the statutory nomination for the recruitment of native civilians, its vindication of the competitive examination as the only mode of entry for the covenanted branch of the service was of little good to native candidates.

The differences between Hindus and Muslims on the mode of native recruitment to senior administrative posts proved to be a blessing in disguise: for it allowed the colonial authorities simultaneously to vindicate the principle of competitive examinations in the abstract and to challenge its validity for native recruitment. The Commission, therefore, recommended abolishing the system of statutory nominations and making the competitive examination the sole mode of entry to covenanted posts; but, at the same time, the disproportionate success of Bengalis and Hindus at the competitive examination provided an excuse to avoid conceding that the competitive examination was equally suitable for native as for British recruitment. In effect, therefore, the discontinuation of the statutory nominations without any compensatory encouragement to native recruitment at the competitive examination only made the covenanted service, that was now newly designated as the Imperial Service (the Secretary of State later changed the name to the Indian Civil Service), into more of a British-dominated *corps d'élite* than before.

Another, closely related, effect of the sectarian definition of colonial masculinity was the mobilisation of the fear of 'Bengali' and 'Hindu' domination of the civil service to guard against any modifications to the competitive examination that would make make it more accessible to native candidates. The two most important modifications to the competitive examination being considered by the Public Service Commission had to do with raising the age for taking the examination and conducting the examination simultaneously in London and in India. Although the Report of the Commission accepted the former and rejected the latter, the underlying theme in both the debates was the same: to mobilise other natives against Bengali and Hindu domination of the civil service with the aim of furthering the Anglo-Indian crusade against greater native access to the competitive examination.

Although the decision of the Public Service Commission to change the current age limit for the examination from nineteen and return to the earlier age limit of twenty-three had all the appearances of a concession to the native civil service agitation, the reason behind the change had nothing to do with improving native chances at the examination.[44] In the debate on the age-question, for example, both Anglo-Indian opponents and supporters of the change appealed to the fear of Bengali and Hindu domination of the service. Although Anglo-Indian opponents of the higher age limit were primarily concerned with preserving British domination at the examination, they raised the fear of 'Bengalis' and 'Hindus' outsmarting all other natives at the examination to make their case against the change. Similarly, the Anglo-Indians who favoured the change supported their decision with the argument that, contrary to general expectations, the higher age limit would in fact reduce the success of the 'precocious Bengali' at the competitive examination. The reason that the colonial authorities accepted the recommendations for the higher age limit, despite considerable Anglo-Indian opposition, was not a concession to native public opinion but a response to the complaints about the quality of the British civil service recruit.

Since up until the Public Service Commission all the changes in the age limit for the competitive examination had coincided conveniently with conditions believed to be less favourable for native candidates, the changes had never aroused the passion provoked by the Commission's recommendation for a higher age limit. Ever since the introduction of the competitive examination in 1855, the age at which candidates could take the examination was consistently lowered, first to twenty-two in 1859, then to twenty-one in 1866, and finally to nineteen in 1876. The ostensible reason given for the change was the improvement in the quality of British candidates: to assert the influence of the great English public schools and 'Oxbridge' over the influence of London 'crammers' on the civil service recruits.[45] But the belief that lowering the age limit would also limit the chances of native candidates, who required extra time to prepare for the examination after the completion of their studies in India, was probably as much a factor in the support for lowering the age limit. C. P. Ilbert, the Law Member during Lord Ripon's Viceroyalty, provided the following gloss on the motives for lowering the age limit to nineteen in 1876:

> Sir Henry Maine has informed me (in a *private* letter) that [the exclusion of natives] had nothing to do with the alteration . . . This denial does not appear to me to agree completely with Lord Kimberley's [Secretary of State] recent admission 'that Lord Lytton had written to Lord Cranbrook [Secretary of State] to get an Act of Parliament passed to prevent natives becoming civil servants. But if that could not be done, then the age for passing the examination should be lowered, which would practically have the same effect.'[46]

Over the years, Indian political organisations had presented several memorials on the age question to the Viceroy in India and to the Secretary of State in London without much effect. In 1884, Ripon and Ilbert, over the opposition of the majority of the Viceroy's Council and the local governments, had written separate minutes to the Secretary of

State, citing the opinion of the Muslim leader Syed Ahmad Khan and the Bengali–Hindu covenanted civilian R. C. Dutt, in favour of raising the age for the examination.[47] The then Secretary of State, Lord Kimberley, had resisted these demands for fear of flooding the service with 'Bengali baboos'.

In so far, however, as the age at the competitive examination affected native as well as British candidates, the fixing of the age limit had to mediate between often different and conflicting priorities. When Kimberley rejected Ripon's proposal to raise the age limit for fear of 'Bengali baboos', for example, there existed a respectable body of opinion in Britain in favour of a higher age limit with British candidates in mind. Benjamin Jowett of Oxford and E. M. Sidgewick of Cambridge had joined with the leading London 'crammers', like Walter Wren and W. B. Scoones, to lead a campaign against the lower age limits. Despite the fact that under the lower age limits successful candidates were required to undergo an additional two-year probation at one of the approved universities in Britain, there was a general impression that the British recruits sent out to India under the lower age limits were too young and 'unformed'. This view was supported in Scoones's letter to Lord Dufferin; Scoones complained that before the age was lowered British recruits who went out to India 'had cricketed in their public school eleven or had rowed in the eight', but under the lower age limit 'lads are sent out [to India] before they have done with the playing field'.[48] The nagging suspicion that somehow 'underdeveloped' schoolboys were being sent to India had come to a head in the revelations about the 'constitutional robustness' of British civilians in 1882–83.

But since the Public Service Commission was prohibited from discussing the conditions for the recruitment of British candidates, the dissatisfaction with the present system could be expressed only through a recommendation for a higher age limit. Therefore, although it was remarkable to find such broad support for the higher age limit from Anglo-Indian witnesses examined by the Commission, the reason for their support had little to do with improving the chances of native candidates at the examination; rather, it had to do with securing, within the ideological terms of the politics of colonial masculinity, the 'best' type of British recruit. Of the 140 Anglo-Indian and Eurasian witnesses examined by the Commission, 110 expressed definite views on the age question. Of the 110, only 13 favoured the present age limit and 97 favoured raising the age limit for the examination.[49] Even those, like Lord Roberts the Commander-in-Chief in India, who were otherwise hostile to any concessions to educated Indians, nevertheless, testified in favour of the higher age limit.[50]

Yet as the proposal for the higher age limit also raised the fear that the rate of success of native candidates at the competitive examination would be enhanced, there were plenty of die-hard Anglo-Indian opponents who were dead set against the change. They typically expressed their antipathy to the change by raising the fear of 'quick-witted Bengalis' who would surpass all their countrymen and flood the covenanted service. Theodore Beck, the Anglo-Indian principal of the Muhammedan Anglo-Oriental College in Aligarh, tried to prejudice Muslim witnesses against any changes that, he argued, could lead to the domination of Muslims by Hindus in general and Bengalis in particular. But in a candid letter to the *Pioneer* on 9 November 1886, Beck admitted his real fears about the change: 'the most patriotic Englishman', he wrote, 'would not risk heavy stakes on John Bull beating the Bengali *Babu* in a competitive examination'.[51] The bad faith in the Anglo-Indian efforts to prejudice other natives against the change was commented upon by the *Amrita Bazar Patrika* of Bengal: '[The] Bengalee may outwit the "dull Britisher" but [it is] yet to be shown he will outwit all other provinces in a competitive examination.'[52]

Since neither side on the age question, however, was sanguine at the prospect of the 'clever Bengali' outwitting the 'dull Britisher' and challenging British domination of the covenanted service in India, it was important to allay what seemed to the colonial authorities to be a legitimate Anglo-Indian anxiety about the change. When Aitchison was asked to defend the higher age limit in the Viceroy's Council, he offered an ingenious twist to the old Anglo-Indian notion that the more 'effeminate' races matured intellectually at an earlier age than the 'manlier' races.[53] He argued that since natives matured earlier than Englishmen, the former had certain advantages over the latter at the lower age limits; these advantages would be cancelled if the age limit were raised and natives deprived of their natural advantage over Englishmen. Aware that he was overturning the standard view that held that it was the higher age limit that was more favourable to native candidates, Aitchison provided statistics on the rates of success of native candidates at various age limits to support his contention. The Home Secretary, A. P. MacDonnell, tried to dispute the statistics with more of his own, but Aitchison's arguments seemed to have convinced the majority of the Council to go along with the recommendation of the Commission.[54] Only two members of the Viceroy's Council, James Westland and Charles Elliott, remained unconvinced that the higher age limit would not lead to a greater influx of 'clever' and 'well-crammed' native candidates at the competitive examination.[55]

Even greater powers of persuasion were needed to convince the Secretary of State and his Council in London; anxiety about the higher age

THE PUBLIC SERVICE COMMISSION

limit in London held up the official response of the Secretary of State, Lord Cross, to the Commission's report for a full year until 1889. James Peile, a retired Anglo-Indian civilian serving in the India Council in London, wrote to Arthur Godley, the Permanent Under-Secretary of State at the India Office, expressing some scepticism of the argument used by the advocates of the higher age limit that the 'native is really better suited to compete at nineteen then at twenty three'.[56] Peile's aim was to garner support against the age increase in London. He referred to the earlier comments of his fellow Council member John Strachey that intellectual development occurred very early among the Bengalis, and, by the same token, also declined very early; Peile expressed the hope that Strachey 'would not be so cynical' as to do 'justice to the native by changing the age to one which is less favourable to him, mainly because the native ignorantly wants what is bad for him'. Strachey, as Alexander has shown, responded by scribbling on Peile's letter that he would indeed have no hesitation in being so 'cynical', but that his decision would be influenced ultimately by more than cynicism alone.[57]

Since the view that the higher age limit would actually be less favourable to the native candidates was still a relatively new and untested principle, the Secretary of State and his Council needed greater assurance that other safeguards existed to prevent natives from flooding the service. The Civil Service Commissioners in London, who were asked for their opinion by the Secretary of State becuse the change affected British and native candidates alike, had responded negatively the change; they expressed their unwillingness 'to undertake the responsibility of advising in favour of raising the age from nineteen to twenty three'.[58] At least four members of the India Council in London, moreover, remained staunch opponents of the change and added strongly-worded Notes of Dissent when the Secretary of State decided to approve the Report. In typical fashion, Anglo-Indian anxiety about native competition was voiced, as in the Note of Dissent written by P. Lumsden, in terms of the irreconcilable differences between various native groups in India: 'the native class [who were represented in the civil service] may to a certain extent, have acquired European education, [but] they belong to a race which has never been dominant in the East and has never displayed any of those qualities required to secure the respect of the Natives which compose our Indian empire'.[59] What finally persuaded the Secretary of State to accept the recommendation on the higher age limit was, perhaps, the warning of the new Viceroy in India, Lord Lansdowne, who suggested that the delay in accepting the moderate recommendations of the Commission was 'politically mischievous'. In assuring Cross on the age question, moreover, Lansdowne wrote that 'I do not doubt for a moment that [the examination] could be so contrived as to secure for European candidates advantages amply sufficient to prevent a wholescale invasion of the service by the sharp-witted and well-crammed Bengalees.'[60] It is not unlikely, therefore, to presume that what Cross was waiting for was precisely the assurance that the examination, despite the increase in the age limit, could indeed be so 'contrived' as to guard against the success of 'effeminate' natives. Cross was also recommending to the Civil Service Commissioners to ensure a more rigorous enforcement of the physical component of the examination.[61] Not surprisingly, the very first casualty of the new rigour in enforcing the physical component of the examination was a native candidate, Aravinda Ackroyd Ghose. Having passed the Civil Service Examination in 1890 with the overall rank of eleventh, he was debarred from the Indian civil service for failing his riding test.[62]

Even more than in the debate on the age question, the pitting of one native group against the other was at the centre of the debate on holding the competitive examination simultaneously in London and in India. For much more than any change in the age limit for the competitive examination, the question of simultaneous examinations was the only modification that could have made a real difference in the success of native candidates at the examination. The demand for simultaneous examinations had been raised by Indian political organisations as far back as the 1850s.[63] During the Public Service Commission, the Anglo-Indian witnesses examined rejected the suggestion almost to a man. The rejection was also reiterated in no uncertain terms in the Report of the Commission; the ground given for the rejection was the preservation of the 'distinctively English character' of the examination, which was meant primarily as a 'test of English qualifications'. With the objective of preserving this 'English' character of the examination, the Commission also rejected other proposals such as one, suggested by the Bengal Government, for conducting a separate examination in England for a fixed proportion of natives and another for increasing the number of marks allotted for Sanskrit and Arabic in the competitive examination.[64] On the most unpopular proposal of all among Anglo-Indians – that of holding simultaneous examinations – the Report provided the following reasons for its recommendation not to conduct the examination in India: the inferiority of the Indian education system compared to the British; the difficulty of maintaining the secrecy of the examination papers because of the constant fear of leaks in India; and the impossibility of conducting adequate *viva voce* tests in India for judging the character of the candidates.[65] Evidence of the importance attached to the question of simultaneous examinations could be seen in the fact that in an otherwise unanimous Report submitted by the Commission, the only note of dissent was recorded on this question. Three of the four

THE PUBLIC SERVICE COMMISSION

Hindu members of the Commission, Mitter, Nulkar, and Mudaliyar, dissented with the Commission's recommendation on simultaneous examinations. The fourth Hindu member, the Raja of Bhinga, and the two Muslim members on the Commission, Syed Ahmad Khan and Shahubidin Khan Bahadur, the former *Dewan* (minister) of Baroda, went along with the majority Anglo-Indian view.[66]

For the colonial authorities, what was relevant was not so much the strength of the native support for simultaneous examinations in the evidence before the Commission, but the provincial and religious breakdown of the native support for simultaneous examinations. Conveniently, the Commission had maintained, apart from the classification of native witnesses by province, a detailed classification of native witnesses by religion: 66 Muslims, 13 Sikhs, 7 Parsis, 238 Hindus, and 5 listed as 'others' had testified before the Commission.[67] As Anglo-Indians were quick to point out, the opinion on simultaneous examinations in the native evidence was split along both provincial and religious lines. The Commission concluded that while the majority of the Hindu witnesses in northern, central, and southern India, and of the Parsis in western India supported simultaneous examinations, the Muslims and 'others with less education' were against the proposal.[68] This breakdown of native responses by religion and by province also provided the indication of the type of native who, as the Anglo-Indians were once again quick to point out, would flood the service at the cost of other more desirable natives if the examination were conducted in India.

The evidence from Bengal confirmed the Anglo-Indian contention that the support for simultaneous examinations was the strongest in what colonial officials called the 'advanced provinces' of India, and that support for it came overwhelmingly from the Hindus. The breakdown of native witnesses in Bengal showed 111 Hindus, 16 Muslims, one Parsi, and 2 identified as 'others'. The Commission had arrived in Bengal at the tail-end of its investigations; Bengalis, therefore, had access to printed copies of replies made by witnesses in other provinces. Dadabhai Naoroji's call for 'Equal Justice and No Favour' in his testimony before the Commission in Bombay was the most widely circulated in Indian political circles in Bengal.[69] On the one hand, the overwhelming majority of the native witnesses in Bengal, mainly Bengali Hindus, supported simultaneous examinations. Among them the only major difference, that reflected the range of views on the subject expressed in the Indian National Congress, was between the 'compulsionists' and 'non-compulsionists'.[70] The former wanted native candidates selected by the examination in India to spend a compulsory probationary period in Britain together with the candidates selected in Britain; this, they argued, would nullify any attempt by the colonial authorities to introduce an invidious distinction between civil servants recruited in India and in Britain. The non-compulsionists were against compulsory training in Britain for candidates recruited in India. On the other hand, Muslim opinion in the province reflected greater ambivalence towards holding a simultaneous examination in India. Although some Muslim leaders in Bengal, like Maulvi Abdul Jubber, favoured the holding of simultaneous examinations, the leading representative of Muslim public opinion in the province, Amir Ali, of the Central National Mahomedan Association and the Muhammedan Literary Society in Calcutta, expressed the more widespread Muslim opposition to holding simultaneous examinations.[71]

The argument that the competitive examination favoured only a 'single class of natives' allowed Anglo-Indian witnesses to suggest that simultaneous examinations would be prejudicial not only to Anglo-Indian interests, but also to the interests of other natives in India. Anglo-Indian witnesses played a major part in fostering such divisions among native witnesses on the question of simultaneous examinations. Theodore Beck's testimony before the Commission in Allahabad was perhaps the most blatant example of Anglo-Indian efforts to prejudice native witnesses in the Punjab and the North-West Provinces, and Muslim witnesses more generally, against competitive examinations. The backbone of Beck's testimony before the Commission was the alleged distrust and dislike of Bengali civilians among other natives. He told the Commission that 'all Bengalee officials in the North West Province were not popular because they treated the natives badly'.[72] He, moreover, accused Bengali officials in the region of extorting money from the locals. When in the cross-examination, however, the Bengali member of the Commission, Mitter, challenged Beck to provide a single example of his complaints, Beck confessed that he was referring only to petty officials, like ticket collectors, and not to the class of native officials relevant to the discussion. Similarly, W. E. Hart, a member of the Governor's Council in Bombay, testified before the Commission that competitive examinations excluded the traditional ruling classes who were the only equivalents to the English governing class in India; any extension of the examination in India, therefore, would produce an undesirable class of native civilians.[73]

That it was really Anglo-Indian professional as well as economic interests that were most threatened by the question of simultaneous examinations was evident in the alarm in the Anglo-Indian community at the very consideration of such a proposal by the Public Service Commission. As was to be expected, Anglo-Indian civilians whose interests were most directly affected by changes in the civil administration were at the forefront of the move to guard against any possible encroachment on their rights and privileges. To defend the rights of Anglo-Indian civilians, a 'Committee' consisting of Anglo-Indian civilians in the Bengal Presidency was formed to prepare all those who would be called to testify before the Commission.[74] Consequently, there was a remarkable similarity in the testimony of the Bengal civilians on the subject of simultaneous examinations. Only a few, like H. J. Reynolds, Henry Cotton, and Henry Beveridge, were willing to support simultaneous examinations. Cotton, however, was considered far too 'radical' in his views because he dared to question the central assumption that the covenanted service was the '*sine qua non* of the Indian polity'; such a centralised system of government, according to Cotton, was outworn especially in the 'advanced provinces'.[75] Beveridge, who was a Sessions Judge at Alipore, was regarded as having gone the furthest in sacrificing 'European agency' for more 'native agency' in the civil service. For he not only approved the idea of simultaneous examinations, but also suggested that he would have no problem if the examination were to be held exclusively in India.[76] The ferocious attack against Beveridge in the cross-examination was led by W. H. Rylands, the uncovenanted civilian member of the Commission who was also active in the Eurasian and Anglo-Indian Association in Bengal. Rylands and other Anglo-Indian members of the Commission found it enough to discredit Beveridge's evidence during the cross-examination by pointing out that he was an 'agnostic' and not 'a proper Christian'![77] What was obviously being suggested here was a parallel between Beveridge's crime against Christianity and his crime against the most sacred of colonial beliefs — Anglo-Indian domination of the competitive examination and consequently of the upper reaches of the civil administration in India — to cast him as a man quite beyond the pale of 'normal' society.

That powerful colonial economic interests were equally at stake in the substitution of 'cheap native agency' for Europeans in the civil administration was evident in the fact that the Anglo-Indian non-official community was not far behind the official community in Bengal in monitoring carefully the activities of the Commission. Sir Alexander Wilson, Sheriff of Calcutta and a senior partner of the firm of Jardine, Skinner & Co., testified before the Commission that any effort to replace 'European agency' by 'cheap native agency' would 'tend to reduce the amount of English capital that was being invested in India'.[78] The non-official community in fact spearheaded the first public criticism of the working of the Public Service Commission in the Anglo-Indian press; the response from the non-official community in India was provoked by the publication of the native evidence from

Bengal, with its overwhelming support for simultaneous examinations. More than in any other province, complained one Anglo-Indian newspaper, 'Bengalis were coming in hordes to give evidence before the Commission'.[79] Of the total of seventy witnesses who voluntarily came to testify before the main body of the Commission, as opposed to those who had been summoned or specially invited to the sessions, thirty were from Bengal. Twenty-five of them were Hindus, three Europeans/ Eurasians, and two Muslims. Ten of the thirty voluntary witnesses in Bengal were uncovenanted civilians.[80] The *Englishman* summarily dismissed these Bengali witnesses: 'only two penny men gave evidence in Calcutta'.[81] Yet powerful Anglo-Indian economic interests in the province were sufficiently alarmed by what one Anglo-Indian newspaper described as the 'great mass of vapid and sentimental doctrine of which the Commission [was] made the channel of advertisement' in Bengal.[82]

W. B. Hudson, an indigo planter from Muzzafarpur and the non-official Anglo-Indian member of the Commission, issued the first formal complaint against the Commission in the Anglo-Indian press. He rebuked the Commission for not conducting a special sitting in places like Muzaffarpur and Bankipore where planters could more easily come to give evidence before the Commission.[83] Hudson's complaint was followed by an official protest from thirty-four leading firms of the Bengal Chamber of Commerce, representing all branches of the trades of the province and all the major industries in which European capital was invested.[84] The protest was jointly endorsed by the Bengal Chamber of Commerce and the European and Anglo-Indian Defence Association, that had been formed during the Ilbert Bill controversy to continue the fight for the protection of Anglo-Indian privileges in India. Perhaps with the question of simultaneous examinations in mind, they complained that the Commission had become an outlet for airing 'proposals calculated to revolutionise the basis of the present administration of India'.[85]

The Public Service Commssion, however, successfully blocked the only real challenge to the British domination of the civil service from the various proposals under its consideration. The categorical rejection of simultaneous examinations, once in the Report of the Public Service Commission and again later when the Secretary of State and the Government of India used their discretion to nullify the Parliamentary Resolution of 1893 in favour of simultaneous examinations, ended any prospect of altering the character of the civil administration in India. The Public Service Commission's rejection of simultaneous examinations in order to preserve the 'English character' of the examination, moreover, effectively tied the meaning of the 'English' character of the competitive examination to blatantly unequal conditions for British and native candidates at the examination.[86]

Finally, the most important result of the sectarian definition of colonial masculinity was the reconstitution of the status of the native civilians *vis-à-vis* their British colleagues. For whereas the majority of the native civilians had always been employed in the inferior uncovenanted branch of the civil service, the reorganisation of the civil service under the Public Service Commission added a new dimension to their inferiority: they no longer were employed to serve in an all-India bureaucracy, but, henceforth, they would be recruited under, and expected to serve in, strictly provincial services. While the Public Service Commission could not afford to ignore the necessity of some expansion of native appointment at the senior levels of the administration, it proposed to confine this expansion to provincial cadres. The Provincial Services replaced the former uncovenanted service. They would be made up of covenanted posts transferred from the schedule of posts previously reserved for covenanted civilians and of senior uncovenanted posts; the 'statutory' civilians who were previously included in the covenanted lists were also expected to be absorbed in the individual Provincial Services. The candidates for the various Provincial Services, moreover, were to be recruited locally and restricted to serve only in the province in which they were recruited. The 'Provincial Service' (the Secretary of State later recommended that the service be referred to as the Bengal Civil Service, the Madras Civil Service, and so on) virtually ended the prospects for the majority of native civilians to serve in an all-India bureaucracy.[87]

The reorganisation of the native civilians along provincial lines was explained in terms of administrative consideration: the necessity to provide for the distinct characteristics of various native groups as well as the alleged mutual incompatibility of these groups. Anglo-Indian witnesses who favoured some expansion of native employment at senior levels of the administration were just as likely to favour the provincial reorganisation of the civil service as those die-hard Anglo-Indians who opposed any expansion in native employment. The testimony of A. C. Tupp, an Anglo-Indian civilian in the North-West Provinces, is instructive in this respect. Willing to support some expansion of native employment, Tupp favoured the fragmentation of the service along provincial lines. According to him, whereas the 'manly' native civilian from the Punjab or the North-West Provinces could serve safely anywhere in India, the effeminate Bengali civilian could serve only in such provinces as Bengal, Bombay, and Madras, but was totally useless for service in the Punjab and the North-West Provinces.[88]

The fragmentation of the native civil service along provincial lines was the logical outcome of a politics of colonial masculinity that attributed fixed and naturalised characteristics to different native 'types'. The consequences of placing weak and effeminate native civilians over a manly but 'lawless' population and the 'natural' hostility that manly natives felt towards effeminate natives were constant refrains in the Anglo-Indian evidence before the Commission. Walter Raleigh, a professor at the Muhammedan Anglo-Oriental College at Aligarh, warned the Commission that the more lawless Muslim populations in the North-West Provinces would welcome the appointment of 'effeminate Bengalis', because the latter would be unable to establish control over the districts under their charge.[89] Similarly, the Anglo-Indian Principal of Lahore College testified that Bengalis were morally and physically unfit to govern 'virile Muslim populations'.[90] Since 'excitable races' required a 'strong hand', Anglo-Indian witnesses argued, it would be disastrous to place them under the charge of effeminate native civilians. In the words of Sir Lepel Griffin, the rule of the 'competition *baboo*' over the 'manly Mahratta' was like placing 'grasshoppers' in charge of an 'army of lions'.[91] Although experienced native covenanted civilians, like De, testified before the Commission that 'too much is made of the dislike which the inhabitants of one Province are said to feel at being placed under the administration of officers who belong to another province', it was the testimony of Anglo-Indian witnesses that ultimately carried greater weight.[92]

The supposed attributes of different native 'types' laid the foundations not only for the fragmentation of the native-dominated service along provincial lines, but also for retaining colonial patronage in the appointment of natives to the Provincial Services. The rationale for continuing with a system of nominations for recruitment to the Provincial Services derived from the widely held scepticism against a test of educational qualifications for selecting natives: it supposedly favoured only the 'effeminate' natives, like the Bengalis in particular and the Hindus more generally. H. W. Bliss, Additional Member of the Board of Revenue in Madras, testified before the Commission that the only remedy against the influx of 'an undue number of a single class of natives' was to limit the number of vacancies to candidates of particular religions and castes.[93] Hence while nominations were discontinued in the Imperial Service, they were retained for native recruitment in the Provincial Services. Yet James Westland in the Viceroy's Council still complained that the Commission had not gone far enough in catering for those natives who did not have adequate educational qualifications: 'the races who dwell in the North West Provinces, in Rajputana, and in the Punjab, all uneducated as comparatively speaking they are, possess a power of commanding men, which is denied to the Bengali – the Public Service Commission has not shown us a way to pick them out'.[94] The

Lt.-Governor of the Punjab, in his comments on the Report of the Public Service Commission, also argued that since the list of BAs and MAs in the universities in Punjab showed 'no Rajput, Pathan, Ghakkar, Sial, Moghul, Aiwan, Biloch, Jat, or any great landholding tribes', a system of nomination rather than competition should be practised for entry into the Provincial Services.[95] The Public Service Commission left the recruitment for the Provincial Services up to the discretion of individual local governments who could choose between nomination and examination, or some combination of the two. The colonial authorities were thus ensured greater arbitrary control over the Provincial Services by retaining the power of patronage for the recruitment of particular castes and religious groups.

Because the sectarian elaboration of colonial masculinity not only deprived the native-dominated service of its all-India or national character but also instituted a less than rigorous mode for the selection of native candidates for the Provincial Services, it served to justify the 'inferior' status accorded the native-dominated services. This inferiority, in turn, provided a pretext for the colonial authorities to undermine further the transfer of certain positions from the covenanted service to the Provincial Services. The Government of India used the argument that the Provincial Service 'will necessarily be mainly recruited with reference to the qualities required for offices of a less responsible and independent character' to block successfully the number and type of posts to be transferred to the Provincial Services.[96] The Report of the Public Service Commission had originally proposed the transfer of 108 covenanted posts to the Provincial Services. Under the earlier 'statutory' rules, natives could already be appointed to ninety-two of these posts; the Commission, therefore, would have made available only sixteen additional posts. By the time the Government of India and the Secretary of State had completed their review of the Report, however, only ninety-three such posts were transferred to candidates of the Provincial Services, making available only one extra post for native civilians![97] The result was described accurately in a Horatian cliché in the pages of the *Bengalee*: 'A mountain was in labour and a mouse has been produced.'[98]

The colonial attitude towards the inferiority of the native-dominated Provincial Services, moreoever, was best exemplified in the debate over the kinds of posts to be transferred. The transfer of the more prestigious posts on the 'executive' side of the civil service was considered the most controversial. Although the Report of the Commission had declared that it was 'unable to proceed on the general assumption that Natives are unfit for District or other Executive charges', the majority of the positions that it recommended for transfer to the Provincial Services were mainly from the less prestigious judicial side of the civil service.[99] When the Superintendent of the Alipore Jails in Bengal testified before the Commission in the presence of Mitter, who had served as the Acting Chief Justice of Calcutta, that natives were as yet unfit even for senior judicial appointments like that of a District Judge, he was asked to apologise to Mitter.[100] For while native appointments in judicial posts had become a little more acceptable, there was still an overall consensus among Anglo-Indian officials that executive appointments should continue to be the preserve of Anglo-Indians. The colonial authorities had long argued that the typical native civilian was more suited for 'judicial' than for 'executive' appointments. Even native covenanted civilians, who were technically free to choose between the executive and judicial line, were usually encouraged by their superiors to choose the latter. Alexander Mackenzie, as Home Secretary, had tried some years previously to persuade Ripon and then Dufferin to prevent a native covenanted civilian, Anandaram Burroah – who Mackenzie described as a 'mere bookworm' – from choosing the executive line; Dufferin was sufficiently persuaded to inform the Bengal Government in a semi-official note that it should do all in its power to discourage native covenanted civilians from choosing the executive branch.[101] Later, in his capacity as the Chief Commissioner of the Central Provinces, Mackenzie testified before the Commission that natives should under no circumstances be allowed to hold executive positions in Divisional and District commands.[102] His view was reiterated by James Henderson, of the jute firm of George Henderson & Co. According to Henderson, the Government should be guided in its use of 'cheaper native agency' in the administration by 'the extent to which that cheaper agency is employed by European houses in India'. During the thirty years in which the jute manufacturing industry had existed in India, he argued, not 'a single native had been found competent to take charge of jute works'.[103]

Mackenzie's stinging criticism of the Commission for putting forward purely 'sentimental and impractical' reasons for transferring even a limited number of executive positions to the Provincial Services gained widespread support among Anglo-Indians.[104] In fact, it was Mackenzie's detailed rebuttal of the Commission's Report that effectively ensured that certain prestigous positions in the civil service remained beyond the reach of native civilians.[105] He argued against opening the charge of a single District, much less a Commission, to the native-dominated Provincial Services. According to Mackenzie, a native, however qualified, would 'revert to his ancestral type' if placed in command of isolated districts. Mackenzie received support from Bayley who, as Lt.-Governor of Bengal, argued that there were no native civilians in Bengal who could be appointed to any of the senior posts:

without an adequate supply of European officers to deal with the special requirements, administration in Bengal will be disastrously weakened, and the reputation of Government imperilled; and unless provision is made for a fair supply of Europeans on the provincial service it will be impossible to cut the cadre of the Imperial Service to the extent desired.[106]

The Government of India and the Secretary of State heartily concurred, even though the Report of the Commission already provided a sufficient safeguard at least on the question of a 'fair supply' of Europeans in the Provincial Services. For the Report recommended cancelling the 1879 circular that limited recruitment for the uncovenanted service mainly to the natives of India; it suggested that European British subjects residing in the Indian provinces be made eligible in common with others for admission to the Provincial Services. Not satisfied with this safeguard alone, the Secretary of State also removed certain positions, such as the Commissioner of Divisions and the Member of the Board of Revenue, from the list of posts that the Commission's Report recommended for transfer to the Provincial Services. To limit even further the scope of the Provincial Services, the colonial authorities also recommended that appointments to a range of other senior positions be made more contingent. The Government of India's report on the Commission stated:

> we are strongly of the opinion that promotion within the Provincial Service to the higher offices (ie. District Magistrates and Sessions Judges) to be transferred from the covenanted service should be altogether special, and that service rules should contain a distinct provision that such promotion is not to be expected and will not be made as a matter of ordinary course, but that in every case selection will be made of the fittest and most capable men without regard to individual standing in the Provincial Service.[107]

The Secretary of State agreed that the chief executive of a district, the commissioner of a division, and administrative offices of still higher rank should not be transferred to the Provincial Service; he also concurred that Provincial Service recruits should not be promoted routinely to covenanted posts except on proof of exceptional fitness.[108] In short, the colonial attitude towards the native-dominated Provincial Service justified Naoroji's bitter description of it as little more than a 'Pariah Service'.[109] The Parsi leader's choice of words to describe the inferiority of the native service also unwittingly points to a problem in the native civil service agitation: its predominantly Hindu and upper-caste orientation.

The recommendations of the Public Service Commission regarding the special departments, like Accounts, Education, Jails, Post Office, and so on, that were connected to the civil administration in India also further institutionalised the inferiority of the native employees. The heads of the various departments, who were invited to Simla to record their testimony on the appointment of natives to higher posts in their respective departments, all testified in favour of the status quo. Appointments in the various departments, they argued, should follow the natural hierarchy between the races: Anglo-Indians were the most qualified, Eurasians were better than the natives, and natives because of a lack of 'pluck' and 'energy' were the least qualified.[110] This view was endorsed by none other than the President of the Sub-Committee on the Special Departments, Sir Charles Turner:

> on the whole as a race Englishmen are more energetic, more self reliant, more fertile in resource, more vigorous in body than Hindus. Indians have better memory and [are] more obedient. For higher services we recommend nobody but men such as Macaulay contemplates, namely gentlemen of finished English education.[111]

In addition, the Commission recommended that the same principles that were used to reorganise the civil service should as far as possible be applied to the reorganisation of the special departments.

The sectarian construction of colonial masculinity thus also effectively blocked any recommendations for the appointment of natives to higher and better-paid posts in the special departments. One example was the recommendation in the Report of the Commission for the appointment of natives as Superintendents of Central and District Jails. The belief that certain types of natives were devoid inherently of the firmness and courage required for the job, however, gave the Government of India the excuse to modify the original proposal: natives, it argued, could be accepted only in the lesser position of Superintendents of District Jails and not in the more senior position of Superintendents of Central Jails.[112] There were numerous other instances when notions about the 'food', 'religious practices', 'natural stamina', 'aptitude', and so on of different native 'types' were used to argue against the extension of certain better-paying positions in the special departments to natives of India.

The sectarian definition of colonial masculinity, furthermore, reinforced an already existing bias in the special departments in favour of the claims of domiciled Anglo-Indians and Eurasians on government employment over that of 'natives of India'.[113] In recent years, the government was increasingly beset by new pressures: the domiciled Anglo-Indians, Eurasians, and 'poor whites' commanded the attention of the government. The domiciled Anglo-Indians and Eurasians often demanded, as in the recent petitions to the government from F. T.

Atkins, President of the United Railway and Government Servants Association at Allahabad, more than equal treatment as 'natives of India'; instead, they called for preferential treatment as 'European British subjects'.[114] Nowhere was the colonial effort to placate domiciled Anglo-Indian interests more evident than in the Commission's response to the controversy sparked off by the evidence on the Postal Department. At the heart of this colourful controversy ignited by the evidence of Motilal Ghose, the joint editor of the *Amrita Bazar Patrika*, were the rival claims of natives and domiciled Anglo-Indians on government employment. In his testimony before the Commission, Ghose accused the Postal Department of 'jobbery'. He argued that even though the Postal Manual declared that appointments in the Department should be restricted to natives of India, most of the appointments were filled by sons, sons-in-law, brothers, and cousins of some of the European officers in the Department. He also complained of the behaviour of the Postmaster General, H. M. Kisch, towards his native subordinates; furthermore, he claimed, that whereas European employees were typically sent to the best postal divisions, natives were sent to the least popular divisions.[115] As President of the Sub-Committee, Turner was reluctant to record Ghose's charges even though neither the Anglo-Indian members of the Commission nor Kisch, who was also present, could answer Ghose's charges or discredit his testimony during the cross-examination. Ghose's evidence was finally recorded, but only in a much modified form.

What shortly came to be known as the 'Eructation Episode', however, deflected attention away from Ghose's criticism of 'jobbery' in the Postal Department; it focused attention, instead, on the 'unmanly' and 'unmannerly' behaviour of the Bengali witness while testifying before the Sub-Committee.[116] Ghose had apparently belched twice during his testimony; he was 'gently rebuked' by Turner for displaying poor manners. Although Ghose himself excused Turner's rebuke as 'paternal' criticism, much was made of the episode in both the Anglo-Indian and the native press.[117] Both sides were eager to make political capital out of Ghose's eructation and Turner's rebuke. Ghose received anonymous letters and threats from Anglo-Indians on the incident: 'It is a wonder that the European gentlemen present there did not apply the toes of their boots to your backside, as they should have done to you . . . You Bengalis are the most degraded race on earth, and you should read Macaulay.'[118] In the meantime, other efforts were being taken by the Anglo-Indian establishment to discredit Ghose's evidence. The contents of a semi-official note written by Kisch to Postmasters General all over India urging them to organise a defence against Ghose's accusations were leaked to the press. The native clerks suspected for leaking the contents of the note to the press were punished by being promptly sent off to remote postal districts.[119] G. J. Hynes, the First Assistant to the Director-General of the Post Office, was deputed to give a detailed reply to Ghose's charges before the Commission. Hynes argued that the Europeans employed in the postal departments technically came under the rubric 'natives of India' and hence their appointments accorded fully with the regulations of the Postal Department Manual.[120] Yet, despite the fact that the glaring evidence of irregularities in the Postal Department had not been fully answered, the Report of the Commission agreed that the charges of 'partiality' brought against the Postal Department were 'unfounded' and based on a 'misapprehension of the rules which regulate promotion to the higher appointments'.[121] On the question of native employment in the Postal Department, as in the other special departments related to the civil administration, the Commission chose simply not to give much weight to native claims for more extensive appointments.

The Public Service Commission was the natural culmination of decades of concern about British and native employment in the civil administration of India. The gist of the Anglo-Indian critique of native employment in the civil administration was summed up in an article in the *Calcutta Review*:

> Government has (already) made a mistake by entrusting administration solely to English educated youths – ignoring the claims of classes and races who owing to their possession of 'character' have refused to be crammed. By this process our Government is being weakened and deprived of the natural masculine strength it might have had.[122]

In the name of securing an adequate supply of 'natural masculine strength', the Public Service Commission deployed a specifically sectarian dimension of colonial masculinity to reorganise the civil administration. The Anglo-Indian critiques of native employment in the civil administration, therefore, were at least partially answered by the Commission in its recommendations for the greater exclusion of natives from the top levels of the administration and the fragmentation of the native service along provincial lines. The Public Service Commission also had an impact on the debate about the quality of British candidates in the civil service. The roots of the critique of British candidates were expressed candidly in 1864 by the then Secretary of State, Sir Charles Wood. Wood, as R. J. Moore notes, was trying to explain why there were more complaints against British civilians in Bengal, the most prestigious of the provinces for civilians in India, than against British civilians in Madras; his explanation offers an interesting testimony to the prejudice against the social and regional backgrounds of British civilians:

The clever well crammed youths from the Irish universities or commercial schools obtain the highest marks and go to Bengal. The University men, who are gentlemen, go to Madras ... It is difficult to say this in public, for I should have half a dozen wild Irishmen on my shoulders and as many middle class examination students.[123]

The changes in the competitive examination throughout the nineteenth century, as several scholars have pointed out, were directed precisely towards remaking the 'clever' Irish and middle-class British competition civilians in the image of the 'Oxbridge' English gentleman. This problem was substantially resolved by the recommendations of the Public Service Commission, which gave to the majority of British civilians in India the veneer of an 'Oxbridge' training. For after 1892, when the higher age limits came into effect, the average British civilian in India, as B. B. Misra has pointed out, was more likely than ever before to be an 'Oxbridge' graduate.[124] Although this did not end the litany of complaints about the inferior social background of many of the British civilians in India, the establishment of a smaller British-dominated, all-India service as well as the threat of native encroachment exerted sufficient pressure to maintain at least a public mythology of the 'manly' virtues of the British civilian in India. As Spangenburg further reminds us, moreover, henceforth the changes in the competitive examinations were motivated not by complaints of the class and regional composition of the British civil service recruits, but by the need to combat the declining popularity of the Indian civil service in Britain.[125]

Nothing, perhaps, better underscores how the Public Service Commission contained the pressure of greater native employment in the public administration in India than the shift in the meaning of the 'Indian' civil service: technically the Indian civil service now referred only to the small British-dominated cadre of the service. While the redefinition of the 'Indian' civilian confined the majority of native civilians to a strictly provincial identification, it provided an imperial identification for the British civilian. The imperial identification of the British civil servant went a long way towards papering over some of the more overt criticisms directed against the varied backgrounds of 'British' civil service recruits. As many scholars have already suggested, within certain limits, colonial employment cemented the ties of different groups within Britain in the British Empire.[126] To borrow a phrase from Graham Dawson, however, it was an 'English-British' masculinity – one that underscored the 'Englishness' in the identity of the 'British' – that was ensconced in the civil service as a result of the Public Service Commission.[127] There is an additional point to be made of the working of the Public Service Commission: that the national representation of a common 'British' masculinity and the provincial and religious differences in the representation of 'native' masculinity in the civil service were part of the same imperial process. The Public Service Commission, therefore, made the basis of British domination of the civil service more than ever before dependent upon a sectarian elaboration of colonial masculinity. Indeed, most important of all, its redefinition of the 'Indian' civil service served the interests of colonial rule precisely because it constructed as the foil for 'Britishness' not 'Indianness', but fragmented and competing provincial native identities.

Notes

1 Resolution No. 34/1573–98 of 4 Oct. 1886. A Copy of the Resolution was sent to the Secretary of State for India. See *India, Home Department, Public Despatch to Secretary of State,* 19 Oct. 1886, No. 53 A, National Archives of India (NAI), New Delhi.
2 T. D. Beighton, 'The Public Service Commission and Judicial Reform', *Calcutta Review,* 88: 175 (Jan. 1889), 171–209. The Report and the evidence were published in eight separate volumes: *Public Service Commission 1886–87: Report and Proceedings of the Public Service Commission,* Calcutta 1888, NAI (Hereafter: *Progs. PSC*).
3 Critical Introduction by Bradford Spangenberg in Spangenberg (ed.), *British Attitudes Towards the Employment of Indians in the Civil Service: Report of the Public Service Commission (1886–87) Headed by C. U. Aitchison* (Delhi: Concept Publishing Co., 1977).
4 *Bengalee* (Calcutta), 31 Dec. 1887, p. 609.
5 For a classic account of British classification procedures in colonial India, see Bernard S. Cohn, 'The Census, Social Structure and Objectification in South Asia', in Cohn (ed.), *An Anthropologist Among the Historians and Other Essays* (Delhi: Oxford University Press, 1987), pp. 224–54. Also see David Ludden, 'Orientalist Empiricism: Transformations of Colonial Knowledge', in C. A. Breckenridge and P. van der Veer (eds.), *Orientalism and the Postcolonial Predicament* (Philadelphia: University of Pennsylvania Press, 1993), pp. 250–78.
6 Arjun Appadurai, 'Number in the Colonial Imagination', in Breckenridge and P. van der Veer (eds.), *Orientalism and the Postcolonial Predicament,* pp. 314–40. Also see Deborah Epstein Nord, 'The Social Explorer as Anthropologist: Victorian Travellers among the Urban Poor', in W. Sharpe and L. Wallock (eds.), *Visions of the Modern City* (Baltimore: Johns Hopkins University Press, 1987), pp. 122–34. For a discussion of the redirection of existing group identities in India under the colonial impact, see Romila Thapar, 'Imagined Religious Communities? Ancient History and the Modern Search for a Hindu Identity', *Modern Asian Studies,* 23 (1989), 209–32.
7 For the 'disciplinary' function of colonial classifications, see Sanjay Nigam, 'Disciplining and Policing the "Criminals by Birth", Part 2: The Development of a Disciplinary System, 1871–1900', *Indian Economic and Social History Review,* 27: 3 (July-Sept. 1990), 257–87.
8 Quoted in Sumit Sarkar, *Modern India, 1885–1947* (New Delhi: Macmillan India Ltd., 1983), p. 2.
9 *Pioneer* (Allahabad), 10 Jan. 1887, p. 5.
10 For the classic account of British civil servants in India, see Philip Mason, *The Men Who Ruled India : The Guardians,* vol. 2 (New York: W. W. Norton & Co., 1989).
11 See Rupert Wilkinson, *Gentlemanly Power: British Leadership and the Public*

THE PUBLIC SERVICE COMMISSION

School Tradition (London: Oxford University Press, 1964); and Philip Mason, *The English Gentleman: The Rise and Fall of an Ideal* (London: André Deutsch, 1982). For the changing Victorian definition of the 'gentleman', see also G. Kitson-Clark, *The Making of Victorian England* (Cambridge: Harvard University Press, 1962), p. 271; and Geoffrey Best, *Mid-Victorian England 1851–1875* (New York: Schocken Books, 1972), p. 165. For the importance of the 'gentlemanly' ideal for civil service reforms within Britain, see Peter Gowan, 'The Origins of the Administrative Elite', *New Left Review*, 162 (Mar./Apr. 1987), 4–34.

12 I am indebted to the following accounts: Bernard S. Cohn, 'Recruitment and Training of British Civil Servants in India 1600–1860' in R. Braibanti (ed.), *Asian Bureaucratic Systems Emergent from the British Imperial Tradition* (Durham: Duke University Press, 1966), pp. 87–140; J. M. Compton, 'Open Competition and the Indian Civil Service 1854–1876', *English History Review*, 327 (Apr. 1968), 265–84; C. J. Dewey, 'The Education of a Ruling Caste: The Indian Civil Service in the Era of Competitive Examination', *English History Review*, 88 (April 1973), 262–85; and Bradford Spangenberg, *British Bureaucracy in India: Status, Policy and the Indian Civil Service in the Late Nineteenth Century* (Columbia, MO: South Asia Books, 1976).

13 Information furnished by the Secretary of State for India to the Public Service Commission regarding natives of India who presented themselves at the open competition for the Civil Service of India; India Home Department, Public, 1 January 1887, Pros. Nos. 129–131 A, NAI.

14 The similarity in the critique of British and Indian competition civilians has been pointed out in, among others, H. M. L. Alexander, 'The Ruling Servants: The Indian Civil Service 1878–1923' (unpublished Ph.D. dissertation, University of Sydney, 1977).

15 [Percy Greg], 'Competitive Examinations and the Civil Service', *Quarterly Review*, 133 (July-Oct. 1872), p. 268. See also J. M. Compton, 'Indians and the Indian Civil Service 1853–1879: A Study in National Agitation and Imperial Embarrassment', *Journal of Royal Asiatic Society of Great Britain and Ireland*, 3/4 (1967), pp. 101–9.

16 Alexander, *The Ruling Servants*, pp. 36–7. Also see Anil Seal, *The Emergence of Indian Nationalism: Competition and Collaboration in the Later Nineteenth Century* (Cambridge: Cambridge University Press, 1968), p. 362.

17 See H. L. Singh, *Problems and Policies of the British in India, 1885–1898* (New York: Asia Publishing House, 1963), pp. 72–3. Native civil servants favoured competitive examinations over nominations in both the covenanted and uncovenanted branches of the service see R. C. Dutt, 'A Plea For Competitive Examinations', *Calcutta Review*, 78:156 (Apr. 1884), 227–34.

18 For the system of 'statutory' nominations, see S. K. Bajaj, 'Indianization of the Indian Civil Service – The Formation of the Statutory Civil Service 1879', *The Punjab Past and Present*, 5:9 (Apr. 1971), 211–26. For a comprehensive history of the civil service in India, see B. B. Misra, *The Bureaucracy in India: An Historical Analysis of Development up to 1947* (Delhi: Oxford University Press, 1977).

19 The Secretary of State was informed of the dissatisfaction against the statutory regulations by the Viceroy, Lord Ripon, India, Home Department, Public Despatch to Secretary of State, 12 Sept. 1884, No. 51 A, NAI.

20 India, Home Department, Public, 1 January 1887, Pros. Nos. 129–131 A.

21 For the predominantly Hindu themes in late nineteenth-century political nationalism, see Barbara Southard, 'Neo Hinduism and Militant Politics in Bengal 1875–1910' (unpublished Ph.D. dissertation, University of Hawaii, 1971). Also Partha Chatterjee, *The Nation and its Fragments: Colonial and Postcolonial Histories* (Princeton: Princeton University Press, 1993), esp. pp. 95–115.

22 India, Home Department, Public, July 1883, Pros. Nos. 59 – 70 A, NAI.

23 Quoted in *Bengalee*, 20 Jan. 1883, pp. 27–8. Anglo-Indian civilians protested this popular characterisation of their physical health; see *Civil and Military Gazette* (Lahore), 11 Jan. 1883, p. 3; and *Pioneer*, 9 Feb. 1883, p. 5.

24 Bayly, India, Home Department, Public, July 1883, Pros. Nos. 59–70 A. The findings of the enquiry were presented to Parliament and compiled in the *Twenty-Eighth*

Report of Her Majesty's Civil Service Commissioners With Appendix Presented to Both Houses of Parliament By Command of Her Majesty, c. 4039, 1884, National Library Annexe (NLA), Calcutta.
25 India, Home Department, Public Despatch to India, 15 July 1886, No. 65 A, NAI.
26 India Home Department, Public, Nov. 1886, Pros. Nos. 111–129 A, NAI.
27 *Pioneer,* 6 Nov. 1886, p. 7.
28 India, Home Department, Public, Nov. 1886, Pros. Nos. 111–129 A ; *Pioneer,* 6 Nov. 1886, p. 1, and 8 Nov. 1886, p. 1. For the hand of conservative officials of the Home Department in the selection of members for the Commission, see Spangenberg, *British Attitudes Towards the Employment of Indians,* pp. 11–13.
29 Cited in S. Gopal, *British Policy in India 1858–1905* (Cambridge: Cambridge University Press, 1965), pp. 164–5.
30 See S. N. Banerjea, *A Nation in the Making: Being Reminiscences of Fifty Years of Public Life* (Calcutta: Oxford University Press, reprinted 1963, first published 1925), ch. 5.
31 Note by A. P. MacDonnell, 30 Aug. 1886 in India, Home Department, Public, Nov. 1886, Pros. Nos. 111–129 A.
32 Spangenberg, *British Attitudes Towards the Employment of Indians,* p. 24. Also India, Home Department, Public, Dec. 1886, Pros. Nos. 36–37 A, NAI.
33 Note by A. P. MacDonnell, 13 Sept. 1886 in India, Home Department, Public, Nov. 1886, Pros. Nos. 111–129 A.
34 See Rajah Oday Pertap Singh, 'The Growth of Radicalism in India and its Danger', *Calcutta Review,* 84:167 (Jan. 1887), 1–10.
35 S. N. Banerjea, *A Nation in the Making,* p. 45. For Syed Ahmed Khan's infamous speech against effeminate 'Bengali' civilians, see *Sir Syed Ahmed Khan on the Present State of Indian Politics, Consisting of Speeches and Letters Reprinted from the Pioneer* (Allahabad: Pioneer Press, 1888), reprinted in J. R. McLane (ed.), *A Political Awakening in India* (Englewood Cliffs, NJ: Prentice Hall, 1970), pp. 42–7.
36 Report of the Public Service Commission Presented to Both Houses of Parliament by Command of Her Majesty in *Great Britain, Parliamentary Papers, House of Commons,* 1888,48, c. 5327 (Hereafter: *Parl. Papers 1888*). Also see Beighton, 'The Public Service Commission', p. 180.
37 Report of Public Service Commission, p. 3, *Parl. Papers 1888.*
38 Quoted in *Amrita Bazar Patrika* (Calcutta), 10 Feb. 1887, pp. 4–5. For similar evidence from Anglo-Indian officials in Bombay, see *Progs. PSC,* vol. 4, Sec. 3, Sub-Sec. B.
39 Quoted in *Pioneer,* 25 Feb. 1887, p. 3; and *Modern Review,* vol. 13 (Jan. 1913), p. 82. Also *Progs. PSC,* vol. 6, Sec. 2.
40 Brajendranath De, 'Reminiscences of an Indian Member of the Indian Civil Service', *Calcutta Review,* 132:2 (Aug. 1954), p. 91.
41 John Beames, *Memoirs of a Bengal Civilian* (New Delhi: Manohar Pub. [1961] reprinted, 1984), p. 303.
42 Quoted in *Pioneer,* 6 Nov. 1886, p. 7.
43 Report of the Public Service Commission, p. 43, *Parl. Papers 1888.*
44 For the recommendations of the Macaulay committee, see B. B. Misra, *The Bureaucracy in India,* pp. 75–8.
45 Spangenberg, *British Bureaucracy in India,* p. 18.
46 29 Mar. 1884, *Ilbert Papers,* vol. 12, India Office Library and Records (IOLR), London.
47 Minute by Viceroy, 10 Sept. 1884, Civil Service Candidates: Correspondence Between the Government of India and the Secretary of State for India Relating to the Age at which Candidates for the Civil Service are Admitted to Competition in England, in *Great Britain, Parliamentary Papers, House of Commons,* 58, c. 4580 (Hereafter: *Parl. Papers 1883–84*).
48 Scoones to Dufferin, India, Home Department, Public, Oct. 1888, Pros. Nos. 188–223 A, NAI. For the importance of the 'Oxford Reformers' in civil service reforms in general, see Jennifer Hart, 'The Genesis of the Northcote-Trevelyan Report', in Gillian Sutherland (ed.), *Studies in the Growth of Nineteenth Century*

Government (Totowa, NJ: Rowman, 1972), pp. 63–81.
49 From Under-Secretary of State for India to Secretary Civil Service Commission, 24 July 1889, p. 86 in Public Service Commission Correspondence Relating to the Report of the Indian Public Service Commission Including Questions as to the Limit of Age For the Indian Civil Service, in *Great Britain, Parliamentary Papers, House of Commons, 1890*, 54, c. 5926,321 (Hereafter: *Parl. Papers 1890*).
50 Spangenberg, *British Attitudes Towards the Employment of Indians*, p. 24.
51 *Pioneer*, 9 Nov. 1886, p. 5. For Beck's evidence, see *Progs. PSC*, vol. 2, Sec. 2, pp. 33–9.
52 *Amrita Bazar Patrika*, 23 Dec. 1886, p. 4.
53 Steuart Bayly, for example, had argued in the Viceroy's Council in 1883 that since natives were 'infinitely quicker' than Europeans at seventeen and eighteen, the result of conducting the competitive examination in India would be that 'at least half the service would be Bengalis', *India, Home Department Public, Oct. 1883*, Pros. Nos. 183–184 A, NAI.
54 Notes by Aitchison and MacDonnell in *India, Home Department, Public, Oct. 1888*, Pros. Nos. 188–223 A, NAI.
55 Despatch from Government of India to Viscount Cross, 9 Oct. 1888, p. 10, *Parl. Papers 1890*.
56 Cited in H. M. L. Alexander, *The Ruling Servants*, pp. 88–9.
57 *Ibid*.
58 From Civil Service Commissioners to Under-Secretary of State, 19 Aug. 1889, p. 89, *Parl. Papers 1890*.
59 P. Lumsden, *Dissents By Members of Council*, vol. 2, 1881–90, p. 270, IOLR.
60 Lansdowne to Cross, 14 June 1889, *Lansdowne Papers: Correspondence with the Secretary of State Commencing Jan. 1889*, IOLR.
61 See *Hindoo Patriot* (Calcutta), 12 May 1890, p. 226; and *Sanjivani*, 27 Sept. 1890, in *Report on Native Newspapers of the Bengal Presidency*, 1890, No. 42 (Hereafter: RNBP).
62 Cited in Brajendranath De, 'Reminiscences of an Indian Member of the Indian Civil Service', *Calcutta Review*, 132:3 (Sept. 1954), 180–1. Also *Civil Service Commission, Open Competition for the Civil Service of India, June 1890:Regulations, Examination Papers, Table of Marks and Statistics*, NLA.
63 See H. L. Singh, *Problems and Policies*, p. 17. Also see Appendix to Minutes of Evidence Taken Before the Royal Commission on the Administration of the Expenditure of India, in *Great Britain, Parliamentary Papers, House of Commons, 1900*, 24, c.130, Appendix F.
64 For the proposal of the Bengal government, see *India, Home Department Public*, Nov. 1886, Pros. Nos. 111–129 A.
65 Report of the Public Service Commission, pp. 39–40, *Parl. Papers 1888*.
66 *Ibid.*, p. 42.
67 *Ibid.*, p. 6–8. Also *Appendices to the Report of the Public Service Commission 1886–87*, Calcutta 1888, NLA.
68 Report of the Public Service Commission, p. 39, *Parl. Papers 1888*.
69 *Amrita Bazar Patrika*, 20 Jan. 1887, p. 6. For evidence from Bengal, see *Progs. PSC*, vol. 6.
70 *Amrita Bazar Patrika*, 3 Feb. 1887, p. 4, and 17 Mar. 1887, p. 4.
71 *Progs. PSC*, vol. 6, Sec. 2, p. 195; and Sec. 3, Sub-Sec. A. Also *Amrita Bazar Patrika*, 3 Mar. 1887, p. 4.
72 *Progs PSC*, vol. 2, Sec. 2, pp. 33–9. Also cited in *Statesman and Friend of India* (Calcutta), 20 Jan. 1887, p. 2 (Hereafter: *Statesman*).
73 *Progs. PSC*, vol. 4, Sec. 3, Sub-Sec. B, no. 3.
74 See Ethel A. Waley Cohen (ed.), *A Young Victorian in India, Letters of H. M. Kisch* (London: Jonathan Cape, 1957), p. 219.
75 Henry Cotton, *Indian and Home Memories* (London: T. Fisher Unwin, 1911), p. 202. Also *Progs. PSC*, vol. 6, Sec. 2, p. 5.
76 *Progs. PSC*, vol 6, Sec. 2. Also cited in *Navavibhakar Sadharani* and *Ananda Bazar Patrika*, 28 Feb. 1887, RNBP, 1887, No. 10; and *Modern Review*, 13 (1913), pp. 86–7.

77 Quoted in *Pioneer*, 24 Feb. 1887, p. 2.
78 *Progs. PSC*, vol. 6, Sec. 3, Sub-Sec. B. Also quoted in *English Opinion on India: A Monthly Magazine Containing Select Extracts from English Newspapers on Indian Subjects* (Poona), vol. 1 (Apr. 1887), p. 105 (Hereafter: *English Opinion on India*).
79 *Pioneer*, 28 Jan. 1887, p. 1.
80 Report of the Public Service Commission, pp. 6–7, *Parl. Papers 1888*.
81 *Englishman* (Calcutta), 23 June 1887, p. 4. See also Lepel Griffin quoted in *English Opinion on India*, vol. 1 (June 1887), p. 234.
82 *Englishman*, 17 May 1887, p. 4.
83 *Pioneer*, 14 June 1887, p. 2; and *Englishman*, 23 June 1887, p. 4.
84 Cited in *Pioneer*, 14 June 1887, p. 2; *Englishman*, 17 May 1887, p. 4; and *Bengalee*, 7 May 1887, p. 222.
85 Quoted in *Pioneer*, 14 June 1887, p. 2.
86 In 1893 the House of Commons in Britain had approved a Resolution by eighty-four votes to seventy-eight in favour of simultaneous examinations; the Secretary of State and the Government of India ensured the Resolution remained a dead letter; see *Lansdowne Collection: Correspondence with Persons in India, July to Dec. 1893*, Letters Nos. 76 and 117; *Letters From Persons in England, Jan. 1893-Jan. 1894*, Letters Nos. 52, 56, 58, and 127. Also *Dissents by Members of Council*, vol. 2, pp. 279–301.
87 Spangenberg, *British Attitudes Towards the Employment of Indians*, p. 13.
88 Cited in *Pioneer*, 10 Jan. 1887, p. 6.
89 Cited in *Pioneer*, 13 Jan. 1887, p. 5. For a similar testimony from an official in the Punjab, see *Progs. PSC*, vol. 1, Sec. 2, p. 4.
90 Cited in *Bharat Basi*, 1 Jan. 1887, *RNBP*, Jan.-June 1887, No. 4.
91 Lepel Griffin's speech at Lashkar, Gwaliar, drew considerable attention; see *English Opinion on India* (Feb. 1888), pp. 25–35.
92 *Modern Review*, vol. 13 (Jan. 1913), p. 84; *Progs. PSC*, vol. 6, Sec. 2.
93 *Progs. PSC*, vol. 5, Sec. 2, p. 284.
94 *India, Home Department, Public, Oct. 1888*, Pros. Nos., 188–203 A.
95 Lt.-Gov. of the Punjab to Government of India, 25 June 1888, p. 47, *Parl. Papers 1890*.
96 Government of India to Secretary of State, 9 Oct. 1888, p. 11, *Parl. Papers 1890*.
97 Seal, *The Emergence of Indian Nationalism*, p. 182. For a testimony to the fears aroused among Anglo-Indians by even the limited changes recommended by the Commission, see Meredith Townsend, 'Will England Retain India?', *Contemporary Review*, 53 (June 1888), 795–813.
98 *Bengalee*, 16 Aug. 1890, p. 387.
99 *Amrita Bazar Patrika*, 31 Mar. 1888, pp. 3–4; and 7 June 1888, p. 4.
100 Cited in *Bengalee*, 5 Feb. 1887, pp. 66–7; and *Pioneer*, 31 Jan. 1887, p. 3.
101 *India, Home Department, Judicial, Jan. 1886*, Pros. Nos. 305–306 A, NAI. For the impact of this racial divide on the 'executive' and 'judicial' line in the Bengal civil service, see, T. K., 'The Bengal Civil Service', *Calcutta Review*, 180 (Apr. 1890), 388–91.
102 *Progs. PSC*, vol. 3, Sec. 1, Sub-Sec. B.
103 Quoted in *English Opinion on India*, vol. 1 (Apr. 1887), p. 105.
104 Chief Commissioner, Central Provinces, to Government of India, 21 Apr. 1888, p. 63, *Parl. Papers 1890*.
105 Mackenzie's 'able Minute' on the Public Service Commission was cited approvingly by the Secretary of State; see Sec. of State to Govt of India, 12 Sept. 1888, p. 98, *Parl. Papers 1890*. Another influence on the Government of India's decision to limit further the proposals of the Commission was the 150-page note written by A. P. MacDonnell on the Report of the Public Service Commission; see Spangenburg, *British Attitudes towards the Employment of Indians*, p. 33.
106 Lt.-Gov. of Bengal to Govt of India, 4 May 1888, p. 28, *Parl. Papers 1890*.
107 Govt of India to Secretary of State, 9 Oct. 1888, pp. 11–12, *Parl. Papers 1890*.
108 Secretary of State to Govt of India, 12 Sept. 1889, p. 94, *Parl. Papers 1890*.
109 Quoted in N. Subba Rau Pantalu, *The Public Service Question in India* (Calcutta:

Thacker, Spink & Co., 1911), p. 11.
110 *Sahachar*, 22 June 1887, *RNBP*, 1887, No. 27. Also see *Progs. PSC*, vol. 7, p. 23.
111 Quoted in *Englishman*, 5 Oct. 1887, p. 4.
112 *India, Home Department, Public, April 1891*, Pros. No. 86 A, NAI. Also see J. P. Misra, *The Administration of India Under Lord Lansdowne, 1888–1894* (New Delhi: Sterling Pub. Pvt. Ltd, 1975), pp. 212–27.
113 For the question of 'poor whites' during the deliberations of the Sub-Committee, see *Amrita Bazar Patrika*, 21 Apr. 1887, p. 3; and 26 May 1887, p. 4. For the problem of poor whites, also see David Arnold, 'White Colonisation and Labour in Nineteenth-Century India', *Journal of Imperial and Commonwealth History*, 11:2 (Jan. 1983), 133–58.
114 See *India, Home Department, Public, July 1886*, Pros. Nos. 26–35 A, NAI; *Progs. PSC*, vol. 7.
115 Cited in *Amrita Bazar Patrika*, 31 Mar. 1887, p. 6 and 14 Apr. 1887, pp. 4–5.
116 *Amrita Bazar Patrika*, 7 Apr. 1887, pp. 6–7. Also see Paramanda Dutt, *Memoirs of Motilal Ghose* (Calcutta: Amrita Bazar Patrika Office, 1935), pp. 54–9.
117 Quoted in *Amrita Bazar Patrika*, 7 Apr. 1887, pp. 6–7.
118 Dutt, *Memoirs of Motilal Ghose*, pp. 54–9.
119 *Amrita Bazar Patrika*, 21 July 1887, p. 4; *Samaya*, 26 Aug. 1887, RNBP, 1887, No. 36.
120 *Amrita Bazar Patrika*, 16 June 1887, p. 5.
121 Report of the Public Service Commission, p. 91, *Parl. Papers 1888*.
122 F. H. Barrow, 'Education and Hinduism in Bengal', *Calcutta Review* 87: 173 (July 1888), pp. 25–6.
123 Wood to Trevelyan, 16 Oct. 1864, cited in R. J. Moore, *Sir Charles Wood's Indian Policy 1853–1866* (Manchester: Manchester University Press, 1966), p. 101.
124 See B. B. Misra, *The Bureaucracy in India*, pp. 101–4.
125 For the dichotomy in the public and private assessment of the civil service at the turn of the century, see Spangenburg, *British Bureaucracy in India*. Spangenburg demonstrates that henceforth the changes in the civil service regulations had to do with shoring up the recruitment of the service in Britain: in 1895 the examination for the Indian civil service was held jointly with the Home Service; in 1896 the Eastern cadetships for the Colonial Service were also included; from 1922 the examination was held simultaneously in Allahabad, India; see Spangenberg, *British Bureaucracy in India*, pp. 28–34.
126 This is the argument made, for example, in Benedict Anderson, *Imagined Communities* (London: Verso, 1983), pp. 84–9. For a recent survey of the role of empire in cementing the Scottish connection, see John M. MacKenzie, 'Essay and Reflection: On Scotland and Empire', *International History Review*, 15:4 (Nov. 1993), 661–880.
127 See Graham Dawson, 'The Blond Bedouin: Lawrence of Arabia, Imperial Adventure and the Imagining of English-British Masculinity', in M. Roper and J. Tosh (eds.), *Manful Assertions: Masculinities in Britain Since 1800* (London: Routledge, 1991), p. 136, n. 10.

CHAPTER FOUR

Potent protests: the Age of Consent controversy, 1891

On 9 January 1891, the Law Member of India, Sir Andrew Scoble, introduced a Bill in the Legislative Council raising the age of consent for sexual intercourse for Indian girls from ten to twelve years.[1] The Bill proposed to define sexual intercourse with married and unmarried Indian girls below the age of twelve as rape, punishable by ten years' imprisonment or transportation for life. The Bill did not interfere directly with the institution of child-marriage in India, but only with the premature consummation of child-marriage. While the upper-caste Hindu practice of child-marriage was fairly common among different caste/class and religious groups all over India, there was a general consensus that the problem of premature consummation of child-marriage was to be found mainly in the province of Bengal.[2] Nevertheless, by the time the Viceroy, Lord Lansdowne, signed the Age of Consent Act on 19 March 1891, the entire country was sharply divided over the measure. Shortly following the passage of the Consent Act, therefore, the Viceroy, on the initiative of Charles Elliott, the Lt.-Governor of Bengal, issued an executive order that made it virtually impossible to bring cases of premature consummation of child-marriage for trial under the Consent Act.[3]

In spite of the passage of the Consent Act, one of the most striking features of the Consent controversy, as many scholars have pointed out, was the massive opposition provoked by the Bill. For not only was the limited nature of the Consent Bill itself a compromise with indigenous upper-caste patriarchal norms and practices, but the colonial authorities were so impressed by the agitation against the Bill that they did not again initiate any major social reform legislation in India until the passage of the Child Marriage Restraint Act in 1929.[4] Indeed, as several scholars have argued, the agitation against the Consent Bill injected into the incipient political nationalism in India a militant strand that was hitherto unprecedented in the history of elite Indian politics.[5] Just as the Anglo-Indian agitation against the Ilbert Bill is credited with consolidating a new mood of aggressivenes in the Anglo-Indian population in India, so also the Indian agitation against the Consent Bill is seen as similarly inaugurating a new phase in the history of elite nationalism in India.

The politics of colonial masculinity, however, serves to recontextualise the impact of the agitation against the Consent Bill on elite nationalist politics in India.[6] It provides a context in which the contribution to nationalist politics of the defence of orthodox Hindu patriarchy in the agitation against the Consent Bill appears as a more complicated matter. Most recent studies of the Consent controversy have focused on the patriarchal politics of the anti-Consent Bill agitation and its role in radicalising nationalist politics. Dagmar Engels, for example, has argued that nationalist politics in Bengal was radicalised in the conflict between two opposing views of controlling female sexuality: the Bengali male control of female sexuality was pitted against the regulation of female sexuality in a Victorian British gender ideology.[7] Padma Anagol-McGinn's study of the Consent controversy in the Bombay Presidency suggests that the nationalist opposition to the Bill also expressed male hostility towards Indian women who organised meetings and public demonstrations in support of the Bill.[8] The question of why the defence of an unreformed indigenous patriarchy served as the medium for revitalising nationalist politics in late nineteenth-century India has been addressed most directly by Tanika Sarkar. Sarkar situates the Consent controversy in the context of the gradual disillusionment of Indian nationalists with the 'public sphere as an arena for the test of manhood'; this disillusionment made 'Hindu' conjugality and domestic social arrangements an intensely politicised arena in colonial and nationalist conflicts.[9] The more crucial point, however, is that the politics of colonial masculinity substantially qualifies the nature of the contribution of the anti-Consent Bill agitation to nationalist politics. For, notwithstanding the bitterness of the conflict over the Consent Bill, the colonial authorities were sympathetic to the claims of native masculinity: not in the demands for a greater military role, as in the native volunteer agitation; nor for a greater administrative role, as in the native civil service agitation; but only in the defence of orthodox Hindu patriarchy in the Consent controversy.

In Bengal, where opposition to the Consent Bill was perhaps the strongest in all of India, a group of orthodox opponents presented the following argument against the Bill in their impassioned *Appeal to England to Save India From the Wrong and Shame of the 'Age of Consent' Act*:

could the Englishman himself, with all his abhorrence of early marriages, tolerate a penal enactment, which made the husband's sexual intercourse with his wife of 15 years of age (for, as has been already said, 12 in India would correspond to about 15 in England) punishable with transportation for life or imprisonment for 10 years?[10]

The strategy of the opponents of the Bill was a deliberate attempt to appeal to the logic of colonial masculinity: on the one hand, it centred the terms of the debate not on the sexual abuse of Indian child-wives, but on the curtailment of the rights of the Indian husband; and, on the other, it represented the defence of orthodox Hindu patriarchy in a more universal patriarchal language of the 'natural' rights of all husbands. The strategy of the Bengali opponents of the Consent Bill – arising in part from the perception of the emasculation of the elite Bengali male under colonial rule – not only re-focused the Consent controversy on the claims of native masculinity, but also connected its claim with the perception of a growing 'crisis' in British masculinity arising, from among other things, the feminist challenges of the 1880s.[11] Indeed, the problematic of masculinity in a colonial situation serves to reframe the agitation against the Consent Bill in two crucial ways: it both underscores the shared assumptions in colonial and nationalist responses to the Consent Bill and situates the Indian Consent controversy in relation to the larger imperial social formation. Although the agitation against the Consent Bill has been typically understood in terms of the rejuvenation of nationalist politics in India, its contribution was far more ambiguous: for the defence of orthodox Hindu patriarchy resulted, above all, in bringing the claims of native masculinity into closer alignment with the agenda of late nineteenth-century colonial rule.

The first indication that the agitation against the Bill was more ambiguous – aligning with, rather than challenging, colonial politics – was the paradoxical impact of colonial masculinity on nationalist politics: it simultaneously empowered the opposition against the Bill as nationalist and recuperated the nationalist challenge by bringing it in closer harmony with colonial politics. Indeed, the politics of colonial masculinity obscured the colonial interests served in the nationalist backlash against social reform. For, on the one hand, the colonial authorities had conceded the indigenous domestic realm as an 'autonomous' site for native masculinity; and, on the other, this construction of the domestic realm also fostered nationalist scepticism toward the reform of the domestic realm as a threat to Indian autonomy. The contradictory impact of colonial masculinity on social reforms resulted from the convergence of colonial and nationalist interests in the late nineteenth century: the withdrawal of colonial support for social reform initiatives converged with the increasingly defensive response to social reform legislations from Indian nationalists. In the decades after 1857, for example, the colonial authorities were committed to a policy of ostensible non-interference in the social and religious affairs of the country.[12] The myth of non-interference was sustained by the demarcation of a supposedly 'uncolonised' space untouched by colonial rule. This 'uncolonised' space, as Sarkar reminds us, was itself a product of the legal framework of colonial rule: it demarcated a separate public sphere of criminal codes, land relations, laws of contract, and so on that was brought under the regulation of British and colonial law and an alternative private sphere of family relationships, family property, and religious practices regulated by separate Hindu and Muslim laws (which were themselves unified and codified under the imperatives of colonial rule).[13] Yet whatever the contradictions haunting the policy of non-interference, the colonial authorities were engaged in a much more self-conscious effort in the late nineteenth century to defer to the authority of indigenous interpretations and of customary practices in all matters designated 'private'. The colonial policy of non-interference, therefore, committed itself in no uncertain terms to the nurturing of orthodox indigenous practices.

In addition, colonial masculinity also forged a connection between the changing imperatives of colonial rule and nationalist politics: it smoothed the transfer of responsibility to Indian men for the indigenous domestic realm. For the gradual reconstitution of the domestic realm as an arena for Indian autonomy also coincided with the imperatives of an emerging 'official' Indian nationalism, which, as Partha Chatterjee has demonstrated, constructed its own unique identity by demarcating a separate domain in which to locate its autonomy.[14] Hence when the Parsi reformer from Bombay, Behramji Malabari, first published his 'Notes on Infant Marriage and Enforced Widowhood' in 1884, his proposal for a government initiative to reform Indian domestic practices received a mixed response both from nationalist Indians and from the colonial authorities.[15] The opinions collected by the colonial authorities on Malabari's 'Notes' in 1885 reflected the strength of orthodox Indian opposition to social reforms as well as the new spirit of caution with which even many Indian social reformers approached the question of government interference in Indian domestic arrangements. The argument that an 'alien government' and an unrepresentative legislature had no right to legislate the 'internal' affairs of the people was so popular with nationalist public opinion that even M. G. Ranade, an influential Hindu reformer from Bombay, justified his support for government legislation on the grounds that there was no harm in seeking government intervention in cases where legislative intitiative coincided so directly with the welfare of Indians.[16] Equally significant in the responses to Malabari's 'Notes' was the colonial Government's anxiety to clarify the limits of its own responsibility: the 'Legislature should keep within its natural boundaries and should not by overstepping these boundaries place itself in direct antagonism to social opinion.'[17]

The crucial point about the impact of the politics of colonial masculinity was that even as it produced a complicity between colonial interests and indigenous orthodoxy, it obscured the colonial role in nurturing the indigenous orthodoxy. The result was that colonial masculinity not only discouraged support for reform, but, even more crucially, it underwrote the very protest against social reform. Colonial politics, moreover, continued to use social reform as a test of native masculinity – a handy stick with which to beat Indian nationalists. This was evident, for example, in the colonial insistence that Indian men should concentrate on social rather than on political reforms and the often insulting attitude adopted by missionaries and colonial officials towards the social problems of India. When Revd W. Milne of the Free Church in Calcutta and Revd K. S. Macdonald, editor of the *Indian Evangelical Review*, wrote Resolution Two of the Calcutta Missionary Conference – which proposed, among other things, that either party in an unconsummated child-marriage should be given the right to dissolve the marriage and marry again – their ostensible aim of getting Indian reformers to support the proposal was undercut by the disparaging tone adopted towards Indians.[18] The proposal not only led to a major split between the European and Indian Christian community in Calcutta and to a spirited defence of Hindu child-marriage by the Bengali Christian G. J. Shome, but it also alienated other Bengali reformers who may have otherwise shared the outrage of the missionaries at the abuses of child-marriage. Bipan Chandra Pal, the author of a series of articles on 'Infant Marriage in Bengal and its Poisonous Effects', and Surendranath Banerjea, a critic of child-marriage in his paper the *Bengalee*, were critical of the tone adopted by the Calcutta Missionaries and apprehensive of government interference in the matter:

> What would Englishmen think, if we wrote strong articles and presumed to hold strong opinions regarding their divorce laws . . . ? Social reform is a matter which eminently concerns those who are the members of the society that needs to be reformed. Any interference from outside is the officious impertinence of strangers, and it can do no good but may do a great deal of harm.[19]

The result of such debates was deliberately paradoxical; it neither committed colonial authorities to encourage social reforms, nor allayed nationalist scepticism against colonial interference in social reform. Herein lay the paradoxical dynamics of masculinity as the site for colonial conflict: it channelled nationalist energies into a protest against social reform, a stance which in fact brought the nationalist challenge into closer alignment with colonial politics.

The paradoxical role of colonial masculinity does indeed recontextualise the meaning of the revivalist–nationalist opposition to the Consent Bill. In the opposition against the Consent Bill, it was not just domestic reform that was sacrificed at the altar of a more militant nationalist politics: rather, nationalist politics itself was sacrificed to a more thorough recuperation within the limited arena of colonial masculinity. The complicity between the revivalist–nationalist opposition to the Consent Bill and colonial politics thus constitutes an important context for the Consent controversy. Although it was the colonial authorities who introduced the Consent Bill, and then insisted on passing it over the opposition of a sizeable Indian public opinion, it was clear from the outset that they were simultaneously anxious to validate the very ground from which the strongest opposition to the Bill was raised. The government initiative to undertake the Consent Bill itself followed only after the public indignation in India over the much-publicised case of Hari Mohan Maitee, which was committed for trial to the Sessions Court at Calcutta on 6 July 1890. Maitee, a man of about thirty-five, was accused of having caused the death of his child-bride Phulmoni in 1889 through brutal sexual intercourse.[20] Justice Wilson, who presided over the case, declared that Phulmoni was eleven years old and, therefore, Maitee could not be tried for rape but only for the lesser charge of committing a 'rash and negligent act'; the Exception to the Fifth Clause of Section 375 of the Indian Penal Code, introduced in 1860, declared that 'sexual intercourse by a man with his own wife not being under ten years of age is not rape'.[21] The Phulmoni case brought to light other cases of 'Hari Maitism' in which husbands guilty of causing the death of their child-brides had been either acquitted by the Courts or else had been awarded relatively minor sentences for causing 'bodily harm'.[22] Scoble, the Law Member, introduced a proposal that drew upon the recommendations that had been formulated earlier by the Bombay reformer, Dayaram Gidumal, for raising the age of consent from ten to twelve years in the Fifth Clause and its Exception in Section 375 of the Indian Penal Code.[23]

Yet after having been forced by circumstances into initiating government legislation to protect child-brides, the colonial authorities were anxious to return to the colonial–nationalist agreement on the domestic realm as the arena of Indian autonomy: thus the colonial justification for the Consent Bill was that it did not interfere with indigenous religious principles. In the speeches that introduced the Bill in the Viceroy's Council, colonial officials were eager to commend the Bill for conforming with orthodox religious practices. In his speech to the Legislative Council, Scoble quoted from the orthodox *Pundit* (priest) Sesadhur Turkachuramani of Bengal to establish that the proposed Bill did not violate the injunctions of the *Shastras* (Hindu scriptures).[24] It was an indication of the extent to which the colonial authorities were cut off from Bengali public opinion when, much to Scoble's embarrassment, the *Pundit* shortly afterwards publicly castigated the Law Member for misrepresenting his opinions, and went on to become one of the leading opponents of the Bill on the grounds of religious interference.[25] It was not until it was fully apparent that the religious opposition to the Bill could not be placated so easily that Scoble eventually appealed to universal principles of humanity and morality to justify the Consent Bill.[26]

The Government, moreover, conceived the nature of its initiative in a manner that compromised with the opponents of reform without in any way encouraging its supporters. Partly out of considerations of political expediency, for example, the Government was willing to go beyond merely reiterating the policy of colonial non-interference to accommodate the prejudices of orthodox Hindu patriarchy. The colonial initiative was thus deliberately designed to be extremely limited in scope. Scoble stressed that the proposed Bill did not create any 'new offence', but was limited only to amending a provision already existing in the Indian Penal Code. The Viceroy, in his speech to the Legislative Council, was careful to dissociate the limited nature of the Consent Bill from the more comprehensive proposals that were being proposed by Malabari and his London Committee.[27] Malabari, having failed to persuade the Indian Government to undertake legislation to protect child-brides, had taken his campaign to Britain to exert the pressure of British public opinion on the colonial Government. On 14 July 1890, Malabari's London Committee, drawing on the support of prominent ex-India hands like Lord Reay, former Governor of Bombay, and C. P. Ilbert, former Law Member of the Government of India, Orientalist scholars like Professor Max Mueller, and British feminists like Millicent Fawcett, had issued a resolution urging the Indian Government to undertake reform legislation. The resolution of the London Committee recommended the raising of the age of consent, the ratification of child-marriages by law, the repeal of the restitution of conjugal rights imported to India from ecclesiastical law in England, and the further encouragement of widow remarriage through the proper implementation of the Hindu Widow Remarriage Act of 1856.[28] In private letters to the Viceroy, however, prominent British members of Malabari's London

Committee, like Northbrook and Reay, drew the Viceroy's attention to their own heroic efforts in diluting Malabari's 'radical' proposals and urged the Viceroy to show similar caution in undertaking any reforms.[29]

Furthermore, the logic of colonial masculinity empowered the arguments of the revivalist–nationalist opponents at the expense of the reformist–nationalist supporters of the Bill. The major nationalist positions on the Consent Bill – in spite of the differences between the reformist support for and revivalist opposition to the Bill – were framed within the politics of colonial masculinity. Even for the most prominent nationalist supporters of the Bill, the autonomy of the domestic realm as the site for native masculinity necessarily competed with any commitment to social reform as the basis for the Bill; they were thus left justifying their support for the Bill by demonstrating that it was sanctioned within Hindu religious principles and entailed no 'new interference' in indigenous practices. Indeed, the colonial mediation of masculinity had produced an acute self-consciousness about accepting colonial legislative interference, as well as providing greater political momentum to the nationalist arguments against the Bill.

The Consent controversy – unlike previous debates on child-marriage, which were concerned primarily with the impact of child-marriage on the development of the race or on the progress of female education in India – made available alarming statistics on the sexual abuse of child-wives; but for the majority of Indian nationalists the sexual abuse of child-wives was not in itself sufficient as a justification for the Consent Bill. This was especially true in Bengal, where reformist concern for the child-wife was most mediated by the constraints of a colonial politics of masculinity. Apart from the men and women of the *Sadharan Brahmo Samaj*, the most radical of the reform organisations in Bengal, and their paper the *Sanjivani*, which publicised cases of brutal rape and sexual assault of child-wives to build support for the Consent Bill, the majority of the reformist–nationalists in Bengal were more equivocal in their support for the Bill.[30] Unlike the approximately 150 women in Calcutta (headed by Kadambini Ganguly, the first Indian 'lady doctor' and wife of *Sadharan Brahmo* leader Dwarkanath Ganguly) who petitioned the government in no uncertain terms to protect the child-wives of India, the majority of the Bengali supporters of the Bill were more ambivalent about endorsing colonial legislative interference.[31] Few, at least, were willing to go as far as the women petitioners of Bengal and of other parts of India who stated clearly that 'our sex is solely dependent on the government for the protection of our rights, the necessity for which has been made more urgent by the opposition with which the Bill has met'.[32]

The majority of the reformist–nationalists were indeed eager to demonstrate that the Consent Bill did not represent an interference with the social and religious practices of the Hindus. Even one of the most ardent champions of reforming government legislation, Malabari, could not afford to ignore the implications of colonial interference in Indian social and religious matters. In August 1890 in the pages of *The Times*, Malabari justified his proposals by arguing that the legislative initiatives he proposed constituted no 'new interference' in the social and religious practices of the Indians, but merely aimed at getting the government to 'undo the wrong it has [already] done'.[33] Malabari couched his proposals in terms of the need to undo the low age of consent fixed by the government in 1860, the importation of the law for the restitution of conjugal rights from Britain to India, and the loopholes in the Hindu Widow Remarriage Act. Other reformist–nationalists were similarly anxious to establish religious precedence in the *Shastras* for the changes proposed in the Consent Bill. The basis for this strategy, as Uma Chakravarti has demonstrated, was already well established in the strand within cultural nationalism which justifed the reform of oppressive social practices as a return to a pristine 'Golden Age' in which the upper-caste 'Aryan' woman was supposedly free from the degradations suffered by contemporary women.[34]

The major weakness of basing the justification for the Bill on the reformist interpretation of the *Shastras* – apart from the fact that its 'script for the past' was exclusively Hindu and elitist – was that it already conceded an important point to the opponents of reform: that the preservation of the domestic realm as an autonomous site for native masculinity was the final arbiter for justifying social reform. It was not surprising, therefore, that the reformist position was the weakest in places like Bengal where the objections to 'religious interference' were the strongest. Commenting on the predominantly Bengali aspect of the religious objections to the Bill, one Anglo-Indian paper pointed out the irony in the non-Brahmin Bengali member of the Legislative Council R. C. Mitter's quoting from the *Shastras* to oppose the Bill, while the high-caste Brahmin member from Bombay, K. L. Nulkar, found no objections to the Bill in the *Shastras*.[35] The Bengali opponents argued that the Bill interfered in the Bengali ceremony of *garbhadhan*, or the 'second marriage' that was performed by the upper-castes after the actual betrothal ceremony to mark the period when the child-bride was considered ready for sexual intercourse. Conceding, at least in principle, the significance of the *garbhadhan* argument, Bengali reformers argued that the better-educated classes in Bengal rarely performed the *garbhadhan* ceremony any more and that the *Shastras* neither enjoined the *garbhadhan* at the very first menstruation of the child-bride nor prescribed a severe penalty for delaying the ceremony. The Calcutta Committee in Support of the Consent Bill, which consisted of forty-four Hindus and eleven Muslims, published a pamphlet entitled *The 'Garbhadhan Vyavastha': Opinion on the Question in Hindu Religion Arising out of Consent* to demonstrate that the *garbhadhanist* argument against the Bill was invalid.[36] Similarly in Bombay and Madras, reformist–nationalists, like K. T. Telang, R. G. Bhandarkar, and Raghunath Rao, engaged in highly publicised debates with the religious orthodoxy to demonstrate that the higher age of consent proposed by the Bill conformed with Hindu religious practices.[37] The reformers were backed by the support of the *pundits* of Benares, the centre of Hindu religious learning; the *pundits*, under the leadership of *Pundit* Ram Misra, issued a categorical statement declaring the Consent Bill to be free from any religious objections.[38] The reformers also cited ancient medical authorities such as Sushruta, Charaka, and Agnibes to show that, unlike the latter-day interpreters of the *Shastras*, ancient medical texts supported a higher age at which Indian girls first menstruated and hence became ready for sexual intercourse. Even the Laws of Manu, the text with arguably the most severe restrictions against women, was mobilised by the pro-reform lobby to show support for a later age of marriage and for consummation of marriage in the *Shastras*.[39]

So long as the logic of colonial masculinity framed the terms of the Consent controversy, however, it favoured the nationalist opponents over the nationalist supporters of the Bill. If, from one perspective, the reformist–nationalist interpretation of the *Shastras* reflected a tactical engagement with the strength of the religious objections against the Bill, then, from another, it also reflected a failure to grasp the arbitrary nature of the religious objections in the service of orthodox patriarchal politics. For the religious objections raised against the Bill were bound by neither the constraints of consistency nor logic. The opponents, for example, dismissed the views of the ancient medical authorities cited by the reformists on the grounds that the experience of the ancient authorities was drawn largely from 'up-country' girls; in the hot and humid climate of Bengal, they argued, girls menstruated at a much earlier age.[40] Those references from the *Shastras* that did not support the arguments of the orthodoxy in Bengal were similarly dismissed on the authority of the sixteenth-century *Pundit* Raghunandan Siromani, whose interpretation of the *Shastras* was considered the most authoritative for Bengalis. Raghunandan, it was argued, had clearly laid down that if the *garbhadhan* was not performed at the first *ritu* (menstruation), then the womb would become impure and children conceived subsequently would be deprived of the right to offer *pindas* (literally: rice balls) or ritual offerings at the death of their parents.[41] Summing up the impact of the opponents of the Bill in Bengal, Alfred

Croft, the Director of Public Instruction in Bengal noted, 'the *pundits* as a class' had 'pronounced what may be called an official opinion against the provisions of the Bill'.[42]

Still another example of how the logic of colonial masculinity favoured the opponents rather than the supporters of the Bill was evident in the inconsistency of arguments of 'colonial interference'; for such arguments were once again manipulated freely by the opponents of reform in the interests of indigenous patriarchal social relations. This had become apparent, for example, in the Rukmabai case of 1887. Rukmabai, after several years of court battles, had been found guilty by the Bombay High Court of failing to fulfil her conjugal obligations to her husband Dadaji Bhikaji.[43] Sensitive to the impact of a law for the restitution of conjugal rights in cases of non-consensual child-marriage in India, Indian reformers supported Rukmabai's right to live apart from her husband and appealed to the Government to repeal the law by which husbands could force their wives to fulfil their conjugal obligations. Since the law was not based on Indian religious texts but had been imported from Christian ecclesiastical law in England, the reformers did not anticipate much religious objection to the change. Nevertheless, the anti-reformist campaign successfully mobilised religious arguments against the change: they produced evidence to demonstrate that suits for the restitution of conjugal rights had their basis in the *Shastras*. They argued that the colonial law was only providing legal recognition to precepts that were already sanctioned in religion.[44] The further point, as Engels shows, is that in the Rukmabai case revivalist–nationalists – despite all their arguments of native autonomy in religious and domestic affairs – had no compunction in turning to an imported colonial legislation if it served to shore up orthodox indigenous patriarchy.[45]

The reformist efforts to demonstrate that the Consent Bill did not constitute any 'new interference' in indigenous practices was no match for the highly exaggerated rhetoric of the opponents: the opponents claimed that the Consent Bill represented an unprecedented interference by the colonial authorities that threatened to rend asunder the entire Indian social fabric. The argument that the Consent Bill was the first real breach of Indian autonomy, as Sarkar has suggested, was the core of the revivalist–nationalist strategy against the Bill; it was based on the dubious claim that previous colonial legislations on *sati* (widow immolation), on widow remarriage, and on female infanticide were of much less significance for the autonomy of the Indian social fabric compared to the present legislation that interfered in marriage practices.[46] The opponents of the Bill absolved even the previous age of consent legislation of 1860 from the charge of such interference; since the Hindu *Shastras* themselves did not sanction pre-puberty consummation of child-marriage and no Indian girl achieved puberty before ten, the 1860 legislation was considered a dead letter. The increase in the age of consent to twelve, however, was presented as a direct interference because Indian girls allegedly attained puberty between the ages of ten and twelve. In interfering with the consummation of child-marriage, therefore, the Consent Bill was portrayed as more odious than any previous colonial legislation. The Consent Bill, it was argued, would destroy the entire social and religous fabric of Indian society and reduce 'Indians to the European levels in matters social and religious' by imposing the 'hateful English marriage system' and importing 'the gross sexual vices of Europe into India'.[47] The final flourish in the arguments against colonial interference was provided by the 'Indian Magna Carta' or the Queen's Proclamation of 1858, which had committed the colonial government to a policy of non-interference.

Perhaps the crowning irony of the Consent controversy was the fact that, within the logic of colonial masculinity, the reformist–nationalists became more vulnerable – despite all their efforts to present the Bill as sanctioned by the *Shastras* and as constituting no 'new interference' with indigenous practices – to charges that they were an elite out of touch with the people. It was, in the first place, the anomaly in the social position of the nationalist political leadership as a whole – reformists and revivalists alike – that framed the Consent controversy in the limited terms of colonial masculinity. Yet although all of the nationalist political leadership was vulnerable to a 'populist' critique for its elite and upper-caste orientation, the terms of colonial masculinity placed the onus of establishing 'proper' indigenous credentials disproportionately on the reformist–nationalist supporters of the Bill. A new alliance of elite groups in Bengal, therefore, coalesced around opposition to the Consent Bill; the alliance was the product of the specious manoeuvring of different factions within the Bengali elite, all equally cut off from a base of popular support. For, as Rajat Ray points out, it was the powerful and orthodox landed magnates of the British Indian Association who allied with the lower middle class and smaller gentry in rural Bengal – whose views were represented in such papers as the *Amrita Bazar Patrika* and the vernacular newspapers the *Bangabasi* and the *Dainik O Samachar Chandrika* – to challenge the reform party identified with the more 'Westernised' and cosmopolitan gentry of the Congress and the Banerjea-led Indian Association in Calcutta.[48] The opposition characterised the reformist–nationalist faction in Bengal as a deracinated elite. When, at a protest meeting against the Bill, the *Maharanee* Surnomoyee – a powerful female *zamindar* (landlord) of Cossimbazar and a noted philanthropist and patron of a hostel for female medical students in Calcutta – chose to indict Bengali reformers as an elite out of touch with their countrymen, who had 'been to England and returned to their mother country with new-fangled ideas', her indictment was very telling: it pointed out the limits in the social position of not just the nationalist supporters of the Bill but, equally crucially, of the nationalist opponents who launched such critiques.[49]

It was precisely such limits in the position of the revivalist–nationalist opponents of the Bill that were conveniently elided by the mediation of anti-colonial struggle by the politics of masculinity. In thus invigorating the opponents of the Bill over its supporters, colonial masculinity also obscured the greater complicity of the former with the politics of colonial rule. Nothing, therefore, better demonstrates the impact of colonial masculinity in empowering the revivalist–nationalist opposition then the injection of a supposedly 'populist' element in the defence of orthodox Hindu patriarchy. Whereas in the Rukmabai case the anti-reformers were content to invoke the upper-caste strictures on divorce in the *Shastras* against the customary recognition of divorce among the carpenter caste to which Rukmabai had belonged, the anti-reformers in the Consent controversy found themselves willing not only to validate the weight of local customs over the prescriptions of the *Shastras*, but also to sympathise with the difficulties of lower-caste men in following the upper-caste prescriptions of the *Shastras*.[50] This strategic retreat from the *shastras* was enabled in part by the recent division in official colonial policy over the respective weight of, on the one hand, the textualised interpretation of Hindu and Muslim religious practices that the colonial authorities had enshrined in the unitary Hindu and Muslim law recognised by the courts, and, on the other, the varied local customs and practices that were not always at one with the textualised codes.[51] The opponents of the Bill were concerned less with validating popular or lower-caste customs – which were typically less restrictive for women then the upper-caste prescriptions in the *Shastras* – than with validating their own interpretations of such upper-caste customs as the *garbhadhan* even against any interpretation to the contrary derived from the *Shastras*.

Although the revivalist–nationalist case against the Consent Bill was embedded in upper-caste practices, it did not stop some opponents of the Bill from invoking the special hardships of lower-caste and labouring men to defend their position. A precedent for such a strategy was once again to be found in colonial policy: in his speech to the Legislative Council on 9 January 1891, Lansdowne explained away his reluctance to repeal the law for the restitution of conjugal rights, recommended by Malabari's London Committee, on the grounds that it was a 'poor man's remedy' and of great benefit to the lower classes in India.[52] Taking a chapter out of Lansdowne's speech, some of the orthodox opponents of the Consent Bill claimed to have the interests of the lower castes at heart in opposing the Bill. Their reasoning was based on the confusion regarding the castes and classes that were most guilty of premature consumption of child-marriage. It was widely acknowledged that although child-marriage itself was prescribed only for the upper castes, its practice was much more widespread: high and low castes as well as Muslims and other communities practised some form of child-marriage. There was less agreement, however, on the question of which castes and class routinely practised premature consumption of child-marriage. H. H. Risley, an Anglo-Indian ethnologist, argued that child-marriage and premature consumption in Bengal was more or less confined to the Bengali upper castes and that lower-caste Gops and Bagdis were free from such practices.[53] Other officials consulted by the Government reported that, unlike child-marriage, the practice of 'consummating marriage before girls attain puberty' was 'more prevalent among the lower than the higher castes'.[54] Mitter, in his Note of Dissent to the Report of the Select Committee, invoked the special hardship that the Consent Bill imposed on poor and lower-caste men to oppose the Bill. Quoting from a pamphlet entitled *The Sisters of Phulmani (or the Child Wives of India)* by T. N. Mukharji, Mitter presented the case against the Consent Bill thus:

> We must not overlook what would be the hard case of thousands of males, chiefly of the low castes. These poor fellows possessing only one little hovel, have to live alone with their child wives because under the existing marriage system they have no chance of procuring grown-up girls recognized by law as adults. All in a day the law will not turn them into saints and it might blight their young lives by seven years imprisonment with hard labour for one single instance of momentary weakness under one of the most trying temptations to which flesh is subject.[55]

The impact of colonial masculinity, therefore, added to the potency of the protest against the Bill: it not only empowered the nationalist opponents over the supporters of the Bill; but also, in the process of empowering the opposition, obscured the level of colonial complicity with the opposition against the Bill.

In so far as the protests against the Consent Bill came to be identified with militant nationalism, therefore, their impact was to recuperate the anti-colonial challenge of the nationalist movement. A nascent elite nationalist leadership, trying to consolidate itself more sharply against colonial rule, could not, because of the contradictions of its own social position, fail to be impressed by the demonstrable proof of public support mobilised by the opponents of the Bill; the price of succumbing to this appeal, however, was not just the consolidation of the nationalist movement around an unreconstructed patriarchal politics, but also the bringing of nationalist politics in closer harmony with a colonial agenda. For the very impressiveness of the protests against the Bill was marked by greater complicity with a certain colonial politics. The protest meetings against the Bill in Bengal invariably drew much larger crowds than the meetings organised in support of the Bill.[56] The 'circus-like' atmosphere at the infamous protest meeting in the Calcutta Maidan on 25 February 1891 attracted an unprecedented crowd from Calcutta and the suburbs for any public meeting in Bengal.[57] The protest meetings, as Amiya Sen's account of Hindu revivalism in the Consent controversy demonstrates, were usually organised by local religious bodies that raised the cry of 'religion in danger' to swell the numbers at the meetings; but the meetings typically attracted crowds made up of different religious denominations, including Hindus, Jains, and Buddhists, as well as Muslims from Calcutta and its surrounding suburbs.[58] The predominantly Hindu religious objections against the Bill, therefore, did not preclude sympathy for the opposition from the public opinion of different religious orthodoxies. Despite efforts of many in the Muslim community to demonstrate that the Bill did not have any bearing on Islamic religious prescriptions, the public opinion in the Muslim community was more divided on the Bill. There was some prominent Muslim support for the Bill: the Muslim members of the Viceroy's Legislative Council supported the Consent Bill; the Secretary of the Muhammedan Literary Society in Calcutta published a pamphlet entitled *A Practical View of the Consent Act for the Benefit of the Mahomedan Community in General* to assure the Muslim community that the Bill did not affect Muslim religious practices. But the *Sudhakar*, a Muslim vernacular newspaper in Bengal, as well as the Central National Mahomedan Association in Calcutta, expressed criticism of the Muslim members of the Council and of Muslim organisations that supported the Bill.[59] Another measure of the popularity of the opposition was the large circulation enjoyed by anti-Bill newspapers in Bengal: of the vernacular newspapers, the anti-Bill newspaper the *Bangabasi* had the highest annual subscription at 20,000 compared to the 4,000 subscription of the pro-Bill *Sanjivani*; the English-language weekly the *Amrita Bazar Patrika* was converted from a weekly to a daily to represent the opposition that was not adequately represented in the two prominent native English-language newspapers of Calcutta, the *Bengalee* and the *Indian Mirror*.[60] Such indeed was the paradoxical role of colonial masculinity that at one and the same time it empowered the opposition against the Bill as nationalist and accommodated it to colonial interests.

Another indication that the agitation against the Bill was less than unalloyed nationalism was that its success in fact depended upon the intersection of the nationalist perception of a 'crisis' of Indian/Bengali masculinity with a growing perception in Britain of a 'crisis' of British masculinity. The responses to these crises were different and even contradictory in India and in Britain; but they intersected – albeit in uneven ways – to reframe the Consent controversy as a referendum on native masculinity. For if one context for the response of the colonial authorities to the Consent Bill was dicated by political expediency and the fear of arousing anti-government feeling from the orthodox Hindu community in India, then another was dictated by the anti-feminist backlash in Britain: both produced greater tolerance for patriarchal institutions in India. There was considerable masculinist anxiety in Britain following the gradual reconstitution of the traditional male public sphere in response to such feminist challenges as the activities of Josephine Butler and the Ladies' National Association for the repeal of the Contagious Diseases Acts in the 1880s and the feminist and purity crusades for the passage of the British Criminal Amendent Act of 1885.[61] This anxiety had its counterpart in the growing admiration for the merits of child-marriage in the writings of several late nineteenth-century commentators in Britain. Whereas Professor Max Mueller, as a member of Malabari's London Committee, was willing to endorse a limited reform of Indian marriage practices, he also published the same year an essentially celebratory account of child-marriage in India.[62] The words of a special correspondent of *The Times*, who wrote a three-part series on 'Child Marriage and Enforced Widowhood' to support Malabari's London campaign, bears quoting at some length:

> For more than a thousand years the supreme need of Hindu women was not independence, but safety. To meet this supreme need the Hindoo marriage system was developed into a powerfully constructed organisation of protection – a system which endeavoured to give the maximum security to Hindoo women as a whole, and which deliberately acted on the principle that their general safety must be insured, even at the cost of hardships to individuals among them. It assured to every woman the protection of a lawful husband and the legal status of wife; and it also assured her of that protection and status as soon as she achieved physical maturity.[63]

For W. W. Hunter, the *Times'* special correspondent, the main objective in reforming Indian marriage practices was clear: 'how to secure for wives and daughters the *old safety of dependence* [my emphasis] with a larger measure of the freedom of modern independence'.[64] By conceding merit to the arguments of orthodox Hindus who cited 'statistics of prostitution in Europe' against adult marriages in India, moreover, Hunter was far from sanguine about the value of his cause. In so far as Hunter was considered one of the more vocal Anglo-Indian friends of social reform in India, his attitude is instructive. The ambivalence towards the Consent Bill in Britain was nicely summed up in the following comment on the Indian Consent controversy: 'England has as much to learn from India [about the control of women?] as she has to teach that country.'[65]

Nowhere, however, was the anti-feminist context for the British response to the Indian Consent Bill more apparent than in the stand taken by the *Saint James Gazette* of London. The *Saint James Gazette*, which defended aristocratic male privileges against feminist challenges during the debate on the Criminal Amendment Act or the British Consent Act of 1885, was also an outspoken critic of the Indian Consent Bill.[66] The paper drew a parallel between the discomfort of orthodox Hindus towards the Indian Consent Bill and its own discomfort at the growing political visibility of single and independent women in Britain: 'what will the English friends of the Indian child wife say if some acute Hindoo moves a resolution denouncing London society on account of the superabundance of unmarried ladies in Kensington? We Hindoos manage these things better, he would argue, very much better in Bengal'.[67] The paper went on to justify the Indian opposition to the Consent Act:

> It is perfectly clear that the strongest and best native opinion is against the Age of Consent Bill promoted in London drawing rooms and praised by globe trotting philanthropists . . . And it is tolerably certain that the rite of child marriage is, in fact, so rarely abused that our consciences need not be very sorely vexed about enormities which we cannot abolish. The most important and significant point is that the women of India are against a Bill professing to protect them.[68]

This was written after at least one newspaper in Britain, *The Times*, carried information about a petition from approximately 2,000 'women living in India' to Queen Victoria in support of raising the age of consent for Indian women.[69] Members of the Legislative Council in India quoted similar petitions in support of the Bill received by the Government of India from Indian women in Ahmedabad, Calcutta, Bombay, Lahore, Poona, and Mymensingh.[70]

The highly publicised criticisms in Britain of the Government of India for undertaking the Consent Bill provided valuable support for the Indian opponents of the Bill. Sir George Birdwood, a retired senior Anglo-Indian official, wrote a series of letters to *The Times* criticising the government initiative; he concluded that 'Hindu family life was of a very high order' and did not require government interference.[71] For Dr Richard Congreve, the High-Priest of Positivism in England, the Consent legislation raised important questions about Indian cultural autonomy: 'with the usual feeling of superiority', he wrote, 'instead of mending ourselves we are but too anxious to intrude our crude actions on others as necessary reforms'.[72] The most vigorous champion of Hindu orthodoxy in Britain during the Consent controversy was Frederic Pincott, whose article 'Hindu Marriage Agitation' in the *National Review* bolstered all of the arguments of the orthodox Hindu opponents of the Consent Bill. So sensitive was Pincott about respecting the 'prejudices of [the] people', that he promised his services to Hindu revivalists to continue the agitation against the consent regulations in Britain after the Consent Bill was passed in India.[73]

Colonial politics, however, mediated the crisis of British masculinity very differently in India. Whereas in Britain the sympathy for the orthodox Hindu opposition to the Bill was expressed freely in public, the Anglo-Indians in India were obliged to express greater unanimity for the government-sponsored Bill. Although some Anglo-Indians in India, including senior officials, did convey reservations about the Bill in private communications, the Viceroy strongly discouraged any impression in public that there were doubts about the Bill among senior government officials.[74] The Anglo-Indian paper the *Statesman* attributed the relative unanimity of Anglo-Indian public opinion in India to the recent changes in the political climate: the ex-India hands in Britain, who were typically members of a pre-Congress generation, felt free to express their reservations about the Bill, but Anglo-Indians in India could not afford to miss the opportunity to embarrass Indian political leaders. In the words of the *Statesman*:

> The advocacy of W. W. Hunter and the English Committee [for the Consent Bill] would have had a dividing effect [on Anglo-India] earlier. Nothing has occurred to modify materially the inner convictions of Anglo-India on such points as these, [but] something has occurred to lead them very generally to subordinate those convictions to considerations of another kind; and that something is the Congress movement. In the opposition to the Bill (embracing as it did some educated Bengalis), [Anglo-Indians in India] saw an unrivalled opportunity to discredit the Congress in the eyes of the public at home. To do this they sink all differences about the Bill among themselves and represent its merits in the strongest possible light, as something which no one with any pretensions to true enlightenment could possibly have any doubt about.[75]

The Anglo-Indian case in India was helped by the position adopted by the Indian National Congress, the most prominent of the Indian political organisations: even though the General Secretary, A. O. Hume, privately assured the Viceroy that at least four-fifths of the Congress members were secretly in favour of the Bill, the Congress refrained from giving an official opinion on the Bill.[76] The fact that prominent Bengali congressmen, like Banerjea and W. C. Bonnerjee, did not rally behind the government to support the Consent Bill gave Anglo-Indian public opinion further ammunition to attack the political aspirations of Indian politicians. The *Englishman* of Calcutta questioned the 'impossible schemes for the reform of the Indian government' promoted by the educated class in Bengal when these same groups were indifferent to 'the social problems that await solution in their country as they are pleased to call India'.[77] The cynical manipulation of the Consent controversy was openly acknowledged in the pages of the *Daily Chronicle* in London, which pointed out that Indian opposition to the Bill was 'useful in a way' because it served to discredit thoroughly Indian political aspirations.[78]

It was thus in the context of the political climate of India that Anglo-Indian public opinion turned to the colonial distinction — by now profoundly over-determined — between 'manly' and 'effeminate' natives. They used this distinction to mediate between the imperatives of an embattled British masculinity and support for the Indian Consent Bill. Despite the more unanimous support for the Consent Bill among Anglo-Indians in India, therefore, the distinction made by colonial officials between the practice of child-marriage among 'manly' natives and the practice of premature consummation of child-marriage among 'effeminate' natives preserved a certain ambivalence towards the reform of orthodox Hindu patriarchy. This distinction both limited the nature of the challenge to orthodox Hindu patriarchy and associated the challenge more narrowly with the 'effeminacy' of the Bengali male. When Lansdowne sent Scoble's proposals for comment to local officials in 1890, the reports of the colonial officials underscored the difference between child-marriage as it was practised among the 'manlier' races of India and the premature consummation of child-marriage as practised among the 'effeminate' Bengalis. The Lt.-Governor of Bengal, Steuart Bayly, reported as follows:

> It is a general practice for Hindu girls after they are married but before puberty is even indicated, much less established, to be subjected to more or less frequent acts of connection with their husbands. The custom appears to be widespread. . . . [It] prevails generally over Bengal Proper, especially over Eastern and Central Bengal. It does not extend generally to Behar, nor is it prevalent in Orissa, and the aboriginal tribes are apparently free from it.[79]

It was more widely held among Anglo-Indians that in the Punjab, where 'the work of women in the fields was valuable', a father, 'though marrying his daughters off before puberty, after ancient custom, would keep them from their husbands' house as long as possible'.[80]

The image of native effeminacy did in fact perform an important ideological function in the Consent controversy: the distinction between the results of premature consummation and of child-marriage was used to reinforce colonial contempt for the class from which came most of the India's nationalist politicians and intellectuals as well as to limit the full implications of the brutal murder of Phulmani. The work of Risley, the well-known amateur ethnologist of the Bengal Civil Service, provided the scientific basis for distinguishing between child-marriage and premature consummation of child-marriage: 'in different parts of India', he argued, 'infant marriage prevails in two widely different forms, one of which is at least free from physiological objections, while the other deserves, from every point of view the strongest condemnation'.[81] In an article in *Blackwood's Magazine* in December 1890, Risely commented on the impact that the two systems of child-marriage had on the physique of the people of India:

> as we leave the great recruiting ground of the Indian Army and travel south eastward along the plains of the Ganges, the healthy sense which bid the warrior races to keep their girls at home until they are fit to bear the burden of maternity, seems to have been cast out by the demon of corrupt ceremonialism ever ready to sacrifice helpless women and children to the traditions of fancied orthodoxy.[82]

Risley's opinions were confirmed by other Anglo-Indian officials with ethnological experience, like Denizel Ibbetson, who argued that, at least in the Punjab, child-marriage was free from the harmful effects found in Bengal: 'No one who has seen a Punjabi regiment march past, or has watched the sturdy Jat women lift their heavy water jars at the village well, is likely to have any misgivings as to the effect of the marriage system on the physique of the race.'[83] The focus on native effeminacy thus restricted the Consent controversy to a referendum on native masculinity in which the physical and moral deterioration of the race occupied at least as much attention as the sexual abuse of child-wives.

The stereotype of Bengali effeminacy during the Consent controversy, moreover, drew its strength precisely from the varied contexts in which the discourses of masculinity were deployed. One context for Bengali effeminacy was the political climate in India; it suggested connections with the distinctions Anglo-Indian public opinion made between 'loyal' and 'disloyal' natives. The *Pioneer* concluded of the Indian responses to the Consent Bill: the 'agitation which has been set on foot will not command the sympathy of the more manly races which are free from the outrage upon child wives'.[84] The Private Secretary to the Viceroy expressed relief that the public protests against the Consent Bill were confined mainly to the 'effeminate' native races; commenting on a circular advertising a protest meeting to be held in Calcutta, he wrote that 'a less timid race might have been aroused to acts of violence by the exaggerations and misrepresentations of this Circular'.[85] Another context for Bengali effeminacy suggests connections with what Jeffrey Weeks has identified as a new development in scientific and medical discourses in the late nineteenth century: the emergence of the concept of the homosexual.[86] The tone, however tentative, was set in the link between sexuality and 'unmanliness' suggested by the *Indian Medical Gazette*: early sexual intercourse among Bengalis was linked to 'physical deterioration', 'effeminacy', 'mental imperfection' and 'moral debility'.[87] A more direct allusion to popular theories of the aetiology of homosexuality was suggested in the discussion of masturbation and its consequences for the effeminacy of the Bengali male.[88] Hume, who was not unsympathetic to the political aspirations of the educated community in India, found in the prevalence of masturbation among Bengali men the connection between early sexual intercourse and their physical and moral debility. According to Hume, therefore, the 'disgusting habit' of masturbation which was 'one of the reflex consequences of the premature sexuality engendered by the early marriage and consummation system' had become 'universal in Lower Bengal'.[89] He further stated that the answer to the question why 'diabetes is so prevalent amongst all Bengalis' is to be found not in the Bengali diet of rice but in the Bengali vice of masturbation.

The most telling example of the overdetermined context for 'Bengali effeminacy', however, was the popular colonial accusation that Bengali 'manhood' had succumbed to the undue influence of Bengali women by opposing the Consent Bill. This view was supported by the belief, common among many a 'manly' Anglo-Indian and Indian official alike, that it was the female members of the Indian household who were chiefly responsible for encouraging the 'scandal' of the premature consummation of child-marriage. Older female relatives, it was argued, took tremendous delight in encouraging sexual intimacy between a young couple.[90] The Bengali man's effeminacy, therefore, was attributed to the inability of Bengali men to stand up to the recalcitrant women of their families. In a letter to the *Statesman*, Hume declared that Indians 'who know or think, that their womankind will not abandon [their role in encouraging premature consummation of child marriage] and who are not *masters of their own houses* [my emphasis]' are behind the opposition to the Bill.[91]

THE AGE OF CONSENT CONTROVERSY

It is thus, in such an overdetermined context for native effeminacy, that the revitalised Indian masculinity in the opposition to the Consent Bill appears in its full ambiguity: much more closely allied to the context of an embattled British masculinity than at first appears. B. G. Tilak, one of the most prominent nationalist opponents of the Bill, responded to Hume's portrait of the Indian opponents as inadequate 'masters of their own houses' by questioning the masculinity of Indian reformers who, because they were unable to 'manage their [own] household affairs', had appealed to the Government for help.[92] The *Mahratta*, edited by Tilak, commented that it was the Indian reformers who were 'unmanly' because they had shown themselves to be 'so helpless as not to be able to protect their daughters from their sons-in-law or their daughters-in-law from their own sons'; instead, they 'pray Government to keep a watch in their private rooms'.[93] So long as the colonial legislature was unrepresentative of Indian public opinion, the opponents of the Bill argued, the support that Indian men demonstrated for government legislation was a symbol of effeminacy and not of masculinity. Despite the fact it was based on a fierce opposition to the Consent Bill, the revitalised Indian masculinity did in fact converge quite nicely with colonial apprehensions about challenges to British masculinity.

That the nationalist triumph claimed on behalf of the revitalised Indian masculinity was based on a disregard of the plight of the child-wife is perhaps an obvious point; but the further point is that the revitalised Indian masculinity was scarcely even a nationalist triumph. The apparent resurgence, indeed, was based on its greater affinities with the agenda of colonial rule. For it was the uneven ways in which colonial politics mediated the crises of British and Indian masculinities that allowed revivalist–nationalists to claim their revitalised Indian masculinity as an unambiguous nationalist triumph: a supposed reversal of the colonial emasculation of the Indian male. This was evident, for example, in the apparent victory of the revivalist–nationalist challenge to one of the favourite colonial arguments: the eugenics-based distinction between child-marriage and premature consummation for the physical and moral development of the race. The Standing Committee of the Sobhabajar protest meeting in Calcutta published a document with medical evidence from thirty-four Indian medical practitioners and one Anglo-Indian Surgeon, Major J. F. P. McConnell, the Medical Inspector of Emigrants, to refute the connection that the advocates of the Bill made between early sexual intercourse and racial deterioration. Contradicting the dominant Anglo-Indian medical establishment, Dr Juggobandhu Bose of Calcutta University declared that there was no medical proof to establish that early childbirth hindered the development of an organism and so caused a permanent injury to the physical development of either the mother or the offspring.[94] Taking up this logic, Raja Rajendra Lala Mitra, the President of the Asiatic Society of Bengal, informed the Chief Secretary of the Government of India that the link that was being drawn between early sexual intercourse and the physical weakness of the race was at best 'pseudo-scientific':

> In the case of racial determination the reporters who have written on the subject are peculiarly unscientific. In a question of biology, or physiology, every thing must depend on statistical information and in this respect we have not a single fact to show that like mortal sin, improper consummation is visited in the race several generations after the first offender.[95]

Nabogopal Mitter, the editor of the *National Paper* and the founder of the National Training Academy for the physical development of Bengali youth, provided further concrete examples of young Bengali married men from his academy who had impressed even Europeans with their physical prowess.[96] Others, while conceding that the Bengali male had become physically enervated, argued that to emphasise only the physiological circumstances for the physical development of the race would be to apply the 'laws of cattle breeding' to human beings. The editor of *Hope*, an anti-reform paper in Bengal, put it thus: 'the forces which lie at the root of racial development are so many and varied, the intellectual and moral ones presumably predominant in the case of man, who is more a spiritual and moral being than an animal for purposes of exhibition.'[97] In any case, as the revivalist–nationalists argued with the impeccable logic of colonial masculinity, a government that still adhered to the Arms Act and persisted in refusing to enrol Bengalis as volunteers could hardly be credited for showing concern about the 'conversion of Indians into a nation of sturdy men'.[98]

No single issue in the Consent controversy better captures the strange dynamics that invested the revitalised Indian masculinity with the misleading appearance of a militant nationalist politics than the objections to the marital rape clause. For the controversy over the marital rape clause exposes, on the one hand, that the colonial advocates of the Bill and its most bitter opponents shared a common commitment to a certain definition of masculinity; and, on the other, that this shared commitment was obfuscated in a bitter conflict mediated by colonial politics. With the issue of marital rape, the opponents of the Consent Bill actually broadened their defence of orthodox Hindu patriarchy; for they appealed to the one privilege guaranteed men by the patriarchal laws of most countries: the legal exclusion of marital rape. While it was true that the Indian Penal Code was long an exception to this legal

THE AGE OF CONSENT CONTROVERSY

exclusion of marital rape, the opponents of the Bill politicised the issue anew in the context of the nationalist crisis over the emasculation of the Indian male. There was in fact one point on which most nationalists – reformists and revivalists – were agreed: if sexual intercourse between a husband and wife was to be penalised, then the crime should be characterised as 'criminal assault' and not rape.

It was of considerable interest, moreover, that the objections raised about the marital rape clause acquired a nationalist significance precisely because of the contrast with Britain, where the legal exclusion of marital rape remained unchallenged. The imperial controversy over marital rape complicates seriously the standard interpretations of the contributions of both the Indian and British Consent Acts. When the first Indian Law Commission, under Lord Macaulay, drafted the Indian Penal Code in 1837, it recommended that the Indian Penal Code follow the law in Britain in declaring that 'sexual intercourse by a man with his own wife is in no case rape'.[99] In Britain, the legal 'justification for the marital rape exception' was expounded in the famous declaration on the subject in the seventeenth century by Sir Matthew Hale: 'the husband cannot be guilty of rape committed by himself upon his lawful wife, for by their mutual matrimonial contract the wife hath given up herself in this kind unto her husband which she cannot retract'.[100] Since then there had been nothing to challenge Hale's opinion on the legal exception of marital rape in Britain. The Criminal Amendment Act of 1885 in Britain not only retained the legal exception of marital rape, but went even beyond Hale: it extended the legal right of a husband to have sexual intercourse with his wife without her consent to forcing her into sexual intercourse with others.[101] The British Consent Act only made 'unlawful and carnal intercourse' with a girl under thirteen a felony and under sixteen a misdemeanour; but since the law applied only to 'unlawful' intercourse, a husband, by virtue of the matrimonial contract, always had lawful access to his wife.[102] The status of the legal exemption of marital rape in Britain was clarified in a famous case tried in 1888. Although the husband in this case was not charged with rape, but only with causing 'bodily harm' for having sexual intercourse with his wife after he was suffering from a venereal disease and had withheld the information from her, the case reiterated the legal position in Britain on the question of marital rape. For Judge B. Pollock took this occassion to clarify the status of marital rape in Britain: 'The husband's connection with his wife ... is done in pursuance of the marital contract and of the status which was created by marriage and the wife ... has no right or power to refuse her consent.'[103] According to the law in Britain, therefore, a husband was not criminally liable for having sexual intercourse with his wife of twelve years of age, the legal age of marriage for girls in Britain.[104] Even as the law in Britain raised the age of female consent, it not only retained but reinforced the irrelevance of female consent within marriage.

When the Indian Penal Code first departed from the British law on the legal exemption of marital rape in 1860, there were hardly any objections from Indians. The recommendation for the inclusion of marital rape was first made by J. C. Thomas, a member of the Law Commission of 1846; but the official Anglo-Indian consensus was against any departure from the law in Britain.[105] Thomas argued that the prevalence of child-marriage in India made it necessary to include married with unmarried girls in the age of consent clause of the Indian Penal Code. J. M. Macleod, who had also served in the first Law Commission under Macaulay, did not approve the change. The *Report of the Law Commission of the Year 1846* recorded Macleod's dissent and his claim that Macaulay had agreed with him in defending the original draft of the Bill. He contended that even if the exclusion of married women was considered faulty, it erred on the side of safety.

In response to the growing attention focused on the abuses of child-marriage in India, colonial officials decided finally to incorporate Thomas's suggestion in the Fifth Clause in the Exception to Section 375 of the Indian Penal Code. In the 1850s the Bengali social reformer and architect of the Hindu Widow Remarriage Act of 1856, *Pundit Ishwarchandra Vidyasagar*, wrote an article in the *Sarvasubhakari Patrika* urging his followers to take a pledge against early marriage. In 1855 the government was further urged to intervene in the practice of child-marriage by the initiatives of the *Brahmo* reformer A. K. Dutt.[106] The Government responded to all these efforts with the inclusion of married girls in the age of consent clause in the 1860 Penal Code. The nine years age of consent originally proposed by Thomas was raised to ten and made to apply to both married and unmarried Indian girls.[107] The change was widely supported by Indian reformers; Vidyasagar, among others, was prominent in the campaign to get the 1860 Penal Code accepted in India.

It was only when the Law Member introduced the Consent Bill in January 1891 – with the dual objectives of protecting young girls from immature prostitution and child-wives from premature consummation – that the distinction between married and unmarried girls in the consent provisions became a highly charged issue. For in the past there was not much objection raised by Indians to the inclusion of married girls in the age of consent regulations. Nor was there much Indian interest in the initiative of missionary women's organisations to raise the age of consent in India for unmarried girls only. Missionary women's organisations were bringing the concern with child-prostitution that

THE AGE OF CONSENT CONTROVERSY

motivated the British consent regulations to bear on their demands for changes in the consent regulations in India. The Calcutta Missionary Conference for the Protection of Young Girls and the World's Women's Christian Temperance Union in Calcutta, under Mary E. Leslie, had for some time urged the Government to adopt a British-style consent legislation that would raise the age of consent only for unmarried Indian girls. Leslie, as the President of the Calcutta Branch of the World's Women's Christian Temperance Union, favoured raising the age of consent for unmarried Indian girls to sixteen.[108] The colonial Government, as well as Indian society, largely ignored the petitions from the missionary women's organisations. After the introduction of the 1891 Bill, however, the popular view in the reformist and revivalist circles was that Indians were willing to accept an even higher age, such as fourteen or sixteen for unmarried girls, if necessary, but were not willing to have married and unmarried girls treated the same in the consent provisions.

It was the mediation of colonial conflict by 'masculinist' politics that gave the inclusion of the marital rape clause in the Consent provisions in India – as well as its exclusion from similar provisions in Britain – a new political significance. The marital rape clause was valuable to the opponents of the Bill precisely because it turned the spotlight on the colonial advocates of the Bill: it invoked the patriarchal compromise in Britain that ensured the exclusion of married girls from the general consent provisions of the British Consent Act. The Bengali barrister Manomohun Ghose, well-versed in British law, provided the most detailed objections to the Indian Consent Bill on the grounds of the marital rape cause.[109] Ghose, unlike his brother Lalmohun Ghose, was a strong opponent of the Consent Bill; he used his knowledge of British legal deliberations on marital rape to complicate Bengali public opinion on the Indian Consent Bill. By comparing the Indian Consent Bill to the British Consent Bill, he argued that there was no moral or legal justification for the inclusion of marital rape in the former and its exclusion from the latter. Ghose dismissed the idea that the prior inclusion of the marital rape clause in the Indian Penal Code of 1860 was sufficient grounds to retain the clause in the 1891 Bill; the earlier provision, he argued, had led to not a single successful prosecution of an Indian husband on the charge of marital rape. He argued, moreover, that since a child-wife was already sufficiently protected by the existing provisions of the Penal Code that held a husband criminally liable for various acts which constituted an offence against his wife if she were under twelve years of age with or without her consent – such as for committing a 'rash and negligent act', for causing 'hurt simple and grievous', and for 'assault' – there was no need to reinforce the provision of marital rape in the Penal Code.

What made the marital rape issue so significant as a nationalist symbol of protest was that it went beyond the blatant defence of orthodox Hindu patriarchy. In the hands of Ghose, an erstwhile supporter of female education in Bengal, the objections against marital rape were a more ambivalent issue: for they simultaneously furthered the patriarchal agitation against the Bill and pointed out the patriarchal contradictions of colonial policies in India. According to Ghose, the colonial authorities had a devious plan in insisting on the marital rape clause; for they were not committed to challenging patriarchal privileges as such, but only to making a symbolic attack on the 'honour' of the Indian male. On the one hand, therefore, he highlighted the fact that in the marital rape clause the Indian husband was being denied the 'lawful access' to his wife that was guaranteed to the British husband by the matrimonial contract. This complaint had immediate resonance for the Bengali male. The sense of humiliation at the emasculation of the Bengali male, for example, motivated such objections to the Bill as that expressed by a Ramottam Ghose in his letter to the *Statesman*: '[we are at] a loss to understand from what standpoint – rational, moral or legal – the lustful seducer of a guileless and yielding virgin, and the passionate husband of a loving wife are to be placed under the same category and alike to be branded as a criminal of the blackest dye'.[110] In the words of another opponent of the Consent Bill, the Bill was the biggest insult to the Indian male: it was tantamount to placing all Bengali *jamais* or sons-in-law in barracks and allowing them to visit their wives only with the permission of the Government.[111] But, on the other hand, Ghose also demonstrated that the colonial law undercut any real challenges to a husband's patriarchal privileges by assuring to every Indian husband the absolute right to the company of his wife. Ghose thus pointed out the anomaly of the Consent Bill in penalising a husband for sexual intercourse with his under-age wife when at the same time other laws forced the Indian wife to cohabit with her husband. In Case Twenty-Three WR 178 of Katiram Dukani *v*. Musst. Gendlum and others, moreover, the Calcutta High Court had recently upheld the legal right of a husband to insist on the company of his bride immediately after the marriage ceremony was performed, regardless of the age of the wife.[112]

Of greatest significance, perhaps, was the fact that the marital rape controversy brought together the two different positions from which Indian nationalists could oppose the Consent Bill: from a straightforward defence of orthodox Hindu patriarchy and from a closer alignment of Hindu patriarchy with British patriarchy. For at the same time as Ghose, using the pretext of the marital rape clause, objected to the Consent Bill, he also argued in favour of a civil law that would directly address the issue of child-marriage. He complained that the current Bill left the performance of child-marriage intact.[113] Ghose argued that a civil law against child-marriage would raise no more objections than the present law and would additionally secure the approval of many reformers currently ambivalent about the merits of the Consent Bill. The *Sudhakar*, which had criticised the Muhammedan Literary Society in Calcutta and other Muslims for supporting the Consent Bill, also echoed Ghose's sentiments that a 'law for the prevention of early cohabitation' was much 'more mischievous' than a 'law for the prevention of early marriage'.[114]

Whether Ghose's proposal for marriage reform was a 'red herring' in the path of reform, as colonial authorities considered it to be, or a genuine effort to align Indian patriarchal norms with British patriarchal norms, he was perhaps correct in pointing out that many erstwhile social reformers in Bengal might have preferred a measure that would address directly the issue of child-marriage over the current Bill.[115] Banerjea, for example, presented the following defence for his lukewarm support of the Consent Bill: 'I entirely sympathize with the object it has in view viz. to afford protection to child wives, but I should have preferred a measure which more directly dealt with one of the worst evils of child marriage, vis. premature consummation by declaring marriage void under a certain age.'[116] The *Indian Mirror*, the most prominent English-language *Brahmo* daily in Calcutta, was more supportive of the Government-sponsored Consent Bill, but it too expressed a preference for a civil law regulating child-marriage over the current Bill. Just prior to the introduction of the Consent Bill in the Council, the *Indian Mirror* had commented that raising the age of consent 'without raising the age at which Hindu girls, at least, should be given in marriage' was 'like putting the cart before the horse'.[117]

The broad nationalist coalition that developed over the issue of marital rape, however, had the ultimate effect of legitimising even the most uncompromising agitation against the Consent Bill as nationalist. The recommendations to the Government to modify the rape clause cut across both supporters and opponents of the Bill. A report in the *Bengalee* on 14 March 1891 notes the significance of the marital rape controversy for the nationalist response to the Bill in Bengal: 'The strongest supporters of the Bill, as well as its strongest opponents, are all at one in pressing upon the Government the desirablity of introducing at least this one modification [i.e. the removal of the marital rape clause]'.[118] Many supporters of the Bill were persuaded to recommend modifications of the marital rape clause because, given the logic of colonial masculinity, it only mobilised formidable objections against the Bill. Even some of the Indian women petitioners, who offered perhaps the most unqualified support for the Consent Bill, relented on the rape clause in the case of sexual intercourse between husband and wife.[119] The Calcutta Committee in Support of the Consent Bill also called upon the government to modify the marital rape clause. The *Bengalee* concluded that the Bill would have attracted many more adherents in Bengal had the colonial authorities acceded to Indian wishes and compromised on the marital rape clause: 'if the law had declared that offence as between husband and wife should not be rape, and had included the modifications which are now made [in the Government Circular following the passage of the Act], the opposition to the measure would not have been half as strong as it has unfortunately been'.[120] Even if the *Bengalee* was underestimating the opposition to the Consent controversy, it is perhaps safe to assume that the marital rape clause contributed in no small way to weakening support for the Consent Bill in Bengal.

The controversy over the marital rape clause epitomised the significance of the revivalist–nationalist opposition against the Bill: given the overdetermined context of colonial masculinity, the controversy allowed the defence of orthodox Hindu patriarchy to appear as a nationalist symbol of protest. It is a further comment on the complicity between the protest against the Bill and a broader colonial agenda that the colonial authorities refused to relent on the marital rape issue during the Consent controversy, but were quick to issue an executive order as soon as the Bill was passed that basically guaranteed that there would be no convictions under the charge of marital rape.[121] For the most part, the objections to the marital rape clause gave orthodox opponents of the Consent Bill a pretext to trivialise the sexual abuse of child-wives. The Bali Sadharani Sabha in Bengal, for example, adopted a cavalier attitude towards underage sexual intercourse between a husband and wife: 'sexual intercourse with wives between 10 and 12 may at worst be regarded as a vice (a vice of which both husband and wife are in most cases equally guilty) – and a vice not at all of such disastrous consequences as drinking for instance; and a vice like this should not be treated as a heinous crime'.[122] Similarly Mitter, who claimed he was opposed to child-marriage but did not favour the Consent Bill, argued for leniency in cases of mutually desired sexual intercourse between husbands and their under-age wives if they involved no physical injuries. According to Mitter, classifying such acts as 'rape' would unjustly punish husbands and unnecessarily deprive wives of the company and protection of their husbands.[123] The possibility that the child wife may be sexually abused by her husband completely disappeared from the picture of marital sexual relations put forth by the defenders of the 'honour' of the Indian husband. The irony, however, is that this patriarchal reassertion of native masculinity was not very nationalist either: for the overdetermined context of colonial masculinity revealed a far greater affinity between the colonial advocates of the Bill and its opponents than was apparent in the rhetoric of militant nationalism.

The best indication of the ambiguous nature of the agitation against the Indian Consent Bill was in the complex and contradictory impact of the British consent debate on the consent debate in India: the efforts to recuperate the feminist challenges to British masculinity converged with the revivalist–nationalist efforts to reassert Indian masculinity. Each reinforced the other by limiting and narrowing the terms of the Indian consent debate. Following on the heels of the British consent debate, the debate over female consent in India became a means of containing any radical potential in the redefinition of female consent. In Britain, the feminist and purity crusaders – who were provoked by sensationalised cases of child-prostitution – mobilised women as a group in the British consent debate of 1885 to define a new public discourse of sexuality. The mobilisation of women by the purity movement was undoubtedly limited and contradictory: it paved the way, as various scholars have pointed out, for the involvement of middle-class women in social regulation and class-disciplining in Britain. Yet the moral discourse of purity in the British consent debate, as Frank Mort among others has suggested, was a 'battleground on which conflicting aims and intentions struggled for space': it opened the way, on the one hand, for further coercive regulations of sexuality; on the other hand, it also provided for middle-class women's challenges to male sexual double standards and for a definition, however limited, of their own image of female sexuality.[124]

It was precisely the recuperation of this possible redefinition of female consent and female sexuality in Britain that made allies out of colonial and orthodox indigenous interests in limiting the terms of the Indian Consent debate. When the purity movement confronted directly the context of marital sexual relations in the Indian Consent debate, therefore, its contradictions in reconstituting patriarchal privileges were more thoroughly exposed. For, as we have seen, the British Consent debate not only retained but reinforced the irrelevance of female consent within marriage for British women. The more crucial point, however, is that the challenge of the British Consent debate was recuperated in the revitalised colonial masculinity of the Indian Consent debate. If an important contribution of the purity crusaders in Britain, as Mort points out, was their intervention in 'speaking out' about sex, the opposite was true in the contributions of the colonial advocates of the Indian Consent Bill. In the dialogue between 'puritanical' reformers and the Hindu orthodoxy, for example, their significant disagreements did not mask their shared investment in the logic of colonial masculinity. According to the Bengali orthodoxy, as Engels points out, moral purity was a matter of ensuring male control of female sexuality. The view was expressed in the pages of the *Bangabasi*, a staunch opponent of the Consent Bill; it predicted a terrible scenario of 'females in groups hurrying from door to door begging males to gratify their lust' if the Bill were passed.[125] More dire consequences were predicted by a *pundit* of the *Hindu Sabha* who believed that a wife was bound to 'go astray' if she was 'in heat' and her husband did not satisfy her, just as her husband would 'go astray' if his wife 'who has attained her puberty, that is accessible in the provision of nature, cannot cohabit with him'.[126]

Although 'puritanical' opinion in the Indian Consent controversy did counter the male sexual double standard in the orthodox Hindu view, it nevertheless also discouraged 'speaking out' about sexuality, which could pose a challenge, however limited, to male prerogatives. On the one hand, for example, the *Pioneer* lambasted Mitter for criticising the advocates of the Consent Bill for excessive 'sexual moralism'. The paper pointed out that Mitter's arguments for a more lenient attitude towards sexual intercourse between a young couple was nothing but the 'selfish gratification of voluptuous men'; it countered Mitter's charge of 'puritanism' with the argument that 'male persons are bound to exercise self restraint in this matter [and all] truly civilized persons [could not condone the] self indulgence excused by Mitter'.[127] On the other hand, however, the *Pioneer*, along with other Anglo-Indian papers, was equally critical of any public discussion of sex. Much of the criticism was directed at 'Hindu women' who supposedly 'delighted' in talking about sexual practices:

> such is the debased atmosphere of the domestic life in which Hindu women move that they are aware of no impropriety in openly discussing subjects, the merest mention of which a more enlightened civilization would lead them to shun. The much talked of 'garbhadan' ceremony is to them a subject of delighted conversation. . . . The subject of the garbhadan ceremony is too odious for description in a newspaper read in respectable households.[128]

For Lionel Ashburner of the Bengal Civil Service, it was the Indian widows who were the 'chartered libertines' who 'declined to be reformed by philanthropic legislation and thus relinquish the Bohemian freedom of an amateur member of the "Demi Monde"!'[129]

The surprisingly limited terms of the debate on female sexuality in the Indian consent controversy is best reflected in the similarity between two opposite responses to the Bill: one by the Bengali *Brahmo* reformer, P. C. Majoomdar, who supported the Bill; and the other by the Bengali Christian Inspector of Girl's Schools in Calcutta, Manhomini Wheeler, who opposed it. Majoomdar favoured the Consent Bill, but was opposed to adult marriages. In fact, he supported the Consent Bill precisely because it did not directly challenge child-marriages. The Consent Bill could prevent 'familiarity with sex' – which he believed was responsible for polluting the imagination of Bengali boys in early youth – without risking the sexual immorality attendant with allowing men and women to marry at a later age.[130] In contrast, Wheeler was opposed to the Consent Bill, but favoured a law to prohibit or discourage child-marriage. In two separate letters to the Lt.-Governor of Bengal, she recorded her dissent against the Bill for encouraging sexual immorality among girls. Since 'continence is not in (the) blood' of Bengali girls, she argued, the prohibition against consummation cannot be enforced without first prohibiting child-marriage.[131]

The Indian Consent debate reveals much more in common between the Indian opponents of the Bill and its colonial advocates than has been assumed from the bitterness of their conflict. For together their efforts to offer a revitalised colonial masculinity served to marginalise the public contributions of Indian women as a group. The dominant debate on the Consent Bill, as Anagol-McGinn has demonstrated, ignored the 'gendered critique for the raising of the age of consent' expressed in Indian women's journals and in their support for the Consent Bill in petitions and in separate public meetings, at least in the Bombay Presidency.[132] The perspective of Indian women was largely overwhelmed by the claims of colonial masculinity that recuperated the implications of redefining female consent in an imperial social formation. Indian women activists, like Pandita Ramabai and Rakhmabai Modak, organised women in support of the Consent Bill in Poona and Bombay respectively; many prominent male advocates of the Bill even acknowledged the contributions of Indian women in supporting the Bill. Yet the very logic of a revitalised politics of masculinity rested on the erasure of the public contributions of Indian women as a group; as the *Liverpool Post* in Britain wrote, 'no one thinks of assuming that a Hindoo or Mahomeddan woman should be capable of knowing what is best for her own welfare'.[133] The crucial point, however, is not that Indian women's role was erased because their contributions were simply overlooked; but, rather, that the logic of colonial masculinity precluded visibility for certain kinds of contributions from Indian women. For, as in the case of the *Saint James Gazette*, the opponents of the Bill were often pleased to note that some Indian women were opposed to the Consent Bill. The press in Bengal recorded the support to the opposition from ordinary housewives who lined the streets of Calcutta on the occassion of the

Mahapuja (prayer ceremony) held at the *Kalighat* on 16 March 1891 to protest against the Consent Bill.[134] In similar vein, there was much talk about the contribution of the nameless older female relatives who supposedly encouraged young couples in the practice of premature consummation. It was the public contributions of women representing women as a group that were antithetical to the logic of the assertion of masculinity on colonial terms.

It was in Bengal that the intersection between the colonial recuperation of the redefinition of female consent and the nationalist 'crisis' of Bengali masculinity most effectively marginalised women from the debate over the Consent Bill. While Kadambini Ganguly, together with some 150 Hindu, Christian, Brahmo, Buddhist, and Muslim women, officially endorsed the Consent Bill; and though at least one other meeting of women was held in Calcutta in support of the Bill, there was a relative absence of more public contributions from elite Bengali women to the Consent controversy. It may be plausible, as Anagol-McGinn suggests, that the *bhadramahila*, or middle-class Bengali woman, was less conspicuous in the public debate on the Consent Bill than her counterpart in the Bombay Presidency because upper-caste Bengali women suffered greater orthodox restrictions than women in Bombay; but a more plausible explanation lies perhaps in the constraints of the terms of the Consent debate in Bengal.[135] For although there was a long tradition of women's writings on child-marriage and early maternity in Bengal, as in Bombay, the Bengali female periodical literature, as Ghulam Murshid has demonstrated, was curiously silent about the Bill throughout the Consent debate. It was only in 1894 when the *Bamabodhini Patrika*, one of the leading journals for women in Bengal, was celebrating its thirtieth jubilee that Murshid finds a passing reference to the Consent Act. Mankumari Basu, in her article *Bigata Shata Barshe Bharat Ramaniganer Abastha* (The Situation of Women in the Last Hundred Years), listed the Consent Act as one of the legislative initiatives that aimed to benefit the position of women in Bengal.[136] The terms of the Consent controversy thus not only overwhelmed the recognition of Indian women's actual contributions, but also discouraged their fuller participation in a debate that was strictly limited to revitalising the claims of masculinity.

Given the limited agenda of the debate, the colonial advocates and nationalist opponents of the Bill marked the differences in their positions by highly exaggerated claims – claims that, nevertheless, expressed a surprising similarity in their attitudes towards women. The definition of female consent, for example, was tied, by almost universal consensus, to the reproductive capacity of women: the age at which women could be considered physically fit to bear healthy children without injury to themselves or to the future of the race. The dominant Anglo-Indian view, as expressed in the report of the Calcutta Medical Society, coincided with the orthodox Hindu view: puberty, as defined by the onset of the first menstruation, declared a woman fit for sexual intercourse.[137] The dissenting voice in the Anglo-Indian medical establishment came mainly from European 'lady doctors' associated with the National Association for Supplying Medical Aid by Women to the Women of India, also known as the Lady Dufferin's Fund.[138] Although Edith Pechey-Phipson, who had served seven years as a 'lady doctor' in Bombay, accepted a physiological criterion for determining female consent, her definition of puberty and physical maturity at least made a case for a much higher age of female consent.[139] Within the dominant terms of the debate, however, the differences between the supporters and opponents of the Bill was reduced simply to a disagreement over the average age of menstruation of girls in India.

Confronted with conflicting evidence on the average age of menstruation, the supporters of the Bill invoked the medical authority of Dr Cheevers, who in his 1856 *Manual of Medical Jurisprudence for Bengal* had argued that Bengali girls were often deliberately 'ripened' for sexual intercourse through the 'artificial stimulation' of their sexual organs and the excitation of their sexual instincts.[140] Accordingly the colonial advocates of the Bill suggested that few Indian girls menstruated 'naturally' and that 'unaided menstruation' was an especially 'rare event' in Bengal. Furthermore, Anglo-Indian officials laid the blame for this primarily on the 'female members of the bride's family' who adopted 'measures to hasten menstruation'.[141] The opponents of the Bill bitterly contested the consensus in the Anglo-Indian medical establishment on the average age of menstruation for Indian girls; but they too reserved their greatest contempt for women: the European 'lady doctors'. The *Dainik O Samachar Chandrika*, for example, singled out the 'lady doctors' for criticism; it wrote disparagingly of the 'characteristic irrepressibility of their sex', which did not make the 'lady doctors' hesitate in giving their opinion 'on a subject on which even the learned Surgeon-General, Dr Cornish, has not been able to pronounce himself confidently'.[142]

For all their differences, both sides on the debate over the Indian Consent Bill constituted mutually reinforcing rather than oppositional positions in eliding the real implications of the redefinition of female consent. The advocates of the Bill made available alarming statistics of the physical injury done to child-wives. Morelle Mansell, an American medical missionary, and forty-nine other 'lady doctors' publicised cases of the sexual abuse of child-wives in India in their petition to the Viceroy on the Consent Bill.[143] The Calcutta medical establishment further substantiated these statistics with medico-legal returns of the sexual abuse of Indian girls between the ages of seven to twelve.[144] Yet the attention on the sexual abuse of child-wives seldom led to an exploration of the broader sexual exploitation of women; instead, as one official in the Viceroy's Legislative Council declared in a telling comment, the information shed light on 'fiendish husbands' whose 'moral depravity' was to be pitied. For their part, revivalist–nationalists converted the information into an affront to national pride. They charged that the statistics about sexual abuse were unrepresentative because the information was collected from the criminal population. In what was perhaps one of the more ingenious arguments adopted by the opponents of the Bill, Dr Juggobandhu Bose, an MD from Calcutta University, alleged that the European system of 'honeymoon' was far more injurious to a virginal girl than the Indian system of child-marriage. For on the authority of Dr Lawson Tait's *Diseases of Women and Abdominal Surgery*, Bose argued that injury during sexual intercourse had to do with the 'disproportionate size of the male organ' provoked by sexual excitement; and it was adult women more than child-wives who produced sexual excitement among males.[145] Bose and other opponents of the Bill tried to dignify opposition to the Bill as a sign of national independence. The real irony was that, notwithstanding professions to the contrary, it was the opposition against the Bill that remained most dependent on colonial masculinity.

The politics of colonial masculinity in the consent controversy did not provide a model for a more militant nationalist politics against colonial rule. Rather, it recuperated the energies of the nationalist movement and brought them into closer harmony with colonial rule. The ambiguity of the consent controversy thus suggests the need for recontextualising the relationship between nationalism and other emancipatory political projects. For even a militant critique of colonial rule, if it remains oblivious to the intersection of different contexts, may mask a far deeper complicity with a colonial agenda. The paradoxical role of colonial masculinity in the Indian consent controversy had as much to do with the politics of the imperial social formation as a whole as with colonial–nationalist politics in India. This overdetermined context for colonial masculinity is not unique: it suggests that the intersection of the imperial and the national not only frames the politics of race, class, gender, and sexuality, but is also constitutive of their very meaning.

Notes

1 *Abstract of the Proceedings of the Council of the Governor General of India, Assembled for the Purpose of Making Laws and Regulations 1891*, vol. 30 (Hereafter: *Abstract*), India Office Library and Records (IOLR), London.
2 For the extremely high incidence of child-marriage in Bengal, see Census Report of 1881 quoted in *Selections from the Records of the Government of India in the Home Department, No. 223: Home Department Serial No. 3, Papers Relating to Infant Marriage and Enforced Widowhood in India* (Hereafter: *Selections Home Department*), IOLR. Also *Parliamentary Papers: Moral and Material Progress and Condition of India During The Year 1890–91 and the Nine Preceding Years*, vol. 59, Paper 43, p. 91, IOLR. For the belief that premature consummation of child-marriage was also common in Bengal, see *Abstract*, p. 10; also Meredith Borthwick, *The Changing Role of Women in Bengal, 1849–1905* (Princeton: Princeton University Press, 1984), p. 128.
3 The Government of India Circular of March 1891 adopted Elliot's circular on the Bill; *India, Home Department, Judicial, April 1891, Pros. Nos. 103–104 A*, National Archives of India (NAI), New Delhi. Also *A Collection of the Acts Passed by the Governor General of India in Council in the Year 1891* (Calcutta: Government Printing Press, 1892).
4 For a history of child-marriage reform in India, see Geraldine Forbes, 'Women and Modernity: The Issue of Child Marriage in India', *Women's Studies International Quarterly*, 2:4 (1979), 407–19. Also Charles Heimsath, *Indian Nationalism and Hindu Social Reform* (Princeton: Princeton University Press, 1964); and 'The Origin and Enactment of the Indian Age of Consent Bill, 1891', *Journal of Asian Studies*, 21: 4 (1962), 491–504.
5 See especially S. Natarajan, *A Century of Social Reform in India* (Bombay: Asia Publishing House, 1962).
6 For an earlier formulation of this point, see Mrinalini Sinha, 'The Age of Consent Act: The Ideal of Masculinity and Colonial Ideology in Late Nineteenth Century Bengal', in T. K. Stewart (ed.), *Shaping Bengali Worlds: Public and Private* (East Lansing, MI: Asian Studies Center, 1989), pp. 99–127; and in slightly different form, see 'Gender and Imperialism: Colonial Policy and the Ideology of Moral Imperialism in Late Nineteenth Century Bengal', in Michael Kimmel, *Changing Men: New Directions in Research on Men and Masculinity* (Berkeley: Sages, 1987), pp. 217–31.
7 Dagmar Engels, 'The Age of Consent Act of 1891: Colonial Ideology in Bengal', *South Asia Research*, 3:2 (Nov. 1983), 107–32.
8 Padma Anagol-McGinn, 'The Age of Consent Act (1891) Reconsidered: Women's Perspectives and Participation in the Child-Marriage Controversy in India', *South Asia Research*,12:2 (Nov. 1992), 100–18. In Calcutta 'Brahmo ladies' who supported the Bill were subject to considerable ridicule; see *Reis and Reyyet* (Calcutta), 28 Mar. 1891, p. 149.
9 I am indebted especially to the account of the Age of Consent controversy in Tanika Sarkar, 'Rhetoric Against Age of Consent: Resisting Colonial Reason and Death of a Child-Wife', *Economic and Political Weekly*, 28:36 (4 Sept. 1993), p. 1870; also her 'The Hindu Wife and the Hindu Nation: Domesticity and Nationalism in Nineteenth-century Bengal', *Studies in History*, 8:2 (1992), 213–35. It is significant for my argument that in a footnote in her article 'Rhetoric Against Age of Consent', Sarkar points out that the camps that articulated the strongest nationalist case against the Age of Consent Bill were in the Swadeshi Movement of 1905–08 'quiescent, even loyal to the authorities'; see p. 1877, n.1.
10 *An Appeal to England to Save India From the Wrong and the Shame of the 'Age of Consent Act'* (published by Bali Sadharani Sabha, 1891), p. vi (Hereafter: *Appeal*).
11 For the perception of a crisis of British masculinity in the late nineteenth century, see Judith R. Walkowitz, *City of Dreadful Delight: Narratives of Sexual Danger in Late-Victorian London* (Chicago: University of Chicago Press, 1992). For a historical perspective on such 'crises' in Britain and the US, see Michael S. Kimmel, 'The

COLONIAL MASCULINITY

Contemporary "Crisis" of Masculinity in Historical Perspective', in Harry Brod (ed.), *The Making of Masculinities: The New Men's Studies* (Boston: Allen & Unwin, 1987), pp. 121–54.

12 See Heimsath, *Indian Nationalism and Hindu Social Reform*.
13 Sarkar, 'Rhetoric Against Age of Consent', p. 1871. For the 'invention of tradition' and its impact on social reform, see Lata Mani, 'Contentious Traditions: The Debate on Sati in Colonial India', *Cultural Critique*, 7 (Fall 1987), 119–56.
14 P. Chatterjee, 'The Nationalist Resolution of the Women's Question', in K. Sangari and S. Vaid (eds.), *Recasting Women: Essays in Indian Colonial History* (Brunswick, NJ: Rutgers University Press, 1990), pp. 233–53. Chatterjee's argument of the identity-crisis of 'official' Indian nationalism arising out of its 'derivative' project of modernity is made most forcefully in *Nationalist Thought and the Colonial World: A Derivative Discourse?* (London: Zed Books, 1986). In his later work, Chatterjee emphasises that the 'originality' of Indian nationalism lay in the imaginative task of constructing a community in the 'spiritual' or cultural realm; see *The Nation and its Fragments: Colonial and Postcolonial Histories* (Princeton: Princeton University Press, 1993).
15 *Infant Marriage and Enforced Widowhood in India: Being a Collection of Opinions For and Against Received by B. M. Malabari From Representative Hindu Gentlemen and Officials and Other Authorities* (Bombay: Voice of India Printing Press, 1887); also see *Selections Home Dept*.
16 12 Feb. 1885, *Selections Home Dept*, pp. 92–3. For an account of the consent controversy in Bombay, see Meera Kosambi, 'Girl-Brides and Socio-Legal Change: Age of Consent Bill (1891) Controversy', *Economic and Political Weekly* 26:31–32 (3–10 Aug. 1991), 1857–68.
17 *Selections Home Department*, p. 2.
18 G. A. Oddie, *Social Protest in India: British Protestant Missionaries and Social Reforms 1885–1900* (New Delhi: Manohar, 1979), pp. 84–5.
19 *Bengalee* (Calcutta), 9 July 1887, p. 329.
20 Scoble to Lansdowne, 6 July 1891, *Lansdowne Papers: Correspondence with Perons in India*, July to Dec. 1890, Letter No. 20 (Hereafter: *Lansdowne India*), IOLR. The colonial authorities believed that there was sufficient public indignation against 'Hari Maitism' in the 'native press' in the 1890s. See *India Legislative Proceedings, Nos. 1–73, Act 10 of 1891 and Connected Papers, April 1891*, Pros. No. 5 (Hereafter: *Proceedings*), IOLR.
21 Wilson's opinion was cited in Scoble's speech, 9 Jan. 1891, *Abstracts*, pp. 10–11.
22 For other cases of 'Hari Maitism', see Scoble's speech, 19 Mar. 1891, *Abstracts*, pp. 79–80.
23 See Dayaram Gidumal, *The Status of Woman in India: Or a Handbook for Hindu Social Reformers* (Bombay: Fort Printing Press, 1889). For Gidumal's contribution, see V. A. Narain, *Social History of Modern India: Nineteenth Century* (Meerut: Meenakshi Prakashan, 1972), pp. 140–1.
24 Scoble's speech, 9 Jan. 1891, *Abstract*, p. 10.
25 The *Pundit's* letter contradicting Scoble was printed in the *Statesman and Friend of India* (Calcutta), weekly edition, 17 Jan. 1891, p. 1 (Hereafter: *Statesman*). The gaffe was discussed in the *Statesman*, 4 Feb. 1891, p. 1.
26 Scoble's speech, 19 Mar. 1891, *Abstracts*, pp. 81–2.
27 Viceroy's speech, 9 Jan. 1891, *Abstracts*, pp. 21–4.
28 Malabari set up a Standing Committee in London at 37 Wimpole Street at the residence of a Mrs Jeune; see *Pioneer Mail and Indian Weekly News*, 17 Sept. 1890, p. 356 (Hereafter: *Pioneer*). For the involvement of Fawcett, see *Bengalee*, 29 Nov. 1891, p. 548. For the contribution of the private meeting at Jeune's residence, see *Proceedings*, No. 10. The Committee's Resolution is quoted in Lord Reay to Lansdowne, 1 Aug. 1890, *Lansdowne Papers: Correspondence with Persons in England*, Jan.-Dec. 1890, Letter No. 51 (Hereafter: *Lansdowne England*), IOLR.
29 Reay to Lansdowne, 4 July 1890, Letter No. 43; Reay to Lansdowne, 7 Aug. 1890, Letter No. 51; Northbrook to Lansdowne, 7 Aug. 1890, Letter No. 52; Lansdowne to

THE AGE OF CONSENT CONTROVERSY

Northbrook, 6 Sept. 1890, Letter no. 58, *Lansdowne England*, Jan.-Dec. 1890.
30 The *Sadharan Brahmo*, Dwarkanath Ganguly, who was also Assistant Secretary of the Indian Association, volunteered an independent endorsement of the Bill because the official response from the Indian Association expressed some reservations about it. See Appendix V, *Proceedings*, No. 38; and his letter to the *Statesman*, 17 Jan. 1891, p. 1. For the isolation of the *Sadharan Brahmos* in Bengal during the Consent Controversy, see also the memoirs of another *Sadharan Brahmo*, Bipan Chandra Pal, *Memories of My Life and Times*, vol. 2, 1886–1900 (Calcutta: Yugayatri Prakashak Ltd, 1951), pp. 114–18; also *Statesman*, 7 Mar. 1891, p. 1. This is also discussed in Engels, 'The Age of Consent Act', pp. 115–20.
31 See *Papers Relating to Act 10 of 1891*, pp. 677–80, cited in Rajendra Singh Vatsa, 'The Movement Against Infant Marriages in India 1860–1914', *Journal of Indian History*, 49 (Apr./Aug./Dec. 1971), p. 295.
32 Quoted in Scoble's speech, *Abstracts*, pp. 79–80. For some of the petitions from women's organisations, see *Proceedings*, No. 31, No. 54, No. 55, and No. 61.
33 Letter to *The Times* (London), 30 Aug. 1890, p. 13; for other letters, see 20 Aug. 1890, p. 3 and 4 Sept. 1890, p. 12.
34 Uma Chakravarti, 'Whatever Happened to the Vedic Dasi? Orientalism, Nationalism and a Script for the Past', in *Recasting Women*, pp. 27–87.
35 *Englishman*, (Calcutta) 17 Jan. 1891, p. 2. Also Lansdowne to Cross, 14 Jan. 1891, *Lansdowne Papers: Correspondence with Secretary of State*, from Jan. 1891, Letter No. 2 (Hereafter: *Lansdowne Sec. of State*), IOLR.
36 The pamphlet by Ramnath Tarkaratna and Nilmani Mukherjee was reprinted from the *Reis and Reyyat*; see *Tracts on Indian Marriage Customs 1887–1891*, no. 12 (Hereafter: *BM Tracts*), British Museum (BM), London.
37 See the debate between Bhandarkar and Tilak on the *Shastras* reprinted from *The Times of India* (Bombay), B. G. Tilak, *Express Texts of the Shastras Against the Age of Consent Bill* and R. G. Bhandarkar, *A Note on the Age of Marriage and its Consummation According to Hindu Law*, in *India Office Library Tracts*, vol. 711 (Hereafter: *IOR Tracts*), IOLR. Also see K. T. T. [Telang], *Notes on Consent, BM Tracts*, No. 13; and N. G. Chandavarkar, *The British Government and Hindu Religious Customs – A Plea For Consent, BM Tracts*, No. 10.
38 Scoble's speech, *Abstracts*, pp. 82–3. Also Appendix 17, *Proceedings*, No. 60.
39 See Nulkar's speech, *Abstracts*, p. 110. Also Kosambi, 'Girl-Brides and Socio-Legal Change', pp. 1859–60.
40 Cited in Amiya Sen, 'Hindu Revivalism in Action – The Age of Consent Bill Agitation in Bengal', *The Indian Historical Review*, 7:1–2 (July 1980-Jan.1981), p. 171.
41 For the defence of Raghunandan's interpretation of the *garbhadhan*, see Appendix 5, From Babu Bhudeb Mookerjee; and for a challenge to the significance of the ritual, see Note from Rash Behary Ghose, *Proceedings*, No. 38. Also the pamphlet by Sarat Chandra Some, *Glory Unto Loyalty – An Open letter to the Empress Not to Interfere With Religion, BM Tracts*, No. 11.
42 Appendix A 16, *Proceedings*, No. 59. Croft noted that even the famous Bengali reformer *Pundit* Ishwar Chandra Vidyasagar was opposed to the Bill.
43 For the Rukmabai case, see Sudhir Chandra, 'The Problem of Social Reform in Modern India: The Study of a Case', in S. C. Malik (ed.), *Dissent, Protest and Reform in Indian Civilization* (Simla: Institute of Advanced Studies, 1977), pp. 250–67; and 'Whose Laws? Notes on a Legitimising Myth of the Colonial Indian State', *Studies in History*, 8:2 (1992), 187–211.
44 V. S. Apte, *The Law for the Restitution of Conjugal Rights, IOR Tracts*, vol. 711; for a dispute between Hindu *pundits* on whether Section 260 of the Civil Procedure Code, dealing with the restitution of conjugal rights, accorded with Hindu *Shastras*, see *The Hindu Marriage Question – Correspondence Between R. Raghunath Rao and Pandit Shyamji Krishnavarma*, IOR Tracts, vol. 711.
45 Dagmar Engels, 'The Limits of Gender Ideology: Bengali Women, the Colonial State and the Private Sphere, 1890–1930', *Women's Studies' International Forum*, 12

(1989), 425–37.
46 Sarkar, 'Rhetoric Against Age of Consent', p. 1876.
47 Quoted in *Appeal*, p. 4.
48 Rajat Kanta Ray, *Social Conflict and Political Unrest in Bengal, 1875–1927* (New Delhi: Oxford University Press, 1984), pp. 89–95, 125–7.
49 The *Maharani's* telegram was sent to the protest meeting organised by the Sovabazar Rajbari; see *Statesman*, 24 Jan. 1891, p. 4; for her role, also see Paramanda Dutt, *Memoirs of Motilal Ghose* (Calcutta: Amrita Bazar Patrika Office, 1935), pp. 74–5. Another female *zamindar*, the *Maharanee* Bhivasundari of Dighapatia, also organised protest meetings against the Bill; cited in Sen, 'Hindu Revivalism in Action', p. 173.
50 For the upper-caste argument of revivalist–nationalists during the Rukhmabai case, see Sarkar, 'Rhetoric Against Age of Consent', p. 1873.
51 *Ibid.*; see also Lucy Caroll, 'Law, Custom and Statutory Social Reform: The Hindu Widows Remarriage Act of 1856', *Indian Economic and Social History Review*, 20:4 (Oct.-Dec. 1983), 363–88.
52 *Abstracts*, pp. 21–4; also Lansdowne to Benjamin Jowett, 3 Feb. 1891, Lansdowne *England*, From Jan. 1891, Letter No. 15. For the use of such suits in litigation, see Jim Masselos, 'Sexual Property/Sexual Violence: Wives in Nineteenth-Century Bombay', *South Asia Research* 12:2 (Nov. 1992), 81–99.
53 Quoted in *Statesman*, 10 Jan. 1891, p. 3.
54 Cited in *Abstracts*, p. 78.
55 R. C. Mitter, Note of Dissent, *Proceedings*, No. 63. Mitter was quoting from T. N. Mukharji, *The Sisters of Phulmani (Or the Child Wives of India)* (Calcutta:Indian Nation 1890), pp. 20–1.
56 Natarajan, *A Century of Social Reform*, p. 84. Also see Prem Narian, 'The Age of Consent Bill (1891) and its Impact on India's Freedom Struggle', *Quarterly Review of Historical Studies*, 10:1 (1970–71), 7–21.
57 *Bangabasi*, 25 Feb. 1891, *Report on the Bengal Native Press*, 1891, vol. 17, No. 2 (Hereafter: *RNBP*), IOLR.
58 I am drawing from Amiya Sen's account of the impressive strength of the Hindu revivalist agitation against the Bill. See Sen, 'Hindu Revivalism in Action', esp. pp. 170–5.
59 For Abdool Luteef's pamphlet on behalf of the Muhammedan Literary Society, see *BM Tracts*, No. 5. For Muslim opposition to the Bill, see *Sudhakar*, 13 Feb. 1891, *RNBP*, No. 8; and Lansdowne to Reay, 14 Jan. 1891, *Lansdowne England*, From Jan. 1891, Letter No. 7. The Calcutta-based Muslim paper, *Ahmadi*, was also against the Bill. See Narian, 'The Age of Consent Bill (1891)', p. 14.
60 Extract from *Amrita Bazar Patrika* (Calcutta), 9 Aug. 1890, *Proceedings*, No. 5. For the tremendous popularity of the *Bangabasi*, see Shyamananda Banerjee, *National Awakening and the Bangabasi* (Calcutta: Amitava-Kalyan Publishers, 1968).
61 See Walkowitz, *City of Dreadful Delight*; also *Prostitution and Victorian Society: Women, Class and the State* (Cambridge: Cambridge University Press, 1980). Also see Mary P. Ryan, *Women in Public: Between Banners and Ballots 1825–1880* (Baltimore: Johns Hopkins University Press, 1990). For the changes in the construction of 'masculinity', see Jeff Hearn, *Men in the Public Eye: The Construction and Deconstruction of Public Men and Public Patriarchies* (London: Routledge, 1992).
62 Max Mueller, 'The Story of an Indian Child Wife', *Contemporary Review*, 60 (Aug. 1891), 183–7. For a discussion of the admiration of Indian patriarchal institutions in Englishwomen's writings on India during this period, see Janaki Nair, 'Uncovering the *Zenana*: Visions of Indian Womanhood in Englishwomen's Writings, 1813–1940', *Journal of Women's History*, 2:1 (Spring 1990), esp. pp. 18–21.
63 Part 1, *The Times*, 13 Sept. 1890, p. 8.
64 See Part 3, *The Times*, 7 Oct. 1890, p. 8. The identity of the author is mentioned in the *Bengalee*, 11 Oct. 1890, p. 486. Also cited in Kosambi, 'Girl-Brides and Social-Legal Change', p. 1860.
65 Quoted in Kosambi, 'Girl-Brides and Social-Legal Change', p. 1864.

66 I am grateful to Professor Walkowitz for drawing my attention to this connection. The paper was also an outspoken critic of the Indian National Congress in India. For mention of its role in the Consent controversy in Britain, see Michael Pearson, *The Age of Consent: Victorian Prostitution and its Enemies* (London: Newton Abbot, David & Charles, 1972), p. 156.
67 *Saint James Gazette* (London), 20 Jan. 1891, p. 4.
68 *Ibid.*, 2 March 1891, p. 4. The *Dainik O Samachar Chandrika* was pleased to note the *Saint James Gazette's* support to the opposition, 12 Sept. 1890, *RNBP* 1890.
69 *The Times*, 13 Jan. 1891, quoted in *English Opinion on India: A Monthly Magazine Containing Select Extracts from English Newspapers on Indian Subjects*, No. 2 of March 1891 (Hereafter: *English Opinion*). The petition signed by approximately 1,600 'women living in India' was sent in December 1890; see Appendix N, *Proceedings*, No. 31; also *India, Home Department, Judicial, February 1891*, Nos. 155–159 A, NAI.
70 *Abstract*, pp. 79–80, 125.
71 *The Times*, 11 Feb. 1891, p. 4.
72 Quoted in *Appeal*, p. 40. His support was welcomed by Bengali Positivists in Calcutta; Jogendra Chundra Ghosh, one of the most famous Bengali Positivists, was the author of an anti-Consent Bill pamphlet, *Listen Slowly, Age of Consent, BM Tracts*, No. 14. For the impact of Positivism in Bengal, see Geraldine Forbes, *Positivism in Bengal: A Case Study in the Transmission and Assimilation of an Ideology* (Columbia, MO: South Asia Books, 1975).
73 Cited in *Amrita Bazar Patrika*, 9 Nov. 1891, p. 3; 1 Sept. 1891, p. 2; 25 Aug. 1891, p. 2.
74 Lansdowne expressed his displeasure at the prospect of the new Lt.-Governor of Bengal appearing less than enthusiastic about the Bill; see Lansdowne to Scoble, 21 Feb. 1891, *Lansdowne India*, Jan.-June 1891, Letter No. 144. For dissenting opinions from senior government officials, see Lord Connemara (Governor of Madras) to Lansdowne, 23 Oct. 1890, *Lansdowne India*, July-Dec. 1890, Letter No. 313. Also *Proceedings*, No. 38; No. 47; No. 51.
75 *Statesman*, 21 Mar. 1891, p. 1.
76 Quoted in *Englishman*, 11 Feb. 1891, p. 4. Also Hume to Lansdowne, 10 Feb. 1891, *Lansdowne India*, Jan. – June 1891, Letter No. 159.
77 *Englishman*, 21 July 1890, p 7; 23 Feb. 1891, p. 4. *Pioneer*, 12 Feb. 1891, p. 199. Rudyard Kipling wrote in the *Contemporary Review* in September 1890 of Indian political leaders: 'they talk about the cow but the protection of women is a new and dangerous idea', quoted in *Bengalee*, 27 Sept. 1891, p. 461. Lansdowne was obviously disappointed not to receive the support of Congress stalwarts like Banerjea and Bonnerjee on the Bill, Lansdowne to Ilbert, 4 Feb. 1891, *Lansdowne England, From Jan. 1891*, Letter No. 16.
78 *Daily Chronicle* (London), 3 Jan. 1891 quoted in *English Opinion*, No. 2, Mar. 1891.
79 Bayly's views were collected in Aug. 1890; quoted by Scoble, *Abstracts*, p. 10.
80 This was to become the dominant Anglo-Indian view on the impact of child-marriage in India, see Flora Annie Steel, *The Garden of Fidelity:Being the Autobiography of F. A. Steele, 1847–1929* (London: Macmillan & Co. Ltd, 1929), p. 161.
81 Sir Herbert Risley, *The People of India* (Calcutta: Thacker, Spink & Co., 1908), p. 185.
82 Quoted in *Statesman*, 19 Jan. 1891, p. 3.
83 Quoted in Risley, *People of India*, p. 185.
84 *Pioneer*, 29 Jan. 1891, pp. 134–5.
85 3 March 1891, *Lansdowne Sec. of State, From Jan. 1891*, Letter No. 26.
86 Jeffrey Weeks, *Coming Out: Homosexual Politics in Britain From the Nineteenth Century to the Present* (London: Quartet, 1977); *Sex, Politics and Society* (London: Routledge & Kegan Paul, 1981); and *Against Nature: Essays on History, Sexuality and Identity* (London: Rivers Oram Press, 1991).
87 Sept. 1890, *Proceedings*, No. 3. For the links between 'unmanliness' and 'homosexuality' in popular perceptions, see David Hilliard, 'Unenglish and Unmanly:

Anglo-Catholicism and Homosexuality', *Victorian Studies*, 25:2 (Winter 1982), 181–210.
88 For popular attitudes that linked masturbation with homosexuality, see R. P. Neuman, ''Masturbation, Madness and the Modern Concepts of Childhood and Innocence', *Journal of Social History* (Spring 1975), 1–27; and V. L. Bullough and M. Voght, 'Homosexuality and its Confusion with the "secret sin" in pre-Freudian America', *Journal of the History of Medicine and Applied Sciences*, 28:2 (1973), 143–55. For the Anglo-Indian belief that Indian men were particularly prone to masturbation, see Ganga Din, *The Young Man's Guide: Medical Companion*, p. 12, in *IOR Tract*, vol. 735.
89 Hume to Lansdowne, 10 Feb. 1891, *Lansdowne India*, Jan.-June 1891, Letter No. 159.
90 Bayly to Lansdowne, 5 Oct. 1890, *Lansdowne India*, July-Dec. 1890, Letter 257. Also see letter to *Bengalee*, 31 Jan. 1891, p. 53.
91 *Statesman*, 31 Jan. 1891, p. 1.
92 *Mahratta*, 12 Apr. 1891, *Report on Bombay Native Press*, 1891, IOLR.
93 *Ibid*.
94 The most detailed medical argument against the Bill was presented by the Standing Committee of the Sobhabajar meeting in Bengal. See *Full Proceedings of a Public Meeting Held on 22 Jan. 1891 to Protest Consent Bill, BM Tracts*, No. 4. Dr Juggobandhu Bose, a distinguished MD of Calcutta University, was the most active in leading the rebuttal against the medical arguments for the Bill; see *Appeal*, p. 2–3.
95 Appendix 5, 7 Feb. 1891, *Proceedings*, No. 38. Also Alok Ray (ed.), *Counterpoint*, vol. 2 (Calcutta: Riddhi India, 1975), pp. 283–6.
96 Cited in *Statesman*, 14 Mar. 1891, p. 1.
97 Quoted in *Statesman*, 31 Jan. 1891, p. 1.
98 *Sakti*, 10 Feb. 1891, *RNBP* 1891, No. 8.
99 See Appendix V, *Proceedings*, No. 38.
100 Quoted by Manomohun Ghose, 6 Feb. 1891, *Proceedings*, No. 38.
101 See Jennifer Temkin, *Rape and The Legal Process* (London: Sweet & Maxwell, 1987), pp. 46–7. According to one Anglo-Indian account, however, the only occasion on which the husband of a young girl in Britain came under the purview of the new British Consent Act was if he procured a third party to have sexual intercourse with his wife under thirteen years of age. See *Englishman*, 12 Sept. 1890, p. 5.
102 Appendix 5, *Proceedings*, Pros. No. 38; *Dacca Gazette*, 29 Jan. 1891, *RNBP* 1891, No. 4; *Dainik O Samachar Chandrika*, 10 Feb. 1891, *RNBP* 1891, No. 8.
103 Quoted in Temkin, *Rape and Legal Process*, p. 47.
104 From Justice Ghosh and Justice Bannerjee, High Court of Calcutta, 2 Mar. 1891, Appendix 10, *Proceedings*, No. 53.
105 23 July 1846, *Notes on the Report of the India Law Commission on the Indian Penal Code*, p. 42, IOLR. Also Appendix 20, Mitter's Note of Dissent, *Proceedings*, No. 63.
106 Heimsath, *Indian Nationalism and Hindu Social Reform*, pp. 79, 91–2.
107 *The Indian Penal Code Being Act 45 of 1860 Annotated With Rulings of the High Court in India and Supplemented With a Copious Index By D. E. Cranenburgh* (Calcutta: Government of India, 1882), p. 155.
108 *India, Home Department, Judicial, July 1888*, Nos. 129–132 A; *India, Home Department, Judicial, March 1888*, Nos. 79–81 A; *India, Home Department, Judicial, June 1889*, Nos. 105–106 A; *India, Home Department, Judicial, July 1889*, Nos. 258–260 A, NAI.
109 Appendix 5, 6 Feb. 1891, *Proceedings*, No. 38. Also Appendix 10, 2 Mar. 1891, High Court of Calcutta, *Proceedings*, No. 53. Mitter and Ghose made parallel arguments against the marital rape clause in the Consent Bill but favoured a civil law against child marriage; see Mitter, *Proceedings*, No. 63.
110 *Statesman*, 17 Jan. 1891, p. 1.
111 *Bengal Exchange Gazette*, 14 Jan. 1891, *RNBP* 1891, No. 2.
112 Appendix A 4 from W. E. Ward, Judicial Commissioner Lower Burma, 9 Feb. 1891, *Proceedings*, No. 47.
113 Appendix 5, *Proceedings*, No. 38.

114 *Sudhakar*, 23 Jan. 1891, *RNBP* 1891, No. 5.
115 This was also repeated by Hume to Lansdowne, 10 Feb. 1891, *Lansdowne India*, Jan.-June 1891, Letter No. 159.
116 Appendix A 16, 12 Feb. 1891, *Proceedings*, No. 59.
117 *Indian Mirror* (Calcutta), 14 Sept. 1890, p. 2.
118 *Bengalee*, 14 Mar. 1891, p. 125.
119 Cited in Anagol-McGinn, 'The Age of Consent Act (1891) Reconsidered', p. 116.
120 *Bengalee*, 2 May 1891, p. 208.
121 There were a couple of well-publicised cases soon after the Consent Act was passed; but very soon most people were agreed that the Act was just a 'dead letter', see *India, Home Department, Judicial, July 1892*, Pros. Nos. 278–291 A, NAI. In 1893, the Government of India decided that since 'there have been very few cases indeed under the Age of Consent Act' it was time to discontinue the annual reports on the working of the Act; *India Home Department, Judicial, Aug. 1893*, Pros. Nos.187–196 A, NAI.
122 *Appeal*, p. 64.
123 Appendix 20, *Proceedings*, No. 63. For a similar view, see U. C. Shome, *No Necessity For Consent Act, BM Tracts*, No. 8.
124 Frank Mort, *Dangerous Sexualities: Medico-Moral Politics in England Since 1830* (London: Routledge & Kegan Paul, 1987), p. 126. Also see, Judith Walkowitz, 'Male Vice and Feminist Virtue: Feminism and the Politics of Prostitution in Nineteenth-Century British History', *History Workshop Journal*, 13 (Spring 1982), 77–93; and Deborah Gorham, 'The "Maiden Tribute of Modern Babylon" Re-examined: Child Prostitution and the Idea of Childhood in Late Victorian England', *Victorian Studies*, 21:3 (Spring 1978), 353–79.
125 *Bangabasi*, 7 Mar. 1891, *RNBP*, 1891, No. 1.
126 Appendix M, A. Sankariah, President Founder Hindu Sabha, Trichoor, *Proceedings*, No. 30. Also see reference to the pamphlet *Ain! Ain!!Ain!!! Bhayanak Bipad!! Sarbanaser Katha!!! Kamalkamini o Sureshbhamanir Kathopkathan* (Oh! Oh!! Oh!!! Terrible Calamity!! Tale of Destruction!!! Dialogue Between Kamalkamini and Sureshbhamini), cited in Borthwick, *The Changing Role of Women in Bengal*, p. 127; and also N. N. Sircar, *A Note on the Age of Consent Bill* (Calcutta 1891), IOLR.
127 *Pioneer*, 26 Mar. 1891, p. 396. Also *Statesman*, 17 Jan. 1891, p. 1. For a more successful deployment of a 'purity' argument for child-marriage reforms in the 1920s and 1930s, see Mrinalini Sinha, 'Nationalism and Respectable Sexuality in India', *Genders* (1995).
128 *Pioneer*, 26 Mar. 1891, p. 396.
129 Cited in Narain, 'The Age of Consent Bill (1891)', p. 20 n. 32.
130 Quoted in *Pioneer*, 19 Mar. 1891, p. 359.
131 Wheeler's letters of 2 and 3 Mar. 1891 are quoted in Elliott to Lansdowne, 6 Mar. 1891, *Lansdowne India*, Jan.–June 1891, Letter No. 232.
132 Anagol-McGinn, 'The Age of Consent Act (1891) Reconsidered', p. 106.
133 *Liverpool Post* (Liverpool), 27 Jan. 1891 in *English Opinion*, No. 2 of Mar. 1891.
134 See reports of the *puja* in the pro-Bill newspaper, *Reis and Reyyat*, 28 Mar. 1891, p. 149. Also see Amiya Sen, 'Hindu Revivalism in Action', p. 173.
135 See Anagol McGinn, 'The Age of Consent Act (1891) Reconsidered', pp. 116–17.
136 Ghulam Murshid, *Reluctant Debutante: Response of Bengali Women to Modernization 1849–1905* (Rajshahi: Rajshahi University Press, 1983), pp. 184–5.
137 The ninth meeting of the Calcutta Medical Society on the 'Nubile Age of Females in India' was held on 10 September 1890; the majority view of Brigade Surgeon K. Macleod that puberty was determined by first menstruation was upheld over the minority view of Major C. H. Jourbet, Professor of Midwifery; see Transactions of Medical Societies, Oct. 1890, *Proceedings*, Nos. 3 and 4; also see Appendix B, 9 Aug. 1890, From C. H. Jourbet, *Proceedings*, No. 13. This was also the view reiterated by Scoble; see *Abstracts*, p. 10.
138 *India Home Department, Judicial, Feb. 1891*, Pros. Nos. 155–159 A, NAI.
139 Quoted in *The Times*, 7 Nov. 1890, p. 6.
140 Extract from the *Indian Medical Gazette*, Dec. 1890, p. 51, *Proceedings*, Pros. No. 14.

For the quote from Dr Cheevers, see Nulkar's speech, *Abstract*, p. 119.
141 E. E. Lowis, Commissioner Rajshaye Division, 18 Oct. 1989, *Proceedings*, No. 13. This view of menstruation among Indian women is also given credence in M. E. Staley, *Handbook For Wives and Mothers in India* (Calcutta: Thacker, Spink & Co., 1908), pp. 66–7.
142 *Dainik O Samachar Chandrika*, 17 Nov. 1890, *RNBP* 1890, p. 1051. Also see *Amrita Bazar Patrika*, 30 Aug. 1891, p. 2. In addition, opponents of the Bill came up with the recommendation of substituting 'puberty' for the age of twelve in the consent regulations; they argued the present Bill made 'children out of mature girls'; see *Dainik O Samachar Chandrika*, 14 Jan. 1891, *RNBP*, 1891, No. 2. Even more 'liberal' papers like the *Bengalee* and the *Sanjivani* supported this change.
143 Memorial of Lady Doctors in India (sent to the Viceroy in Sept 1890), 27 Feb. 1891, Appendix A 15, *Proceedings*, No. 58. The memorial received wide publicity; see *The Times*, 8 Oct. 1890; 7 Nov. 1890; 29 Nov. 1890, p. 6.
144 The Report of the Civil Surgeon of Bengal for 1868–69 demonstrated that out of forty-eight cases of rape half the victims were under ten years of age, in two under five, and in seventeen between six and ten; the Report for 1870–72 established that out of 372 cases of rape, 51 per cent of the victims were below ten and 89 per cent below fifteen; Quoted in *Englishman*, 12 Sept. 1890, p. 6. The most sensational was the alarming interpretation of the disproportion in the ratio of the sexes during the first four years of child-marriage in the 1881 census in Mukharji, *The Sisters of Phulmani*. Mukharji, however, used the statistics to argue against child-marriage and not as support for the Consent Bill. For the concern over the disproportion of the sex ratio in the Indian Census returns, see Caroline Ifeka, '"Spiritual" and "Statistical" Models of the Sexes in British India, 1871–1931', *South Asia* 5:1 (June 1982), 16–28.
145 Bose, *Appeal*, pp. 2–3.

CONCLUSION

The study of the historical formation of colonial masculinity touches upon two broader questions that concern political criticism in our own times: one, how to go beyond the reductive choices offered in political critiques concerned only with one or another isolated aspect of social relations; and, two, how to recast the historiographical unit of both metropolitan and colonial histories to recognise their interaction in the age of imperialism. The first way in which the history of colonial masculinity can open up fresh possibilities is by providing the basis to reconsider the relationship between anti-colonial and feminist politics. Since contemporary political movements all over the world continue to be bedevilled by what is often presented as a stark choice between feminism and various cultural nationalisms, it has become all the more urgent today to demonstrate the inadequacy of either feminist or anti-colonial politics in isolation. The study of colonial masculinity demystifies the grounds for such excruciating choices. At one level, it extends the current scholarship on anti-colonial nationalisms: for it not only expands the field of gender in nationalist politics, but, even more crucially, reconsiders the connection between nationalist and patriarchal politics. Although the scholarship on elite nationalism in colonial India has gone well beyond the nature of its impact on women or of the history of women's contributions to nationalism, and has arrived at much more sophisticated analyses of the constitutive role of gender in Indian nationalism, it has, nevertheless, remained centred on the figure of the Indian woman.[1] The history of colonial masculinity, however, simultaneously exposes the patriarchal politics of nationalism and the limits of the anti-colonial claims made on behalf of such patriarchal politics. It appears likely that a systematic study of the formation of masculinities in relation to nationalisms will show that the anti-colonial agenda has in fact been limited or subverted by patriarchal politics. It is precisely because colonial masculinity reveals not only the patriarchal politics of the nationalism of indigenous elites, but also the limits of a nationalist politics based on the defence of indigenous patriarchy, that it has the potential for intervening in the current impasse between feminisms and nationalisms. Further scholarship on the politics of colonial masculinity, therefore, can demonstrate even more conclusively the impossibility of separating the feminist from the anti-colonial nationalist agenda.

At another level, the study of colonial masculinity revises the

CONCLUSION

boundaries of feminist criticism. Feminist scholarship has had little trouble in identifying the patriarchal gender system that has sustained the masculine sense of loss expressed in various nationalisms.[2] Yet feminist criticisms of the patriarchal politics of masculinity have only scarcely begun to grasp the full implications of colonial masculinity. For the widely dispersed arena for the construction of colonial masculinity disrupts any stable equation between gender identity and sex difference: it demonstrates that masculinity had as much to do with racial, class, religious, and national differences as with sex difference.[3] Hence even an expanded politics of gender – one that recognises the imbrication of gender in a variety of different axes of power – may still fall short as the starting-point for a feminist critique of colonial masculinity. Indeed, the politics of colonial masculinity points out the need for the kind of materialist–feminist analysis that Rosemary Hennessy recommends as the basis for rethinking the nature of feminist critique: for such a critique does not proceed from a priority given to gender, however modified and expanded to include other social relations, but from its particular mode of enquiry into the entire domain of social relations.[4] In so far as the study of colonial masculinity extends the scholarship on anti-colonial nationalisms as well as expands the terms of feminist criticism, it may contribute to a more productive dialogue between feminisms and nationalisms in our own times.

The second way in which the study of colonial masculinity can open up fresh possibilities is by recasting the unit of study for both metropolitan and colonial histories. For the contextual study of the interaction between the 'manly Englishman' and the 'effeminate Bengali' in the late nineteenth century provides a heuristic model, the imperial social formation, for the study of national histories: it demonstrates that metropolitan and colonial histories were both constituted by the history of imperialism. This model of the imperial social formation underscores the following points: on the one hand, the different trajectory of metropolitan and colonial histories and, on the other, the mutual implication of both these histories in the 'uneven and combined development' of the global political economy.

From such an integrated perspective, the history of metropolitan Britain and the history of colonial India may raise interesting questions for each other. One such question, for example, is the 'problem' of bourgeois hegemony in Victorian Britain and colonial India. On the one hand, historians of Britain have continued to debate the identity of the hegemonic faction of the ruling class in Britain: while Perry Anderson and Tom Nairn have identified this faction as 'archaic' and 'patrician' in character, E. P. Thompson has warned against underestimating the cultural achievements and the real power of the 'bourgeoisie'.[5] The debate, which originated as a way of explaining the relative economic decline of Britain from the nineteenth century onwards, has since left its mark on such questions as the analysis of the social structure of Victorian British society and the impact of this structure on British 'overseas expansion'.[6] Since the debate has also touched on definitions of Victorian British manliness as either dominantly 'aristocratic' and 'chivalrous' or 'bourgeois' and 'respectable', the context of colonial masculinity suggests at least one possible site from which the debate may begin to be recontextualised.[7]

On the other hand, Ranajit Guha's perceptive account that demonstrates the 'spurious hegemony' of the British and indigenous bourgeoisies in colonial India has typically not been examined in the context of the debate over bourgeois hegemony in Britain. Guha's analysis, which comes as a timely warning against de-historicised versions of the impact of 'colonial discourse' that erase the specific dynamics of colonial Indian history, explains the exercise of power in colonial India as 'dominance without hegemony.'[8] Guha demonstrates that the colonial authorities' ultimate recourse to the coercive mechanisms of the colonial state, backed by the colonial military establishment, qualifies any effort to characterise the dominance of colonial rule as hegemonic – that is, as based on the consent of the subject populations. Similarly, he also demonstrates that the anomalies in the struggle of the nationalist elites qualifies any effort to characterise the dominance of the indigenous bourgeoisie as hegemonic – that is, as representing the will of all the people of India. Guha suggests that the failure to establish hegemony in colonial India by the British as well as the Indian bourgeoisies and the consequent survival, albeit in much altered form, of pre-colonial or semi-feudal modes of power constitute the limits of the rule of capital. For Guha the 'universalising tendency' of capital, having performed its historical role in Britain, confronts its limit under colonial conditions: feudal or pre-capitalist norms do not disappear, but disrupt the universalising goals of the bourgeois project.[9]

What if the problem of 'bourgeois hegemony' in metropolitan Britain and colonial India were rethought in the context of a historiographical unit reconstituted as the imperial social formation? Would such a revised context provide a new meaning for the supposedly 'aristocratic' character of the ruling class in Victorian Britain?[10] Similarly, would such a context also qualify the assessment that the reliance on pre-colonial modes of power in India represented an 'outside' limit of the rule of capital?[11] It is questions such as these that might be illuminated further by a historical and materialist analysis of the imperial social formation, as has been attempted in this study of colonial masculinity.

What I am suggesting, therefore, is that, as scholars of Britain or of

CONCLUSION

India, of women or of men, we cannot afford to ignore the intersection between the different components and the different levels of the imperial social formation. In these pages I have attempted to examine colonial masculinity as a historical phenomenon that responded to the economic, political, and cultural shifts in the imperial social formation in the late nineteenth century. The attendant stereotypes of the 'manly Englishman' and the 'effeminate Bengali' thus operated not only in many different and often contradictory historical contexts, but also as part of the same historical process: the changes of a global political economy.

Notes

1 Apart from the scholarship already cited in the preceding pages, see T. Sarkar, 'Nationalist Iconography: Images of Women in Nineteenth Century Bengali Literature', *Economic and Political Weekly*, 22:47 (21 Nov. 1987), 2011–15; Jasodhra Bagchi, 'Representing Nationalism: Ideology of Motherhood in Colonial Bengal', *Economic and Political Weekly*, 25:42–43 (20–27 Oct. 1990), WS65-WS71; Samita Sen, 'Motherhood and Mothercraft: Gender and Nationalism in Bengal', *Gender and History*, 5:2 (Summer 1993), 231–3; Indira Chowdhury-Sengupta, 'Mother India and Mother Victoria: Motherhood and Nationalism in Nineteenth-Century Bengal', *South Asia Research*, 12:1 (May 1992), 20–37. Also see the rich variety of essays on women, colonialism, and nationalism in the following collections: J. Krishnamurty (ed.), *Women in Colonial India: Essays on Survival, Work and the State* (Delhi: Oxford University Press, 1989); K. Sangari and S. Vaid (eds.), *Recasting Women: Essays in Indian Colonial History* (New Brunswick NJ: Rutgers University Press, 1989).

2 See especially the discussion in Cynthia Enloe, *Bananas, Beaches, and Bases: Making Feminist Sense of International Politics* (Berkeley: University of California Press, 1989).

3 This point has also been made in Rosemary Hennessy, *Materialist Feminism and the Politics of Discourse* (New York: Routledge, 1993), p. 79.

4 See Hennessy, *Materialist Feminism*, esp. ch. 3. A similar argument, but from a somewhat different theoretical perspective, is made in R. Radhakrishnan's discussion of 'relational articulation'; see R. Radhakrishnan, 'Nationalism, Gender and Narrative', in Andrew Parket et al. (eds.), *Nationalisms and Sexualities* (New York: Routledge, 1992), pp. 77–95.

5 The classic debate on this question between Perry Anderson and E. P. Thompson goes back to the 1960s; the original Anderson–Nairn thesis was restated in Perry Anderson, 'The Figures of Descent', *New Left Review*, 161 (Jan.- Feb.1987), 20–77.

6 See W. D. Rubinstein, *Elites and the Wealthy in Modern British History: Essays in Social and Economic History* (New York: St Martin's Press, 1987); and for imperialism, see P. J. Cain and A. J. Hopkins, 'Gentlemanly Capitalism and British Overseas Expansion, i: The Old Colonial System, 1688–1850', *Economic History Review*, 34 (1986), 501–25; and 'Gentlemanly Capitalism and British Overseas Expansion, ii: New Imperialism, 1850–1945', *Economic History Review*, 40 (1987), 1–27.

7 See Martin J. Wiener, *English Culture and the Decline of the Industrial Spirit 1850–1980* (Cambridge: Cambridge University Press, 1981). Wiener's is a mainly 'culturalist' explanation of Britain's decline and of the supposed failure of its capitalist classes. For the politics of 'manliness' in the formation of the middle class, see L. Davidoff and C. Hall, *Family Fortunes: Men and Women of the English Middle Class, 1780–1850* (Chicago: University of Chicago Press, 1987); and George Mosse, *Nationalism and Sexuality: Respectability and Abnormal Sexuality in Modern Europe* (New York: H. Fertig, 1985).

CONCLUSION

8 See Ranajit Guha, 'Dominance Without Hegemony and its Historiography', in R. Guha (ed.), *Subaltern Studies 6: Writings on South Asian History and Society* (Delhi: Oxford University Press, 1989), pp. 210–309.
9 The classic statement of the expansion of capital – both in its drive to create a world market and its revolutionary role in subjugating earlier or prior modes of production to production based on capital – is found in Marx's *Grundrisse*, cited in Guha, 'Dominance Without Hegemony', pp. 222–9.
10 I owe this suggestion to Alex Callinicos, 'Exception or Symptom? The British Crisis and the World System', *New Left Review*, 169 (May-June 1988), 97–107.
11 For a critique of locating the site of resistance 'outside' that which is to be resisted, see Madhava Prasad, 'The "Other" Worldliness of Postcolonial Discourse: A Critique', *Critical Quarterly*, 34:3 (Autumn 1992), 74–89; and 'On the Question of a Theory of (Third World) Literature', *Social Text* 31/32, 10: 2–3 (1992), 57–83. I am indebted for this point both to Prasad and to Arun K. Patnaik, 'Reification of Intellect', *Economic and Political Weekly*, 25:4 (27 Jan. 1990), PE12–PE19.

INDEX

Ackroyd-Beveridge, Annette, 58–61
age for Civil Service Examination, *see* civil service
Age of Consent Act, 1, 10, 12, 18–19, 22–3, Ch. 4 *passim*
  see also Criminal Amendment Act (British Consent Act)
agrarian unrest, 5, 90
Ahmad, Aijaz, 14
Alexander, H. M. L., 105, 117
Althusser, Louis, 28 n.35
Amrita Bazar Patrika, 6, 16, 24, 61, 62, 93, 116, 129–30, 149, 152
Anagol-McGinn, P., 139, 169, 170
Anderson, P., 95 n.10, 182
Anglicist, 3–4
  see also Orientalist
anglocentric, 103
  see also Ireland
Anglo-Indian
  definition, 23
Appadurai, Arjun, 27 n.28, 102
Arms Act, 71, 94, 160
  see also volunteer movement
Arnold, David, 27 n.28, 66 n.24, 97 n.26, 137 n.113
Aryan race, 20, 22, 31 n.63, 31 n.73, 92, 146
assaults on white women (real and imagined), 47, 51–4, 59

babu
  definition, 17–19
Ballhatchet, K., 66 n.67
Bamabodhini Patrika, 170
Banerjea, Surendranath, 43, 53, 62, 63, 77, 78, 92, 142, 149, 165
Bangabasi, 149, 152, 168
Basu, Mankumari, 170
Baxter, C., 17
Beames, John, 43, 112
Bengal
  definition, 24
Bengal Chamber of Commerce, 122
Bengal Tenancy Bill, 5, 77

Bengalee, 6, 16, 61, 78, 79, 91, 92, 93, 125, 142, 152, 165, 166
Bengali Ladies Association, 62
Bernal, Martin, 14
Beveridge, Annette Ackroyd-, 58–61
Beveridge, Henry, 48–9, 55, 109, 121
  see also Ackroyd-Beveridge, Annette
Bhabha, Homi, 18–19
bhadralok
  definition, 6
bhadramahila, 11, 46, 61–3, 170
  see also memorial hoax
Bombay, 17, 69, 70, 74, 77, 80, 110, 169–70
Bonnerjee, W. C., 156
Borthwick, M., 65 n.49, 68 n.124, 173 n.2, 179 n.126
Brahmos, 162, 165, 168, 170
  Adi Brahmo Samaj, 21
  Sadaharan Brahmo Samaj, 145, 175 n.30
British Indian Association, 6, 77, 94, 149
Burton, A., 60

Calcutta Committee in Support of Consent Bill, 146–7, 166
Calcutta Corporation, 77, 81
Calcutta Trades Association, 82
Canning, Lord, 74, 84, 85
capital
  capitalism, 13
  capitalists, 33, 34
  European capital in India, 3, 39, 121–2
caste, 8, 16, 22, 27 n.28, 41, 101–2, 127, 138, 146, 150, 151
Central National Mahomedan Association, 94, 120, 152
Chakravarti, Uma, 146
Chandra, B., 25 n.6
Chatterjee, Bankimchandra, 21
Chatterjee, P., 7, 22, 26 n.13, 31 n.74, 141

[187]

INDEX

child-marriage, Ch. 4 *passim*
  British ambivalence, 153–5, 161–3
  impact on race, 156–8,159–60
  see also Rukmabai case
Child-marriage Restraint Act, 138
child-prostitution, *see* Criminal Amendment Act
Civil and Military Gazette, 38, 57, 80
civil service, 9, 36–8, 43, Ch. 3 *passim*
  age question, 115–18
  agitation, 77, 100, 114
  competitive examination,111–15
  'covenanted' branch, 37, 42–3, 104
  executive v judiciary, 125–7
  Indian recruitment, 37, 101, 105–7
  myth, 107–8, 131
  'statutory', 37, 105–6, 111, 123
  uncovenanted branch, 37, 123
Cohn, B., 25–6 n.9, 30 n.60, 132 n.5, 133 n.12
colonial
  colonisers and colonised, 1–2, 22
  discourse, 5, 183
  political economy, 3, 5–6, 39
  race relations, 19–21, 39
  see also 'Orientalism thesis'
communalism, *see* sectarian politics
competitive examinations, *see* civil service
Compton, J. M., 133 n.12, 133 n.15
Congress, *see* Indian National Congress
conjugal rights, *see* restitution of conjugal rights
Contagious Diseases Act (Britain), 153
Cotton, Henry, 109, 121
'covenanted' civil service, *see* civil service
Criminal Amendment Act (British Consent Act), 10, 153, 154, 161, 163, 167
  see also marital rape
Cunningham, Hugh, 71–2

Daily Chronicle, 156
Dainik O Samachar Chandrika, 149, 171
De, Brajendranath, 38, 43, 112, 124
Debi, Jnanadanandini, 46
  see also bhadramahila
Debi, Sarla, 21, 68 n.122
  see also bhadramahila

'demilitarisation', 8, 92, 94
  see also volunteer movement
discourse, *see* colonial
divide and rule, 70–1
  see also sectarian politics
Dufferin, Lord, 53, 69, 71, 76, 82, 88–9, 90, 114, 126
Dutt, R. C., 37, 40, 46, 111 n.12, 115, 133 n.17

East India Company, 2, 4, 72
economy, 3, 5–6, 39, 70
  economic interests, 121–2
  financial burden, 90–1
  global political economy, 184
Engels, Dagmar, 139, 148, 168
English-educated Indians, *see* Western-educated Indians
Englishman, 38, 40, 51, 52, 56, 57, 58, 59, 76, 83, 85, 122, 156
English public schools, *see* public schools
Englishwoman's Review, 34, 60
'eructation episode', 128–30
ethnography, 20–2, 101–2, 157
  see also Aryan race
Eurasians, 23, 71, 72, 73, 74, 75, 83, 85, 86, 115, 121, 128
European and Anglo-Indian Defence Association, 56–8, 122

female sexuality, 167–9
  see also Pigot case
feminist, 144
  anti-feminist backlash, 2, 8, 153
  challenge, 35–6, 70
  scholarship, 11–12, 181–2
  single women, 49, 154
  see also 'New Woman'
Forbes, G., 66 n.66, 173 n.4
Foucault, Michel, 26 n.15

Ganguly, Kadambini, 145, 170
  see also bhadramahila
garbhadhan, 146–7, 150
gender, Ch. 2 *passim*
  category of analysis, 2, 11, 172, 181, 182
gentlemanly ideal, 103–4
gentrified values
  aristocratic disdain, 103–6
  attitude to property, 5, 80

INDEX

debate over, 182–3
Ghose, Manomohun, *see* marital rape
Ghosh, Motilal, *see* 'eructation episode'
Gladstone, W., 38, 57
Great Revolt of 1857, 4, 8, 47, 59, 70, 72–3, 88, 141
Guha, R., 27 n.18, 27 n.19, 183
Gupta, B. L., 36, 37, 38, 40, 46, 64 n.12

Hall, C., 8, 10, 64 n.9, 184 n.7
'Hari Maitism', 143
see also sexual abuse
Hennessy, Rosemary, 2, 30 n.55, 30 n.57, 55, 67 n.110, 182, 184 n.3
Hindoo Patriot, 6, 78
Hindu, 2, 7, 15, 16, 22, 24, 41, 101, 110–11, 113, 116, 119, 152
laws, 141, 150
Hindu Widow Remarriage Act, 144, 146, 162
Hirschmann, E., 63 n.2, 63 n.4, 63 n.11, 67 n.90, 97 n.30
homosexuality, 18–19, 30 n.56, 30 n.58, 158
see also masturbation
Hume, A. O., 53, 76–7, 79, 109, 155, 158
Hume trial, 53–4
see also assaults on white women
Hunter, W. W., 40–1, 46, 153–4, 155
hunting, 42, 65 n.32, 86
see also sports

Ilbert Bill, 1, 5, 11, 12, 22–3, Ch. 1 *passim*, 76, 77, 78, 139
Ilbert, C. P., 33, 76, 85, 114, 144
Indian Association, 6, 63, 77, 94, 149
Indian Christians, 49, 83, 142, 169, 170
Indian civil service, *see* civil service
Indian finances, 3, 90–1
Indian Mirror, 93, 152, 165
Indian National Congress, 16, 70, 94, 119, 149, 155–6
Ireland, 92
Irish, 72, 104, 131
Irish nationalism, 70

Jamaica, 10
Jones, G. S., 72

Khan, Sayyid Ahmad, 111, 115, 119
Kipling, Rudyard, 51, 322 n.77
Kopf, D., 25–6 n.9

labour, 33
Ladies Committee, 56–8
Ladies' National Association (Britain), 153
'lady doctor', 145, 170–1
landed magnates, 70–1, 77, 87, 89, 92
rentier class, 5–6
see also zamindars
Lansdowne, Lord, 86, 117, 138, 150, 156
Law Commission, *see* marital rape
law for the restitution of conjugal rights, *see* restitution of conjugal rights
Loomba, Ania, 59
Lytton, Lord, 54, 104, 114

Macaulay, Lord, 15–16, 26 n.14, 80, 128, 129, 161–2
see also marital rape
MacKenzie, John, 9, 137 n.126
McLane, J. R., 25 n.6, 25 n.7
Madras, 69, 70, 77, 80, 100, 109, 123, 124, 130
Madrasis, 16, 86
Madras volunteer affair, 83–4
Maine, Henry, 19, 37, 114
Malabari, Behramji, 141, 142, 144, 146
Malabari Committee, 144, 150, 153
Mani, Lata, 26 n.12, 31 n.72, 44
marital rape, 162–6
see also sexual abuse
marriage, *see* child-marriage
martial race theory, 8, 27–8 n.28, Ch. 2 *passim*, 70–1, 86–9
Martin, B. Jr., 26 n.11, 69, 83
masturbation, 158, 178 n.88
see also homosexuality
memorial hoax, 61–3
menstruation, 146–8, 171
Metcalf, Thomas, 26 n.10
Mill, James, 15
Misra, B. B., 131, 133 n.18
missionaries, 44
women, 49–52, 162–3
see also Pigot case
Mitra, Raja Rajendralal, 78, 160
Mitter, R. C., 38, 110, 119, 126, 146,

[189]

INDEX

151, 166, 168
mofussil, 33, 36–8, 42, 51, 69, 84
Mohanty, C., 25 n.2
Moore, R. J., 130
Mort, F., 167
Mueller, Max, 144, 153
Muhammedan Anglo Oriental College, 111, 116, 124
Muhammedan Literary Society, 120, 152, 165
Murshid, G., 65 n.49, 170
Muslims, 16, 101, 110–11, 113, 116, 119, 120, 150, 152
   laws, 141, 152
mutiny, *see* Great Revolt of 1857

Nair, J., 68 n.113, 176 n.62
Nandy, A., 7, 30 n.56
Naoroji, D., 78, 110, 119, 127
native
   definition, 23–4
'New Woman', 2, 55, 59, 63
   see also bhadramahila
non-interference policy, 140–1, 144
non-martial, *see* martial race theory
non-official Anglo-Indians, 2, 6, 23, 36, 65 n.31, 121–2, 126
Nulkar, K. L., 110, 119, 146

'Orientalism thesis', 12–14, 19–20, 22
   application in India, 30 n.60
Orientalist, 4, 19
   see also Anglicist
'Oxbridge', 8, 9, 104, 114, 115, 131

Pal, Bipan Chandra, 142
Parsis, 16, 17, 74, 86, 96 n.23, 119, 127, 141
Patnaik, A. K., 185 n.11
patriarchal, 59, Ch. 4 *passim*
   see also feminist
peasant, 5, 42, 90
   see also agrarian unrest
Permanent Settlement, 5
Phipson-Pechey, E., 171
Phulmoni, 143, 157
Pigot case, 49–50
Pigot, Mary, *see* Pigot case
Pioneer, 40, 55, 57, 77, 102, 116, 157, 168
planters, 42, 75, 122
Poona, 69, 77, 169

'poor whites', 49, 128–9
   'European loafers', 41
   labourers and artisans, 74–5
   'shop-girls', 49
   see also 'eructation episode'
Positivism, 155
Prasad, M., 185 n.11
prostitution, *see* child-prostitution
puberty, 148–9, 151, 171, 179 n.137
   see also menstruation
public schools, 8, 9, 10, 41–2, 81, 112, 115
Public Service Commission, 1, 9, 23, Ch. 3 *passim*
public sphere and women, 8, 11–12, 34–6, 54–60, 61–3, 139, 153, 167
   see also 'separate spheres'
Punjab, 69, 76, 87, 102, 109, 120, 123, 124, 157
Punjabi, 46, 101, 157
purdah, 44, 46
purdahnashin, 49
'purity', 48, 163, 167–9

Queen Victoria, 54, 57, 61, 78, 154
Queen's Proclamation, 38–9, 149

race
   assaults, 42, 65 n.35
   blame for racism, 47
   disqualification, 36–7, 83–4
   theories, 14, 18, 19–20
   see also colonial
Radhakrishnan, R., 184 n.4
railways, 3, 86
   corps, 74
   employees, 75, 76, 129
   guard, 53
Ramabai, Pandita, 169
Ramusack, B., 60, 67 n.105
Ranade, M. G., 141
rape, *see* marital rape
Ray, R. K., 6, 25 n.7, 26 n.17, 149
Reform Acts (Britain), 72
Reis and Reyyet, 61
restitution of conjugal rights, 144, 148, 150–1, 164, 176 n.52
   see also Rukmabai case
Ripon, Lord, 38–9, 52, 76, 77, 114–15
Risley, Herbert, 20, 42, 151, 157
   see also ethnography
Rosselli, J., 15, 29 n.43

INDEX

Rukmabai case, 148, 150
  see also restitution of conjugal rights
Russian war scare, 69, 78–9, 82, 90

Said, Edward, 12–14, 29 n.42
  see also 'Orientalism thesis'
Saint James Gazette, 154, 169
Sangari, K., 11, 75 n.3, 30 n.59, 68 n.125, 70
Sanjivani, 145, 152
Sarkar, S., 25 n.7, 27 n.20
Sarkar, T., 5, 6, 7, 27 n.19, 91, 139, 141, 148, 173 n.9, 176 n.50, 184 n.1
sati, 148
Scott, Joan, 29 n.36
sectarian politics, 23, Ch. 3 *passim*
Sen, Amiya, 152, 175 n.40, 176 n.58
Sen, Kamini, 63
'separate spheres', 8, 34–5, 47, 64 n.9
servants, 48, 52–4
sexual abuse, 140, 143, 171–2, 180 n.144
  see also 'Hari Maitism'
sexuality, see female sexuality and homosexuality
Shastras, 144, 146–7, 149, 150
shikar, see hunting
Sikhs, 16, 40, 119
social reform, 45–6, 60–1
  history, 140–1
  reformers, 141–3, 145–7, 149–50
  see also 'woman question'
Spangenburg, B., 101, 131, 134 n.32, 136 n.87, 136 n.105
Spivak, G. C., 60
sports, 21, 31 n.70, 41–2, 82, 91
  see also hunting
Statesman, 48, 53, 155, 158, 164
Stephen, Fitzjames, 38–9
Stoler, A., 25 n.1, 47
Strachey, John, 29 n.45, 102, 111
Subaltern Studies Series, 27 n.25
subalternity, 7
Sudhakar, 152, 165
Suleri, Sara, 30 n.56
Surnomoyee, Maharani, see zamindars

Tagores of Jorasanko, 21
  Tagore, S. N., 37, 40, 43
Temkin, J., 178 n.101, 178 n.103
Thapar, R., 24, 25 n.9, 31 n.63, 132 n.6
Thompson, E. P., 95 n.10, 182
Tilak, Bal Gangadhar, 159
Times, The, 2, 51, 79, 85, 107, 112, 146, 153, 154
Torri, M., 6, 95 n.6
tribal revolts, 90
  see also agrarian unrest
Turkachuramani, Pundit S., 144

uncovenanted civil service, see civil service

Vaid, S., 11, 68 n.125
Vatsa, R. S., 175 n.31
Vidyasagar, *Pundit* I., 162, 175 n.42
Viswanathan, G., 10, 96 n.12
Vivekananda, Swami, 21
volunteer movement, 1, 7–8, 23, Ch. 2 *passim*, 139, 160
  British, 71–2

Walkowitz, J., 173 n.11, 177 n.66, 179 n.124
Weeks, J., 8, 158
Western-educated Indians
  Anglicised, 4–5, 17, 42
  deracinated, 149–50
  employment, 5–6, 106–7
  hostility, 42–3, 103
  politics, 6, 70, 77–8
Wheeler, M., 169
white womanhood, 11, 46–51, 55–6
  see also assaults on white women
'woman question', 34, 44–6
  see also social reform
working class, 2, 35, 70, 72, 75, 89
Wurgaft, L. D., 19

zamindars, 16, 78, 84, 149
  see also landed magnates
zenana, 44–5, 47, 50, 56